I'm D

For

By Carole

AmErica House
Baltimore

First printing

Acknowledgments of permission to reprint already published material is on page 291.

ISBN: 1-58851-741-1
PUBLISHED BY AMERICA HOUSE BOOK PUBLISHERS
www.publishamerica.com
Baltimore

Printed in the United States of America

for
Hubert Perreault

"I asked myself, 'What is the myth you are living?' and found that I did not know. So ... I took it upon myself to get to know 'my' myth, and I regarded this as the task of tasks ... I simply had to know what unconscious or preconscious myth was forming me."

C.G. Jung,
The Portable Jung

Part One

The Turning of the Spindle

"When all the souls had chosen their lives,
they went before Lachesis. And she sent with
each, as the guardian of his life and the
fulfiller of his choice, the daimon that he
had chosen, and this divinity led the soul
first to Clotho, under her hand and her turning
of the spindle to ratify the destiny of his
lot and choice, and after contact with her,
the daimon again led the soul to the spinning
of Atropos to make the web of its destiny
irreversible, and then without a backward
look it passed beneath the throne of Necessity."

Plato,
The Republic X,620e

What if you have a secret shame that rustles like folds of taffeta? And what if the shame is forgotten like black angel dust in the wind? And what if you dream of a strange and beautiful name? Genevra, Augusta, Diantha–the sequence of lusty syllables unpinning your senses, encircling your ears with breathy nuances, charming the perverse air. What if you reject that very first gift of character moulding, that first turning of the spindle? This name is yours, we are told. The sound of who you are is cradled in its chimes, so love it as you would love yourself because it will accompany you throughout your lifetime.

But what if you cannot love yourself?

Isabelle adds the 'e' to her name when she leaves home. Sixteen years of age is a pivotal year filled with young anticipation, but she doesn't like who she is. The 'e' makes her a bit more exotic. The debonair vowel splashes her persona with a soupçon of French.

The next thirty-four years are spent in a solitary and troubled search to find herself, to find meanings to her existence, to uncover the myth that belongs to her alone for you cannot live another's story without losing your own soul. The path that lays itself out for her weaves and twists its way along like a weft of delicate ivory silks worked into a warp of rough and coloured wools to form a splendid tapestry wrought of life itself. The journey is a difficult one. When her myth awakens, Isabelle struggles to understand its substance as it reveals its truths in remembering the past. This is Isabelle's story.

The name of the village is Bruce Crossing. It's a tiny place. The population register lists four hundred persons. Most have ancestors who emigrated from Scotland to this little corner of rural eastern Ontario in the 1830's, but a large number trace their roots back to great-great-grandparents who crossed the sea from Ireland around the same time. No matter. The bloodlines have intermingled. Today, in Bruce Crossing, 'Mc' or 'Mac' prefacing a surname does not mark one as died-in-the-wool Irish or Scottish. The industriousness of the island people has, however, survived undiluted through the generations of change. The hard-work ethic is as strong now as it ever was. This is where Isabelle and her sister spent their early years. Anna is two and a half years younger, very fair and sprite-like, a picture of carefree innocent childhood wanting protection for being so delicate, wanting protection in the way one wants to immortalize the scent of honeysuckle or dustmotes in a sunbeam. Jealousy must be slithering inside Isabelle when she socks Anna in the face. She hauls back her right arm and lays in a good one with her fist while they pose for a photograph to add to the family keepsakes. The two sisters, one on either side of the father, are wedged between him and the wide curving arms of an overstuffed living room chair covered with green flowered upholstery, a gaggle of legs and hard leather shoes greeting the camera lens. The mother stands in front of them looking down into the viewfinder on the Brownie, which she steadies by pressing firmly to her waist. "Get ready, get set," she warns, then, "Smile for the birdie!" and she clicks the button. Isabelle punches her sister just after the picture is taken. Here's the photograph. Look at the smiles. How lovely! There's Daddy with his two girls. Mummy's missing but everyone knows that Mummy took the picture and it's okay because she'll be in the next one. What a lovely addition to the family album! That was about forty-four years ago. It was winter. Both girls were wearing tartan skirts and long beige cotton stockings. Wool was warmer on cold days, and more expensive, but the short bristly fibers prickled the tender skin at the top of your legs and the back of your thighs, and you ended up scratching and making a mockery of your upbringing. Isabelle's stockings are baggy around the knees. It's probably a Sunday. In all likelihood, the family arrived home from church fifteen minutes ago and now they're waiting for dinner to come out of the oven–a shoulder portion of beef with plenty of potatoes and carrots surrounding it and cooked slowly in a spotted black enamel roasting pan. No onions. The father doesn't like onions. Everyone will keep on his or her good clothes for most of the day. The mother thinks that's the way it ought to be, Sunday being Sunday.

Anna is wailing now, angry as a wet cat, eyes scrunched up like tissue paper, little three-year-old orifice of a mouth open as wide as a barn door. Without another moment's hesitation, the father puts Isabelle across his knee and gives her a spanking for the misdemeanour. The bloom fallen off the rose on the vine, she stands up, humbled, sad, and mad all in the same instant, looks askance at the mother who doesn't say a word, then runs upstairs to her room.

Here's another photo from the early 'fifties. Isabelle is standing in front of their modest home covered with asbestos shingles. It's summertime in Bruce Crossing. She's dressed in a pretty cotton dress with a tight bodice, rounded collar, and tiny cap sleeves edged with ribbon, ruffles of the same patterned cloth cascading down each side of the full skirt. Starched crinolines hold the fabric away from her skinny bare legs, a giant flowered mushroom. I imagine the flowers to be pale mauve with dark green leaves on an off-white background, a popular combination of colours in 1954. There's an odd expression on her face and a lock of hair is hanging across one eye. Whoever took the picture must have waited too long to snap the shutter. You were supposed to straighten your hair, stand still, look at the camera, and say 'cheese,' or smile for the birdie, but her eyes are straining off to one side, as if she's expecting someone to spring out of the hydrangea bush in the corner of the snapshot. In all probability, she was playing tag or hide 'n seek in her party dress, a no-no, and had to interrupt the game to pose for this photo.

And there are others. A wide stand-up bow decorates her hair more often than not. So sweet. So spic 'n span. There's not a speck of dirt to be seen in what has been preserved for posterity, yet the girl likes to play in the mud and climb trees, or hang upside-down by her knees on a branch and look at the sky through the patchwork of fluttering leaves.

"Landsakes! Isabell Joan! Come down from there!" The mother doesn't approve.

"Why?" a slow response, as if she doesn't want to be disturbed.

"You'll get all dirty."

"No, I won't," she chirps back in a high voice.

"You'll be black as a monkey."

"I don't care. I like monkeys."

"Well, I don't. Now do as you're told and come down at once."

"Oh, all right."

"Lickety-split, now."

"Just another minute and then I'll come down."

"You're going to land on your head one of these days and won't that be a pretty sight, now. For the life of me, I can't figure out why you don't keep your feet on the ground where they're supposed to be."

The mother is fond of shopping. Even though the family isn't well off, they're not impoverished and there are plenty of shops with reasonable price tags in nearby Cornwall. So one fine day in early autumn when the babysitter is available to look after little Anna, mother and elder daughter drive the twenty-five miles, through the changing countryside and two or three other village corners, to the city. They continue into the downtown section and leave the car in a parking lot near the shopping district. Isabelle is between two and a half and three years old, so the father says. The mother doesn't remember. While she looks through the collection of new dresses hanging on a presentation rack, Isabelle wanders out of the store, onto the sidewalk, passes between two parked cars, crosses the busy street, and begins walking down the sidewalk on the other side. Going somewhere on your own at this age is a thrill, a peak experience like climbing Mount Everest or your first lick of ice-cream when the cool silky sweetness springs alive on your aroused tongue and engraves a memory on your small soul. Eyes wide open so not to miss a thing, she walks along in the bustle of the afternoon street crowd, a young penguin discovering its water wings, absorbed in the adventure and delighted with the feel of this new place. Each of her senses vies for attention: *Look over here! Feel this! What's that stink? Taste the city! Listen up!* Colours scream out of store windows. Passersby hurry alongside brushing into her. Sulphurous whiffs of skunky air from the local paper industry wrinkle her nose with the unfamiliar stench. A crust-like residue settles in the back of her throat making her mouth papery and huge. She swallows hard, a septic tarry swallow, not unlike the pickled sand in her sandbox at the end of the season, a taste like burnt tires, licorice gone putrid. Truck brakes and car horns screech and beep. But who's this? A lady wearing a brown fall jacket realizes the girl is alone and offers her hand, a womanly hand soft and warm like a velvet powder puff on your cheek or a marshmallow in hot chocolate, in spite of the late September day. Isabelle is not as interested in the woman as she is in the two black beady eyes in the shrunken head of a thin furry animal around the collar of the woman's coat. She leads the child to a policeman in full uniform who is standing at an intersection supervising the relentless comings and goings of the noon hour traffic.

"Well, hello there young lady," he says, tipping the shiny brim of his cap with a forefinger and the largest thumb Isabelle has ever seen. "And what would your name be?" He slides his formidable hat piece to the back of his head.

"Isabell," she replies after taking a few seconds to gaze at the navy blue bulk leaning down towards her.

"Well, now, that's a mighty nice name for a young lass. Do you have a last name?"

"Yes."

"And can you tell me what it is, Isabell?"

"It's Carberry."

"Where do you live, sweetheart?"

"In Bruce Crossing."

"Are you all alone today?"

"Uh huh."

"Where is your mother, dear?"

"I don't know. Over there."

"You stand right here with your lady-friend, Isabell, if you please. Do you see this grey box that I'm pointing at?" She nods. "There's a radio inside and I'm going to talk on it for a minute or two."

The officer lifts a receiver from the steel apparatus on the hydro pole and broadcasts an announcement over the airwaves, "A little girl, by the name of Isabell Carberry, about three years old, was found lost on Pitt Street in downtown Cornwall at one o'clock this afternoon. Anyone with information…." Just then the mother comes rushing down the street, parcels flying, eyes as focused as darts in mid-flight, coat flaps beating against the wind like an osprey with a mission. The guardian angel-lady with the marshmallow hands continues on her way down the street and the incident is over. Isabelle is scolded a dozen times for running off on her own, but she doesn't remember that part.

Three years later, her girlfriend Sandy walks with her to her first day of school. Isabelle has waited and longed for this great event to happen in her life. It's so hard to wait! Jiminy Cricket. Why does it take so long for something you want so much? In Isabelle's estimation, time is an absurd affair without rime or reason. It lasts an eternity when you want it to pass quickly and whizzes by in a flash when you want it to take forever–a dental appointment is quick in arriving as if time is in cahoots with the dentist and sprouts wings in order to get the long needle into your gum sooner rather than later, while waiting for the snow to disappear or to grow up or the first day of school is never-ending and time is as sluggish as a wet mattress.

Sandy began attending the village school the year before and brought her friend Isabelle along with her on a few occasions. Not one of the villagers raises an eyebrow to what might be considered a questionable practice in the city. The local feeling is that it helps a youngster get used to the idea of learning, there being no kindergarten. And what is the harm if the young 'un can mind his p's and q's and sit quietly without disturbing the others? Not a problem for Isabelle, she's a quiet child. She sits in the class with the others and colours pictures, thinking herself pretty special indeed to be attending lessons before she's old enough.

Now, with just a few months before the end of that first school year, she is finding the mile walk through the village on her way home to be rather long and tedious. Each day, Isabelle passes in front of Fairway's General Store, a storey-and-a-half wood-frame building painted white with green trim, on Main Street. Glassed-in displays of merchandise–from coloured pencils and tin lunch boxes and black jawbreakers to modest attire for the whole family, sewing cloth, work boots, and light tools–are arranged on either side of the entrance into the store. The front door is recessed several feet back from the sidewalk between the plate glass windows where the owner, Mac McAngus, has placed his sale sign. *END OF SEASON. WINTER CLOTHING HALF-PRICE.*

This particular afternoon, a boy about her own age of six years, dressed in dark baggy clothes, is standing by one of the showcases. His appearance is terribly disfigured by bumpy growths of skin the size of walnuts, the lumps protruding all over his face and making the skin so loose that it hangs below his chin. The boy's eyes peer out from the depths of this lurid mask with a sadness that doesn't penetrate into Isabelle's narrow world of the unexceptional. Instead, the unfortunate child's pitiful look threatens to reveal the grotesque and ugliness of the unknown. Horrified and frightened, Isabelle begins to run when the boy makes a movement towards her. Going as fast as her legs will take her, she dares once to glance backwards only to see him lumbering after her with a crippled gait, hobbling along like an ogre in *Grimm's Fairy Tales*. Then she is no longer running along Main Street in Bruce Crossing, she is fleeing a terror in a fearful dreamscape and her legs are giving out on her. There's still about half a mile to the Carberry house. When she turns the corner into her street the boy is nowhere to be seen, has seemingly vanished into thin air.

Arriving on the front porch excited and out of breath, Isabelle tries to tell her mother about this strange boy who has scared her so. The words spill out in a jumble as Verda Carberry stands in the doorway holding the screen door ajar while she listens to her daughter's story. Not overly concerned and impatient to get back to preparing the evening meal in the kitchen, she checks quickly up and down the street, just to allay her suspicions.

"Now, Isabell, don't be silly," she admonishes. "There's no one there and I don't know of anyone of that description in the village. It's just your make-up. I've never seen the likes of it. Run along now, dear, and play with your sister."

"But he chased me! He did! He really did!"

"Isabell, there is no boy like that here. Tell your father when he gets home and see what he says."

"I don't want to. He'll laugh at me."

13

"Well, that's enough then. I don't want to hear another word about it. Anna's waiting for you. I'll call you both when supper's ready."

Anna is in the garage on the east side of the house, which the two girls use as a playhouse.

'Tis true that Isabelle has a big imagination. It needs to be big because she has to deal with the world in her own way. Life happens on the outside and then she has to bring the events inside to process them, to place them in a proper perspective. Others are puppets who people dramas, but they're not her dramas. The stage belongs to someone else and she's merely a spectator. People put her on guard. It could be said that they threaten her but no one has the least intention of doing her any harm, no, it is more her sense of feeling good that is disturbed. If you allow yourself to feel, confusion reigns, takes over your thoughts, turns them into fuzzy buzz. It's better to watch from the outside, thinks Isabelle, then you're still in control. You have the option to push feelings down if they make you too uncomfortable, or leave, which amounts to the same thing. One has to be ever so alert. Everyone knows so much more than she does, even little Anna.

There are more children closer to Anna's age in Bruce Crossing than there are to Isabelle's. Anna spends happy hours romping with her friends, playing at their houses, carrying a small ribboned package to each of their birthday parties, but Isabelle never feels like a child, never feels the happy-go-lucky light-hearted frivolity of play. She likes the Sunday school picnics where she can win the races and get a prize. That's fun. And she likes report card day at school because the teacher always writes compliments in the remarks section and gives her the highest grades in the class. That's fun too because when she gets home her father gives her a dollar for doing so well. And she likes to be in charge. Her efforts at planning and structuring, however, don't always bring about the desired emotion of greatness. Being in control carries its own disappointments and embarrassments, like organizing play-acting with Anna and her playmates.

Play in One Act, by Isabelle. The girls go to the empty lot across the street from the playhouse, run and fool, get into fights, yell at each other, and make each other mad. Then they run back to the playhouse, hurt and wailing, to Isabelle, the good mother. Eight feet tall she is, as she stands watching and waiting for the children to come to her like all the pictures of the Virgin Mary in Sunday school. Her head is bowed and inclined slightly to one side in a position intended to be dignified and noble since she's the oldest and the tallest and this posture is most fitting to her coming line in the play. She is infinite maternal patience. Anna plays Isabelle's child. Her role in the drama is to complain to her mother that her friends play too roughly and have hurt her. At that point, Isabelle, the all-knowing wise one, lays her hand softly on

Anna's shoulder, takes a deep breath because this is the climax, and pronounces in a tone as solemn as she can muster, "Forgive them, for they know not what they do."

"Oh, Pshhoooey!" blubbers Anna, wiggling out from under Isabelle's hand and blowing nonsense air at her older sister. "And tooty-frooty besides." She scampers off shaking her head and muttering, "Stupid sister. Sheesh! Stupid, stupid."

Isabelle is mortified. She hopes the other little girls haven't heard the exchange and glances quickly to see where they are. To her satisfaction, they have resumed their play in the grassy field.

Where does Anna get her information? How is it she is so sure of herself? How does she get to have so many friends? Isabelle knows a few girls her own age but she never laughs and plays about with them the way Anna does with her chums. Isabelle is most comfortable with Sandy. She's a year older, but Isabelle took a liking to her from a young age and she's her best friend.

As a rule, the 1950 high school principals were unstinting disciplinarians, and Sandy's father, Mr. Stewart, the learning master of Bruce Crossing, was no exception to this behavioural code, being very strict with the students as well as his family. Isabelle finds him a touch on the scary side and keeps herself at a safe distance. However, there has to be a face to face confrontation whenever the girls want to arrange an overnighter–eating supper, passing the evening, and sleeping together–at one or the other's house. They have to present a formal request to the intrepid and terribly smart Mr. Stewart before the daily routine can be disrupted by the whims of six and seven year-olds. Sandy and Isabelle put on their best behaviour and stand side by side at attention in front of Mr. Stewart as they have been instructed to do when speaking to a person of his stature. Well prepared with an arsenal of answers, which they have rehearsed ahead of time, the girls hope that at least one will suit him and their plan of companionship will come to fruition.

"And what would you girls be wanting?" he addresses them, glowering from above, twitchy fingers clicking loose coins in one pocket and rattling a ring of keys in the other.

"I got an A+ on my report card and so did Isabell, Daddy."

"We'll be extra good, Mr. Stewart, and real quiet."

"Answer the question you are asked, girls, and don't say 'real quiet,' Isabell, say 'really quiet'."

"Really quiet, Mr. Stewart. Like little mice. Not a peep."

"Heh, heh. You mean squeak, but don't exaggerate."

"We want to play with our new kittens, Daddy. It's okay. Fluffy will let us."

"Is that so! Is that how you girls want to spend your time? Playing with cats?"

"They're babies, Mr. Stewart. I like kittens and I won't get a rash, honest, I won't."

"I see. And what else have you got to say?"

"We collected lots of leaves for a project in Brownies, Daddy, and we want to work on it together, so can Isabell stay here tonight? Please, Daddy?"

"We mean if…"

"Don't interrupt when someone else has been invited to speak, Isabell."

"All I meant was, if it's all right with you, Sir, Mr. Stewart, Sir."

"I see. And what is the purpose of the sleep over?"

"We want to iron the leaves we collected and put them in a book so they'll be flat, Mr. Stewart."

"It's for Brownies, Daddy."

"So you girls want me to think that you're going to do some work together?"

"Oh, yes Sir, Brownies are supposed to lend a hand and we won't make a mess in Sandy's room either, Mr. Stewart. No Sir, not us. We'll work neat, Mr. Stewart," says Isabelle. Both she and Sandy are starting to shift from foot to foot, feeling the weight of the ordeal.

"Don't fidget, girls, and it's neatly, Isabell."

"Yes, Sir. If we do, we'll clean up after and leave it nice and neat… er, tidy."

"Indeed you will."

"Does that mean it's okay then, Daddy? Please, Daddy? Mummy says it's okay with her."

"It's all right this time, girls. But I don't want to put up with any nonsense from either one of you and good little Brownies ought to lend a hand to Mrs. Stewart and help with the dishes after we've finished eating."

"Yea! Whoopee!"

"Yippee!"

"That's enough, girls. Shoulders straight. And don't expect this to become a common occurrence."

"No, Daddy."

"No Sir, Mr. Stewart, not a common…"

"Occurrence, Isabell. Not a common occurrence."

"Yes, Mr. Stewart. I mean, no, Mr. Stewart."

"Off with you then," he says as one would say 'scat' to a chicken or 'shoo' to flies.

Mission accomplished, Sandy and Isabelle settle themselves on the divan in the living room, giving Mr. Stewart a wide berth.

The Stewart's have the first television in the village and the children are allowed to watch one program before Mrs. Stewart puts the meal on the family dining table at six o'clock sharp. Motionless for half an hour in front of the little black and white screen, Sandy and Isabelle sit in a trance, mesmerized by Howdy Doody with his dopey eyes and spotted cheeks until Mrs. Stewart hollers, "Supper's ready!" and rings a little bell, which she uses only on such occasions to amuse the girls.

Isabelle guards her friend for herself. It isn't right or fair that Gloria should ask Sandy to play with her at Gloria's house. And what if Gloria invites her to spend a night, like best friends do? Cooked like a goose. Tossed out like stiff old bubble gum. Gloria is rich. What chance does she have against such a competitor? It's not fair! Her house even smells rich. Sweet cream and spice are in your nose as soon as you walk in the door then Gloria's mother greets you with a big smile and asks you if she could take your coat and would you like a cookie. The Carberry house doesn't have a distinctive odour about it like Gloria's. There's nothing at all noticeable in the air most of the time. Furniture polish and Javel water are the closest scents that Isabelle can find to go with her house, but the rubbing and cleaning odours that make the corners of your nostrils flare out in protest like a rattled cobra don't even come close to smelling like vanilla candy. She wishes her house could have a privileged smell that surrounds you as soon as you step inside the way Gloria's does. Gloria has special things, special dolls with perfect little matching clothes and miniature houses and playthings of their own that no one else in the village has. Sandy might start to like her better than herself. Then what'll she do? "Shove it under the rug," her mother would say if she complained to her, but there's no shoving this under the rug, it's too real, too big a possibility. What's really, really awful, thinks Isabelle, is that they're the same age and in a higher grade at school. That could mean something pretty important, a secret pact maybe, or a private club where they make all the rules and leave me out 'cause I'm too young. They have plenty of time to arrange things for themselves when I'm not around being a nuisance to them. Jumpin' jellybean! Some day I'll show them, Isabelle promises herself. More than one way to skin a cat, she's heard her father pronounce wisely. She doesn't take him seriously, knowing he would never do such an outrageous thing, but she understands what he means.

There's only one girl in her own class she likes. Her name is Maysie. She's different from the others. Her hair is parted in the center and pulled into two stiff braids, the matted and stubby ends held in place with different coloured elastics. Short curly wires of reddish brown hair make a fuzzy halo around her head. Wild-looking and ready to fight at the slightest provocation, a roadrunner on slim pickings, Maysie wears the same faded pink cotton dress, a floppy bow tied at the back of the waist, day in and day out. Her slight form is nothing but skin and bones, but she looks strong, like nothing can get her, an armoured mosquito with a doozy of a sting. Isabelle feels an uncanny attraction to Maysie, to a particular kind of knowledge she can't get anywhere else.

A rose-brown coloured wart, about the size of the tiny eraser on the end of a pencil, is growing on the padded base of Isabelle's left thumb. Little rounded lumps of hardened skin gather about a dented spot in the center. Isabelle thinks it's ever so ugly, a deformity that belongs on the end of a witch's crooked nose with a long black hair growing on the tip, or on the thickened skin of, heaven help us, slimy lipless reptilian creatures that leap about with long intrusive fingers and toes, but the squatter certainly has no place being on her person, no right at all to be there. She looks disgustedly at the little outgrowth with a magnifying glass to see if there's any sign of a dark hair emerging from the unwanted protuberance. When none materializes, she pokes at the brownish pink globes, like sausage innards, with the collection of small instruments in her mother's nail kit. Perhaps if she jabs in just the right way, it might puncture a key bulb of whatever's in there and cause the whole thing to deflate instantaneously, to flatten out right on the spot with nary a sign of ever having been there in the first place. Of course, she's not that demanding and would easily settle for a small scar that would disappear with time.

"Granny Thalie says there are things you should never ever say to grown-ups, things you should keep to yourself like best secrets," Maysie tells her, her squinty green eyes darting from one side to the other as if she's scouting a sacred inner territory and she wants to get the details exactly right.

"But if she's your granny, she's a grown-up too."

"I know. She's old but she's special."

"How come?"

"She's not like an ordinary adult. She's different and she knows things."

"Like what?"

"She tells me things that other grown-ups don't."

Isabelle is impressed since she can't think of a grown-up who tells her about things, just how to do things, mostly how to behave.

"Granny Thalie says most adults are outcasts from the world of magic, unbelievers. Children are closer to magic 'cause they ain't been corrupted."

"What's corrupted?"

"Granny says it's when you don't believe natur'ly. It means your spirit's broke."

"How does it get broke?"

"When someone hurts you."

"But how come children are closer to magic?"

"The hidden world, that's what my Granny calls it, has an energy all its own and adults spoil the spell."

"Huh?"

"They disturb its power 'cause they don't believe in it."

"Oh."

"So never tell a grown-up about magic 'cause they'll ruin what you tryin' to do and they'll look at you like you got rocks in your head," explains Maysie, who has a lot of experience behind her eight years going on thirty. "You'll be sorry if you spout your mouth off." According to Maysie, you'll be labeled a strange child who will amount to no good, one with off-colour tendencies who bears constant keeping an eye on if she's not to get into some kind of trouble. "Believe you me, the old guard will shake their heads with dismay and send you hollerin' to the funny farm, an unteachable," says Maysie (and her Granny Thalie from whom she has learned her lessons well).

"What funny farm?"

"It's an imaginary place where adults put people they don't understand."

"So why do they call it funny?"

"Not funny ha-ha, silly, funny weird."

"What's an unteachable?"

"Somebody who don't learn their rules."

"What rules?"

"The rules they make so everyone will be the same."

"Why?"

"'Cause it's easier for them to understand."

"So if you're different they put you in that funny place?"

"Sort of."

"So if it's imaginary why do you yell?"

"'Cause they don't ask you if you want to go."

"But if it doesn't exist…?"

"Isabell, don't talk, just listen."

Warts need to be reunited with their amphibian relatives, toads and frogs, so they will stop trying to resurrect a resemblance of themselves on humans. This is another of Maysie's secrets that she imparts in confidence to her friend, Isabelle. To exorcize Isabelle's wart, the two girls arrange to meet after school in a grovy brushwood at the back of the schoolyard, a place private enough so the Nosy Parker's won't be apt to find them.

Maysie brings a toad and conducts the proceedings that will invoke the vertebrate to take back its likeness into itself and leave Isabelle's thumb. She hums quietly to herself–Maysie says the humming is how the spirits know when it's all right for them to come–and, after a decent length of time, her frail body begins to weave back and forth, because, you know, the beings

19

from the otherworld enter into you causing the inspired movement and it takes a little time before their presence is felt. They're awfully skittery things and don't like surprises or loud noises, so, while Maysie is humming and weaving, Isabelle stays deathly silent, scarcely breathing, so not to scare them away. Once the swaying and waving are pretty regular and the desired state has been achieved, Maysie, eyes bulging and looking skyward, conjures up the devils with a magic incantation. It sounds like Jabberwocky from *Alice in Wonderland* with a touch of improvisation when needed for a special effect:

Brillig and slithy toves,
Gyre and gimble in the wabe,
Mimsy in the borogoves,
Jubjub birds and Bandersnatch.
Be gone. Be gone.

At the same time as the beings are called upon to perform, Isabelle gathers the strength she needs to meet head-on the enormity of the task at hand–flesh to flesh contact with the dreaded alien. Toes curling into the soles of her shoes like the tight little wood shavings on the floor of her father's workshop, she steadies herself, extends her disfigured hand, palm upwards, to Maysie who rubs the sac-like belly of the toad back and forth over Isabelle's wart, surprising her with the dry velvety feel of the toady skin, and sanctioning the rite of passage.

The ceremony doesn't take long, but it works. In a few weeks, the wart has shriveled into nothing, never to return. Isabelle keeps the secret of its disappearance to herself, her heart bursting with new-found knowledge weighty with exclusivity and privilege, and reserves a respectful place for the unexplainable, for the mysterious, for the wonderful richness of the extraordinary. She would like to spend more time with Maysie, but Jake and Verda Carberry don't like her and watch Isabelle closely to be sure she is with only those friends of whom they approve.

The Skating Rink

Wakeham, Quebec, 1956.

In the fall of that year, the family moves to Wakeham, a quaint rural village of sixteen hundred people. A river flows through the picturesque hamlet dividing it in two. Beginning as a trickle high in the Adirondacks south of the border in New York State, the clear water winds its way downward over one rock and then another, meeting up with other trickles, then feeds into a mountain lake. A stream issuing from the lake gathers momentum as it runs down through the foothills and widens out into a river upon reaching the lower regions on the Quebec side of the frontier. The lush farmlands that rest in the valley have produced prize corn crops and fat beef and dairy herds since the early settlers arrived in this part of Canada in the late 1700's. Wakeham is the hub of the valley.

Jake Carberry is the new manager for the Killam Milk Company. Every morning the local farmers bring their wagon loads of fresh milk to the factory to be tested and separated before being loaded on a freight train and sent to Montreal for processing. Isabelle likes to spend time at the factory watching the men as they work with the steel milk cans, hoisting, washing, filling, weighing, loading, and hammering down lids. The din of banging cans and the clank and roar of the heavy machinery is deafening, an emporium of raw pagan clashes, the inscrutable noises of an approaching cataclysm. It causes the men to yell in each other's ear in order to be understood, the sour ginger aroma of spilt milk on cement permeating the air. Jake shows the girl how he takes samples of milk and how he tests the quality with little coloured strips of paper. He's good at explaining and he tells her, in terms she can understand, why some farmers have better milk than others. "But why is there bacteria in milk, Daddy? I thought milk was pure, Daddy. How did it get in there? How does the paper turn into different colours, Daddy? Is it just milk that makes it change colours? What if I put it in pee? What would happen then, Daddy?"

"Oh, Isabell! That's a wicked thing to say. Wherever did you get an idea like that? I swear it didn't come from your mother or me."

On occasion, and those are the times for which Isabelle waits, he will leave her alone to play in the tiny office of the plant while he goes off to attend to the business of the moment. As soon as the door has closed behind him, the carriage of the old black iron Underwood typewriter starts dinging back and forth, the small brass bell tinkling frantically, and the factory cats head for cover. Then the long-handled adding machine clatters and rattles until her father comes rushing back to see if his office equipment has fallen on the hard floor or just what it is that is causing the commotion. When all of the eighty-pound cans have been loaded on a box-car and shipped out, Isabelle wanders into the factory proper and over to the high narrow corridor of steel rollers that carries the milk cans out of the building to the railroad line. The men have gone home for the day. She climbs to the top of the runway, crouches down, and grasps her knees, making herself into a ball. Then she gives herself a push and slides down the shiny metal rollers on her feet, bumping and jiggling along at a good speed. Her compressed body shoots through the milk can opening in the wall, a fifty-pound flash of pink peddlepushers and flying hair, the bright daylight making her squinch up her eyes, and she jumps off quickly about four feet above the ground before falling onto the railway tracks. Her mother is unaware of the game. Her father chuckles, telling her to be careful not to let herself get hurt, and keeps the secret.

Moving to a new village is lonely at first. Isabelle was born there in 1947 but she was only one and a half years old when the family moved to Bruce Crossing. Even though Wakeham is her birthplace, everything about it is new and she misses her friend Sandy. Isabelle never cries but in the middle of one afternoon Verda Carberry finds her in her room, sitting on the bed and looking out the window at nothing, her eyes filled with tears.

"Now what, pray tell, would be the matter, dear?"

"I miss Sandy."

"Oh, cheer-up! You'll get new friends. You've already met some nice girls your own age."

"But they're not like Sandy."

"It takes time to make friends. Clean up your room and you'll soon forget about it."

"I hate cleaning."

"You can't always do just exactly as you please, you know."

"But it's not fair."

"What's not fair?"

"I don't know."

"Well, how can you fix it, if you don't know what it is?"

"Whatever it is, it's just not."

"Oh, Isabell Joan. What ever am I going to do with you? Why don't you listen to me, dear? You can't make friends sitting here in your room. Me oh my, but you put me in a conflab sometimes, so you do. Now, come downstairs with me, you can help me fold the ironing."

Wakeham Public School is undergoing renovations to the old red brick schoolhouse where every grade, from kindergarten to the end of secondary school, is taught. Classes are held in the industrial building in the fair grounds until the fall nights turn too cold and the children shiver during the early morning classes. Anna is in grade two, Isabelle, in grade four. On the second day of school, the French teacher, Mr. Graves, a big burly English man with an even bigger voice and a hairy beard, asks Isabelle a question in class. He speaks in French and she doesn't know what he wants.

"Qu'est-ce que cela veut dire?" he repeats, his voice harbouring a tone of impatience.

Isabelle holds her breath and waits, feeling red rising on her cheeks, clamps her hands together on the top of her desk so they won't move and anchors her feet flat on the floor.

"Speak up, Miss Carberry! We can't hear you! I won't repeat it a third time!" he yells, his voice booming through the large hall while a raging fit rushes through Isabelle cutting off her ability to understand. Mr. Graves waits for her to respond, his foot tapping out the seconds, but she's so afraid of his angry sound and hates him so much for shouting at her that her emotions mix themselves up and she can't say a word.

At twelve, Isabelle falls in love with a boy called Mathieu. He has the sweetest face, slightly curly blondish-brown hair, and mischievous smiling eyes that reach inside her and make her feelings dance. She's captured, enraptured with a delight that makes her float in a cloud. Mathieu is one year older and has given her his school picture. Isabelle gazes at those eyes, longing to be near him, but he is French and Verda Carberry lets it be known that Mathieu is not a suitable boyfriend. Neither does she want any hanky-panky without saying what she means by hanky-panky. Verda has never spoken to the boy, who happens to be well mannered, and Isabelle has no idea why her mother doesn't like him, except for the French thing, which makes no sense to her whatsoever. To Mrs. Carberry's way of thinking, it isn't necessary to give fruitless explanations to a matter that is plain and simple. She doesn't approve and that's that. Young persons ought to respect their elders, no questions asked.

During the summer, Mathieu and his friend Gilles ride their bicycles up and down the Carberry's street time and time again until Isabelle notices the ballad on wheels going past her front door. Not wanting to disturb her mother at her housework or to unnecessarily arouse her curiosity, she makes her way outdoors on whatever pretext is handy, "I'm going to see if anyone's playing softball. Bye," or "I heard Anna calling. Bye," or "I need some fresh air. I won't be long. Bye," then hurries to join the boys on her bike. Usually, they peddle to the park in the north side of the village and sit on the swings, or climb the chains and play acrobats on the top bar of the structure. On other days, they ride to the edge of town and park their bikes in the bushes growing on a rough hillside that stands at the edge of the old abandoned brickyards. The property has been neglected for years giving it a wild appearance; if not exactly savage or peopled with aliens ready to attack, at least the overgrown terrain is suitable for exploring. No bums or dissolute people are apt to wander through the forgotten acreage and it is certainly unfrequented by grown-ups out for a stroll. Many summer afternoons are spent prodding and probing in the tangled bushes and shrubbery with long sticks in a hunt for signs of a previous life, some artifacts, perhaps, or a rusty jewel meaning that the rest of the forgotten treasure must be buried someplace nearby in the dirt. Gilles knows a little English but Mathieu has none at all, so with the few words in French that Isabelle knows they manage to understand each other. Those splendid hours spent swinging in the park or scouting down in the gully with Mathieu and Gilles are Isabelle's favourite times of the day. If there were something terrible about being together, Isabelle doesn't know what it would be. A whole range of ideas has entered her head when she gives the matter some serious thought, but not one of them is terrible or horrific as far as she can make out. She thinks it's her mother who has missed something, not her.

Every December, a spell of below zero temperatures puts the river in a deep freeze until spring. A well-worn footpath down the steep riverbank leads to an outdoor rink on the river ice, which becomes a denizen of activity every Sunday afternoon. Puffs of hot breath condense immediately into small white clouds in the frosty air. Young eyebrows turn into old-man whiskers dripping with sticky ice that catch each gust of snow that the wind sends drifting into their faces. The local boys, both English and French, are playing hockey. Bundled up against the cold, Isabelle ties her skates together, hangs them over the end of her hockey stick, arranges the blade over her shoulder, and makes her way through the village. She sits in a snowbank by the side of the rink to fasten her skates, hoping against hope that Mathieu will send a glance in her direction—any tiny quick look will do, even a slight shift of his eye counts as a greeting, a recognition. *He likes me! He does! I know he does!* And if she waits long enough, at least one of the boys will tell her to stop staring at them like a doofus dork and join in the game. "Aw c'mon! We're playing short-handed. Anyhow, you're not such a bad skater, for being a girl 'n all, that is." Then the fun begins. And maybe, just maybe, Mathieu will bump into to her as he's chasing the puck. Or maybe he'll lose the puck in the loose snow around the edges of the ice and she'll be the one to find it for him. Oh, the thrill!

On Saturday afternoons and evenings, there is skating for everyone at the large wooden arena in the livestock exhibition grounds. Old Mr. Gillycuddy is the guardian of the ice until the joints in his legs are so filled with arthritis and rheumatism that the job is just too difficult for him and he has to let a younger man take his place. Gullyciddy, as the children call him behind his back, knows all the youngsters as Young Winslow or Young Tremblay or You're Jake's Girl and sharpens all the skates in Wakeham for twenty-five cents a pair. Isabelle never misses a winter Saturday at the skating rink. Her heart leaps straight out of her chest into the bleachers and skips a few beats before returning to its rightful place whenever Mathieu unexpectedly appears beside her and grabs her hand as she is skating along. *Oh! Help! Mathieu! I'm in love! I'm in love!* Both good skaters, they whirl around the arena at top speed, hand in hand, passing everyone. Isabelle is in heaven. *I'd like to stay here forever! Please don't let this come to an end!* Sometimes Mathieu will walk part way home with her and carry her skates slung over his shoulder along with his own. It's worthy of note for Mathieu to be seen walking with a girl, especially an English one, especially in tiny Wakeham. Like a declaration, it is, one that leaves him wide open to a deluge of teasing banter from his rowdy chums. They wait until there's a crowd about, twirl on their tippytoes, waving their arms in the air and falling over themselves, then they whoop and guffaw and sing in a raucous chorus, "Mathieu a une petite amie! Mathieu likes the girls! Mathieu's got a girlfriend!" And Isabelle feels special and grand and tries hard not to let a big smile show on her face.

A year or so later, there is a new romance. Ben is his name. Isabelle has a photograph of him too. Ben sent it to her in a letter that she keeps in a secret place underneath her sweaters in the dresser drawer so Mrs. Carberry won't find it and spoil her daydreams. That little sheet of white notepaper comes out of its hiding place, is read, and reread so many times that the precious piece of writing has ripped along the folds, is soiled with dirty fingerprints and falling to pieces like too dry pie dough. Ben lives ten miles south in the rural countryside of Fall Creek.

The village proper and the surrounding farms lie in the foothills of the Adirondack Mountains, an idyllic place of succulent apple orchards and majestic maple bushes that sprawl over the hilly acres of the rambling terrain. On a clear summer day, from a high point of land, you can see for miles and miles down into the valley below. It lays itself out in a tidy and regular fashion, a cleverly phrased hand-stitched quilt or an oil or watercolour painting admirably rendered by a local artisan. Grassy meadowlands of timothy hay, thick pastures of low alfalfa plants, handsome fields of clover bursting into thousands of bluish pink flowers, shiny plots of bright yellow oats undulating in a gentle rise and fall according to the wind, here and there a neat rectangle of clean dark brown land plowed into soft earthy furrows, vast expanses of emerald cornfields growing in tall straight lines with a narrow dirt path between each row of greenery exactly wide enough for the tire of a farm vehicle to pass without harming a single plant, dense groves of pine and spruce in the blackest of greens, small hardwood forests in brighter paler greens, and the grouped dwellings of scattered villages–all come together to create a country mosaic, a live portrait of district life. Vivid black and white patches on grazing cows and great rounded bales of hay dot the fields. And perhaps, if the time is right, one can see a covered red tractor and bailer stopped at the edge of the land for a short while when a farmer takes a break in the heat of mid-afternoon. Silver roofs on wide barns and tall silos and even taller church steeples dazzle in the sunshine. In the middle of the scene, the old river wanders through the lowlands. Slightly beyond, the Saint-Lawrence River travels on towards the Atlantic Ocean, still a thousand miles downstream. Spanning the far northern breadth of the panorama, the rounded blue forms of the lower Laurentians outline the beginning hills of the rich mountainous regions that dominate southern Quebec. At night the lights of Montreal illuminate any low clouds fifty miles to the northeast, casting the sky with a golden shadow.

It's springtime in the photo. The orchards are ablaze in pink and white blossoms. Delicate petals float freely through the sweet air at the slightest breeze. Ben is standing in front of an old and twisted apple tree in full bloom, a white cowboy hat perched lazily on his head, a plaid shirt tucked loosely into tight black jeans. One look from Ben's dreamy dark eyes peering out between long eyelashes is enough to send Isabelle's head flying clean through the air on a speedy journey and make her forget how to speak. *Oh! Help! I'm going to die right this instant!* They're about the same age of fourteen. Once again, Isabelle is overwhelmed with all-consuming feelings of longing and floating in the clouds. When she is in love, everything is beautiful. Birds sing, trees whisper, mountains move. Ben is her secret. No one else knows about him, except Mrs. Carberry, but her mother doesn't count when it comes to secrets, she always knows anyway. Sitting in the darkness of the coat closet underneath the kitchen stairs, Isabelle talks on the telephone to Ben for an hour about nothing. At least, she won't remember exactly what it is that they talk about–it's the dizziness of the heights she is flying through that stays in Isabelle's memory.

In the winter on Saturday nights, Ben comes from Fall Creek with a carload of friends to the skating rink. They're always late. The interminable waiting always provokes a host of worries. *Are they coming or aren't they?* Waiting is similar to wanting–when you want too much the very wanting seems to push the desired thing further away, forces it just beyond your reach. *Maybe they couldn't find a driver. The roads aren't so hot tonight. Ben's mother probably convinced them not to leave. Or maybe there's something at the school in Fall Creek, a dance, or a skating party on the outdoor rink and they decided to stay with their own gang. Oh no!* A horrible feeling alluding to unthinkable situations would sink into her stomach at this latter thought. Then, finally, like Mathieu, Ben will suddenly be at Isabelle's side and the two will skate together, holding hands, gliding surely over the ice. Ben isn't as good a skater as Mathieu, so they don't swoop in and out and around everyone, they follow the crowd and talk. Isabelle's emotions dance with such exuberance that she has difficulty skating in time with the familiar music that blares across the public address system. A scratchy seventy-eight rpm record of Johann Strauss' Vienna waltzes usually plays over and over– *The Blue Danube Waltz* and *Tales From The Vienna Woods*–any riches of harmonic and orchestral effects lost in the noise long before reaching the crowd of night skaters. After the skate and about to burst with the fervour of the springing and leaping that is going on inside her, Isabelle wants to jump and laugh and cry all at the same time. Of course she wouldn't do that. Everyone might think she's improper. Or silly. Or worse.

Even in these young years, Isabelle loves to extremes. Pure excitement and joy is the state of being on some days, a weightless place of smiling and caring people. On others, pure sadness and melancholy is slated as the order of things, the former airiness smudged and bleary with jealously and doubt and sin. The gauge wavers back and forth between the two poles because she loves with all that is in her heart, but doesn't know if Mathieu loves her, and it is forbidden by her mother. It's the same with Ben. Isabelle is enraptured with an image, but doesn't know how he feels. Ben does kiss Isabelle one time, a long wet sloppy kiss. She doesn't like it at all. Lips all soft and wet, it makes her feel icky. She ignores that kiss, however, in favour of the engulfment of a wonderful place to escape into when she is alone.

Nightmares begin to disturb Isabelle's sleep when the family lives in Wakeham. The same one returns night after night until she leaves home. Waking in the dark and filled with a vast terror, Isabelle finds herself sweating and in the grip of a panic attack. She hasn't been dreaming. It occurs to her that perhaps this is madness or the beginning of it. How can one explain the sudden fright? The house is deathly silent, not a sound can be heard from the sleeping family members. She senses a threatening presence in the room and a creature slowly takes shape, like a storm cloud gathering, when she looks at the upper right-hand corner of her bedroom. The form garners human dimensions, a head only, with large penetrating eyes, dark and unsmiling. The head is hairless and hangs steadfastly in the corner of the ceiling for periods of long duration, the eyes unblinking and fixated into the back of her mind, their pull powerful and unyielding. If she looks away, the thing starts to come closer. By staring hard back at it, she can keep it at a safe distance up in the corner, but when her concentration weakens the apparition advances slowly through the room, a dismembered head floating towards her, closer and closer. She is unable to control the demon's movements and fears it will enter into her space and devastate her senseless. The head approaches. She thinks she can feel it exhale, an icy windless breath, and brushes away at the frenzied empty air with her hands. When there is no hope of avoidance, she screams at the top of her lungs and thrashes around under the bedcovers until Mr. or Mrs. Carberry arrives and tries to quiet her. Sometimes, Isabelle thinks the sudden grip, the hand that grabs onto her, is the head that has caught her and she is seized with fright anew, gasps for breath, and falls to exhaustion.

The next morning is school as usual. Whatever horror has occupied the night before is chewed up into little pieces and swallowed as if it isn't allowed to exist during the day.

Other nights, when the intruder has given her some peace, she sits at the end of her bed and gazes out the window at the stars and into the heavens as far as she can see. There's a game she plays when she can't sleep: try to see how quickly a whole idea composed of words and sentences can be thought, as a flash, as a simple impression. First, get all the words of the idea together. Say it out in your mind, one word after the other, so you're familiar with the intent. Then look far off at a star and compress what you have just understood into an essence, a spark, smaller and lighter than a complete thought. Get rid of the words, leave only a spirit. It's fun. The thoughts grow more complicated as she becomes more proficient at her game. She puts words to God, church words–Father Almighty, Tabernacle on High, Sanctifying Grace, Ten Commandments, Holy Sacraments, Consecration, Seven Deadly Sins, Temperance Union, Trespasses, Communion, Temptation–then she puts Him into a smaller thought, then into a tiny threatening substance. Lastly, she diminishes Him even further into her most subdued contraction. Then she has Him. She has God there in a minute precise point that is within her power and reduced by her means. The heady rush makes her brave, makes her decide to challenge.

"God, if You are for real, if You do exist, listen to me! Damn You! I hate You! I would say to You every bad word that exists but I don't know many. Shit. Damn to Hell. If You are there, strike me dead with a lightning bolt for swearing at You, for hating You. Amen."

Isabelle crawls between the bed sheets and waits for God's reaction. Nothing. A great wind does not blow up-turning each leaf on every tree. Resounding thunder that would rattle the windows and shake every village door does not begin to rumble from a distance announcing its coming. A celestial body does not fall through the indigo sky leaving behind it a trail of bright starlight. No, such is not to be as youthful imaginings might suppose– the plain truth of the matter being that not even a whimper of divine recognition disturbs the quiet of that night. Finally she falls asleep. From that time on, Isabelle doesn't believe in God. The church stories are nonsense, kindergarten stuff. She's on her own.

The Wedding Dress

Isabelle has turned sixteen. She's back in Bruce Crossing, thoughts of a godly nature being of minimal concern to a young girl thinking herself a young woman. But, however far dislodged from her present world the mighty riddle of existence may appear to be, the divine have their own agenda. Far be it for a mortal to question the timing of events, or attempt to push the turning of the universe. No divinity worth its salt can ignore a plea such as the one delivered. It has been called upon to assert itself! And so it will, in time. Although, perhaps 'show' is a better word than 'assert,' but you can be the judge. And please don't give a minute's thought to the idea that God has retreated from the foe just because He is shunned for a spell, banished by an abomination. *Poor God.* What a thing to say to God–Poor God–as if He was a person with human touchiness, slighted because of not living up to expectations, not performing in the way He ought. No Sir. No Ma'am. God doesn't plan revenge for Isabelle's lack of courtesy; He adores irony–a picture of what is and what is not in a brazier of intention, a double whammy. No, God doesn't retaliate for her disrespect. God loves the absurd and the ridiculous, not to ridicule, mind you, but to expose the illusion. And God has the patience of Job, if you will pardon the impertinence. He waits until Isabelle has passed through half a lifetime before hearing from her again. And neither should you think that He sits idly by in the meantime, twiddling heavenly thumbs and heaving great yawns that cause the seas to tilt. He is right there, as sure as death and taxes, or plenty after famine, or the scent of a flower, as are His helpers. One of them appears to be more vocal than the others, putting thoughts into Isabelle's head at opportune moments. I have a feeling she's a head angel of sorts, and, if I've the right information, her name's Winona, like a Scottish maiden.

But we'll find out later, in about thirty years or so, if her name really is Winona. These divine aides, another is a spot of light, are watching and listening and waiting for orders from higher up. Believe me. *God is not dead nor doth He sleep.*

Jake Carberry thinks his daughter ought go to university since none of his family has had that opportunity. The high school in Wakeham goes only as far as grade eleven. Needing another school year to complete the entrance requirements, she stays at Grandfather Davidson's in Bruce Crossing.

Soon after the beginning of school, Isabelle decides that she's too fat. Playing every sport that has been on the go–basketball, hockey, volleyball, softball, track and field, tennis, swimming, and skating–has turned her body

31

into solid muscle, which isn't at all svelte and fashionable, according to her. Popularity is a state of demanding proportions. Very slim in certain places and highly endowed in others are what go together, like her girlfriend, Ruth Ann, or Sophie with the tiny hips and big boobs. The boys fight unsuccessfully to keep their eyes out of her cleavage but, in spite of their good intentions, that's the exact spot in which their stares settle and they talk to Sophie's chest, not to her. And they are always so happy to see her, always wearing a big grin on their faces like hot crossed buns just out of the oven. Isabelle stops eating. Not entirely, but she arranges tiny amounts of food on her plate and she takes forever to eat, chewing until she is chewing only saliva. On weekends back at home, however, half a pan of sweet and delicious walnut dainties that Mrs. Carberry has baked, will mysteriously disappear before Isabelle leaves to go back to Bruce Crossing for the school week. She doesn't eat them at the table with the rest of the family; she eats when no one is around to criticize such a criticizable thing, savouring each sugary bite slowly, giving the creamy icing time to smear and melt into the nuts and coconut before swallowing the yummy morsel. Verda Carberry wonders who eats up her desserts so quickly, but on second thought, she doesn't really mind since it must mean they taste good.

The year passes quickly. School is uneventful except for the English teacher, Mr. Lawson. Under his instruction, literature becomes a dramatic and touching place of searching and longing, not an imaginary or fictional world of outlandish events, but a real place of heartfelt quests for understanding and meaning. The animated world of characters Mr. Lawson creates, is in sharp contrast to the forced memorization and rigid note taking imposed by the shrewish and bitter woman who taught English and History to everyone throughout the high school grades in Wakeham. The students called her Hetta, except to her face. She was hell-bent on disciplining the farm boys into quoting Portia's speech from *The Merchant of Venice*:

The quality of mercy is not strain'd,
It droppeth as the gentle rain from heaven
Upon the place beneath: it is twice bless'd;
It blesseth him that gives and him that takes ...

"Come now, boys and girls, repeat after me. Use the lips, the teeth, the tip of the tongue, and spit those words out." In red high-heeled shoes with pointed toes, Hetta marched up and down the aisles between the rows of school desks, her wooden blackboard pointer waving out the rhythm as she waxed on in a poetic mist. When the boys' snuffles couldn't contain their snickers and chortles any longer, the pointer was suddenly airborne and came zinging down through the air to land with a loud whack on the top of a desk or on the ear of a particularly disruptive boy. Likewise, the infectious merriment of the females was orchestrated by Hetta's performance. If the girls looked at each other their faces turned several shades of red, shoulders jiggled in indiscriminate waves, and muffled spurting noises could be heard erupting throughout the classroom. The unexpected appearance of the sublime simultaneously with a less noble emotion was an incongruous affair rendering its victims as helpless as a fly in a gale or wilted lettuce in any attempt to subdue their amusement at the sight, but the finer sex was spared the flying baton.

Mr. Lawson's sensitive rendering of the human spirit running through the great works of the past grasps Isabelle's imagination. It shimmers like a beacon in her mind, luring her to a lusty planet of mercurial words, and directs her into the study of literature at university.

The medieval atmosphere of the university in Kingston, Ontario, the strength of the past mingled with hope for the future, stir an awe that touches a place deep within. Vaulted archways of weathered limestone span the entrances to turreted buildings; long silent expanses of green hug the shores of Lake Ontario; quiet study halls, the atmosphere intense with late-blooming scholastic efforts, light up the old Douglas Library like a legendary castle in the night; the tall spire of the Grant Hall tower stretches upward into the sky in the center of campus, a symbol of learning and of the idealism of youth to change the world. Isabelle can't help but be moved just to be there. Fitzgerald's ghosts of evening *tune again their lyres and wander singing in a plaintive band down the long corridors of trees.*

Her friends are outgoing, impressive, and sure of themselves, compared to Isabelle's serious and contemplative manner, but everyone is slightly different and she doesn't feel quite so out of place coming as she does from a countrified background. She sews clothes for herself that are modish and irons the curls out of her hair into the current straight look, adapting herself to what's 'in'. She has lots of dates. It's the mid-sixties.

Queen's is a conservative university and the flower power of the make love not war generation hasn't hit with full force. Anti-establishment parties and drug-laced hippies will come along a few years later. Isabelle's fling with radicalism is painting her face flourescent green, donning a bright purple moo-moo, and skipping through campus with a group of avant-garde friends. They dance along in single file, Pied Piper fashion, to the tune of Pan on a flute, the colourful parade of mimers blowing gum bubbles, miming verse and song, gesturing elaborately, and bopping balloons in the air. The plot is to create a diversion to the monotony of studying before the finals, nothing so daring as protesting the immorality of the government. Folk music and hootenannies are the lifeblood then. *The House of the Rising Sun*, Bob Dylan, and Joan Baez speak for everyone's soul. Isabelle's talented roommate, Louisa, has a symphonic voice, intimate and grand, and accompanies herself on piano. Her boyfriend, Jim, plays the flute and he and Louisa often give duet performances at Bitter Grounds, the campus weekend cabaret. When the entertainment is over at two o'clock in the morning, a gang congregates in a boarding house living room and the guitar playing, singing, talking, cigarette smoking, and beer drinking go on until the sun comes up.

Louisa has burnished red hair. Isabelle thinks she's beautiful. Her deep sparkling blue eyes are so unlike her own big round plain orbs, which just don't cut it against mysterious and haunting. Louisa has class, she's someone to be reckoned with. Even her freckles are special, giving her a permanently bronzed appearance. Louisa hates the reddish-brown spots and tries to camouflage them with face powder, but Isabelle envies everything about Louisa–her tall presence, her stunning hair, her Streisand voice, her talented fingers, her loving family, even her face specks. Isabelle begins to bleach her bangs, just a dab of hydrogen peroxide here and there to add a highlight that might cast a shine if it caught the light in just the right way. Mousy brown hair doesn't have a place in her box of definitions anymore. Dull brown tresses belong with other relics of the past like bobby socks and saddle shoes. Passé. By the end of second year, at age nineteen, Isabelle is blonde. The clear perfect skin and the honey brown doe eyes haven't changed, but don't ever speak to Isabelle of brown hair. It has outlived its welcome.

On an early December afternoon of her last year, Isabelle is sitting on the bed studying for mid-term exams when Louisa walks into their room. Mrs. Higgins, a seventy-two year old widow, shares her apartment with the two girls on the second floor at 110 Bagot Street to the east of the campus. If either set of parents had an inkling of what a modern lady Mrs. Higgins really was, of her aloof guardianship, it is very likely that neither Louisa nor Isabelle would be living with her. *See no evil. Hear no evil. Speak no evil.* The hear no evil isn't a problem since Mrs. Higgins is very hard of hearing. The girls think that she sees what she wants to see and nothing else since she has probably seen it all already in her years of boarding college girls and nothing they could do would surprise her in the least. They're right. And Mrs. Higgins chooses not to interfere.

It's unusual for Louisa to return in mid-afternoon as she normally studies at the library until five o'clock. It's only two now and here she is, books under her arm and shivering from the cold and blustery walk. Louisa is just arriving from the medical center where her doctor has told her she is going to have Jim's baby the coming June. Unmarried, the third year of her honours English program in progress, no financial way that she and Jim can support themselves, two sets of parents to meet face to face–neither Isabelle nor Louisa know anything for the moment. All they can see are the shattered dreams of academic success and independence, an interesting career, the traveling to Europe and far places that the girls have been planning for the approaching summer, all dissipating with a stroke of fate into smoky reflections of mere conjecture.

Isabelle wonders how her family would react had that been her story. Discussion is something that never happens in the Carberry household. Either it is or it isn't and that is that. Sex is a hush-hush topic, except when Anna and her girlfriends gather around the kitchen table laughing uncontrollably until their faces are wet with tears and they have to stop to catch their breath. Or, they screech and howl to the deaf ceiling, eyes popping, checking the crotch of their pants for wetness until Mrs. Carberry makes an unexpected appearance, "Now, girls. Behave yourselves." When Anna's friend Claire stays for supper, Anna is kept busy giving Claire short swift kicks under the table to keep her conversation in line. To glean a few bits of information, Isabelle leafs through a dirty book her father has left lying around the house, one that hasn't been discovered yet by Mrs. Carberry and whisked away somewhere out of sight, but it never tells her what she wants to know.

She thought for sure she was pregnant when she was in grade thirteen at Bruce Crossing, although she couldn't figure out how. Her monthlies had disappeared into nothing. Maybe if you think hard enough about having a baby... But if that were true then you could have a baby with practically anyone, and I don't really love anyone enough, she thought, not enough to have their baby. How did this happen to me? I'll not tell anyone because maybe it's all a big mistake. If I breathe a word about it, the stupid thing will probably start up the next day and then I'll look like an aardvark or a foolish dingbat and where will I be after that? But why doesn't it start?

So Isabelle was tortured. Oh, how she was tortured during that time! It nearly destroyed her when she was home in Wakeham one weekend and just had to tell her mother that she had not had a period for several months. Expecting a blasting for wrongdoing, she waited until everyone had left the supper table, the dishes had been collected, and Verda Carberry was busy at the kitchen sink, sleeves rolled up to her elbows and hands immersed in the soapy dishwater. When she broke the news, Isabelle thought it might be easier if her mother had something that busied her and the dishes were right there in her hands for her to scrub all the harder, if she felt so inclined. When she was upset, Mrs. Carberry stayed dead silent for an awful minute while she assessed the situation, then her thin lips began to tremble changing her face into a cross one that Isabelle didn't want to see.

"Have you been with a boy?"

"What?"

"Have you been together with Cordell?" Cordell was Isabelle's old boyfriend from High School in Wakeham.

"Nno-o," Isabelle replied, not exactly sure what was meant by being together, although it probably meant more than just going to a drive-in movie and the touching that went on in the backseat, but she didn't dare broach such a subject to Verda Carberry. Too uncomfortable for words to talk about unmentionable things with her mother. As if the air between them would suddenly be filled with laughing penises and grinning vaginas and bouncing breasts. Downright embarrassing. Isabelle stayed home for a few days into the school week to see the family doctor and have any suspicions confirmed. The waiting was pure anguish. She felt a distancing and unstated judgments coming her way, even though Mr. and Mrs. Carberry spoke not a word about the predicament. Convinced she would have to be operated on for some reason or another, she cultivated a fear that left her not once during those two days of waiting to find out what was wrong.

The doctor said it was just nervous strain and the change of atmosphere and schools that had affected her. "There's nothing to worry about, Mrs. Carberry. Your daughter's period will come back when it's ready," he announced. "This happens to a lot of the young new nurses who come to work here."

What exquisite relief! Overjoyed at the news, Isabelle was proud of the fact that something had actually occurred in her sexual system. It meant she really did have one and it was fairly normal if you stretched your imagination a bit. The period part was pretty disgusting anyway but at least they would be back and she would probably be able to get married and have children sometime. That was a wonderful day. The mental ease was as welcome as the new knowledge. Back to school a little changed, Isabelle dropped a hint at each opportunity that came along that there was something different about her. Had someone asked, she couldn't have explained in enough detail to make any sense, but she let on she knew all about it.

Causing her parents any displeasure is something Isabelle dislikes and the thought of facing them with a story like Louisa's is unthinkable. The two girls sit side by side on Louisa's uncluttered bed, a blue chenille spread reaching the floor on either side, Isabelle's arm around Louisa as she rests her head on Isabelle's shoulder and lets herself cry. They agree it isn't fair. Isabelle is the one who has a dozen boyfriends and is a little wild. Louisa is so reasonable and conscious. Where's the sense in that? "Everything will work out all right, Louisa. It will. You'll see, somehow it will," is all Isabelle can think of to say.

And then the summer of 1968. One to remember. It begins with exams finishing, Isabelle's graduating exams. Shortly afterward, she and her boyfriend, Dan Jeffers, arrive in Wakeham with a U-Haul trailer behind the car. Boxes of clothes, textbooks, and stacks of paper from the school year are unloaded into the house and they immediately begin to repack the U-Haul with old dishes and linens and summer attire. "We're going to Toronto," Isabelle tells her parents, sounding as bright and light as a sliver of new moon on a winter night, the reality behind the façade sending out odious signals redolent of dead fish. "Dan already has a summer job and I'll find one as soon as we arrive." Outwardly, Verda and Jake Carberry appear composed and calm about this unexpected turn of events. Inwardly, their thoughts are catapulting around like buckshot in a tin can or flapping like a pool of slimy grey minnows as they try to piece together an only partly revealed story. "We won't see you for the whole summer? Who is this new roommate? Have you seen the apartment, dear? How are you going to pay the rent before you get a job? Or buy food, for that matter?"

"I'll be okay. Trust me."

Dan and Isabelle finish packing the car and trailer and are soon ready to leave. Mr. Carberry takes snapshots with his Polaroid camera of the two young people so bravely setting out with such an uncertain future. Then nothing will do but that Dan and Isabelle go back into the house and have a drink with Jake and his wife before hitting the road and heading for Dan's farm by the lake near the town of Willow River, Ontario. After all, it's not every day a young person sets out on his own in a strange city with no sure means of survival. So back in everyone goes to sit through a restrained conversation period that ventures nothing that does not want to be heard.

Eventually, Dan and Isabelle leave, waving goodbye to Mr. and Mrs. Carberry who remain standing in front of the house, watching the car and trailer until they disappear from sight. The atmosphere at Dan's place is quite the opposite. His parents seem to know that Isabelle will be living with their son, so it isn't necessary to keep it a secret. What worries Dan's mother, Callah, is that Dan could have a good job working at Andrew Technology in Willow River, live at home, dock his boat in the backyard, water-ski, play golf all summer long, and save some money for the coming school year, while, in Toronto, he will be going door to door selling encyclopedias on commission. So Callah goes through every conceivable possible and impossible reason why Dan should not go to Toronto. "You know, Danny, being offered that job at Andrew Technology is no little thing–it's an opportunity of a lifetime. Scores of young persons would jump at the chance. Who knows where it might lead? People say that company's going places."

"There are others."

"Well, if you don't care about that wonderful job that's right here under your nose and yours just for the asking, do you think you can do as well in Toronto? Think what it could mean for your future, Danny, getting an early start in such a company. And you don't know a soul in Toronto."

"I'll make four hundred dollars for each set of books I sell."

"But even if you do, you're not likely to get a fine reception at every household. It's not like here where everyone knew your grandfather, bless his soul. He was the only eye doctor around in the old days and..."

"I heard already, I heard."

"Well, life in the city is different to what you're used to. Lots will slam the door in your face."

"I know."

"You know? Did you say you know? I can't imagine why you want to do that to yourself. Can you tell me why, Dan?"

"No."

"No? Well, I'm blimey'd because I sure don't know either. What about golf? You've got your handicap down to seven and if you don't keep your game up, Danny, it's going to suffer, isn't it? Mark my words, now."

"I'll play in Toronto."

"Go on! You can't play golf in Toronto! The Toronto clubs are too expensive to join, the fees are outrageous there, so I've heard, and, Perry, the golf pro here, thinks you have such potential."

"He doesn't."

"He does too, Danny. I saw him in town just last week and told him I'd be around to renew your membership one of these days. He's such a nice young fellow, that Perry is. Speaks to me every time he sees me, so he does."

"Good ol' Perry."

"That's right. Good ol' Perry. And I was thinking just the other day, even went out to the shed to have a look at it, that your boat could use a new motor. Do you remember last summer..."

"I've only had that motor for two years!"

"Well, even if it is only a few years old, I was going to call Jack at the marina and ask him if he has a better one for you, one with more power so it won't be so hard for you. You told me it was a devil of a job to get back up on your ski after you take a fall in the middle of the lake."

"That can wait."

"What? Last summer you didn't think it could wait. And Clyde's mother told me he was going to spend some time in Willow River this July. Don't you want to see Clyde, Dan? He was your best friend."

Silence.

"Dan? Answer me."

"I'm tired of this."

"Well, you shouldn't be tired. This is important. What if you're making a big mistake?"

"Everyone makes mistakes."

"So they do. But what if it leads you into something you don't want?"

"You're too old to understand."

"I am not too old to understand. Don't you remember Hans?"

"Pa knows. Why are you whispering?"

"I know Robinson knows and that I don't need to use hushed tones, but there's no point in reminding him, is there now?"

"That was different."

"It wasn't that different, Dan. I loved him but I had to think of the consequences."

"You probably should have done what you wanted and run off with him. Maybe you'd have been happier. Anyway, I want to do this."

"I know it's what you want now but what if you change your mind?"

"Then I'll get out of it."

"It may not be that easy to get out of."

"I'll find a way."

"Oh, I know you'll manage."

Robinson Jeffers, Dan's father, stands tall, proud, and straight. A bushy white head of hair and matching uncontrollable eyebrows make him the spitting image of Jed Clampett on the television series of the 'sixties, *The Beverly Hillbillies.* Startlingly bright blue eyes peer out of his tanned and lined leather face that bears witness to a lifetime spent in the outdoors. Robinson doesn't find the situation tenuous at all, rather amusing instead, so while his wife looks after their son, he offers Isabelle a beer, which she politely declines, then walks over to the fridge in the toolshed to fetch a cold one for himself, kicking a screwdriver that has fallen into the grass out of his way as he goes. The weather is pleasant this day in May, balmy and mild. Robinson returns and makes himself comfortable in a lawn chair under the partial shade of a tall elm. He takes a swallow of beer, lights up a DuMaurier, watches the smoke wreathe above the cinder end, and settles down to listen to the altercation between Callah and Dan, chuckling and giving Isabelle a wink out of the corner of his eye when no one is looking. Finally convinced that there is no way she can get Dan to change his mind, even an offer of a weekly cash stipend doesn't work, Callah takes Isabelle by the hand and offers her every piece of furniture in the entire house should they have need of it.

Just the two young lovers on their own in Toronto for a summer–it's a glorious idea but the idealism of romance turns practical all too soon. Arriving in the metropolis, tired and eager to begin a life together, Isabelle and Dan discover that their apartment has not been cleaned after the previous tenant moved out. The rooms are filthy. An ailing old man who lives alone and smokes robust cigars as his only remaining enjoyment in life isn't concerned about dusty corners or onions growing long green sprouts in the refrigerator or breathing air that reeks of stale tobacco and dirty old sock stink. Isabelle spends the first week in grub clothes airing out the apartment and scrubbing layers of brownish yellow grime off every inch of their new dwelling. Once scoured, the location right in downtown Toronto makes it impossible to keep the place clean. The air is thick with smog and exhaust from the constant traffic and heavy black particles settle in again on every surface as soon as they are wiped clean.

Dan's job begins right away and keeps him out on the streets of Toronto until nine or ten every evening. Isabelle doesn't begin her job as a sales clerk in the downtown Holt Renfrew store until three weeks after they arrive in the city. Being in the midst of high fashion and trendy know-how isn't as glamorous as she imagined and getting up to go to work soon becomes a chore. Waiting on a fussy rich madam with her nose in the air and her voice in her nose galls Isabelle somewhere between envy and hate.

Mr. and Mrs. Carberry have spent a week of anxious fretting over the whole affair and are fed up with puzzles. They know a good part of the truth has not been told and they don't like the drowning rank feeling that comes from surmising the missing piece. Their daughter did not lie to them; she told the truth and had indeed gone to Toronto, but she went with a boy barely a man whom they didn't know from Adam, and there was a wide girth around the measly knob of truth at the center. In fact, truth had become slovenly and viscous and sloshed around like egg albumen. It was this untidy element that was disturbing enough to cause sleepless nights and that had dealt a severe blow to the Carberry's social conscience. Jake and Verda find it most uncomfortable to be in a position where word might get out that their daughter is living with a man, unmarried, in an apartment in Toronto. Telephone calls are unpleasant. The word 'apartment' scarcely wants to be spoken, as if her mother is saying 'den of iniquity' instead of 'apartment,' vice strangling the word in her throat. Her father won't speak to her over the telephone, allotting the task of negotiating and establishing the rules of the game to his wife. Nor will Mrs. Carberry speak Dan's name. The conversation begins, "Is *he* there still?" And when *he* is still there, Isabelle is ordered to move out the very next day into a room in a boarding house. Jake and Verda will pay the rent and any other expenses.

"No. I'm staying with Dan," Isabelle tells her mother, a great lump of emotion swelling in her throat.

"Well, dear, your father is not pleased."

"How do you mean that?"

"He's going to drive to Toronto next Sunday to bring you home."

"I won't go."

"I don't think you'll have a choice."

Tears are welling up in Isabelle's eyes. Before her mother called, she and Dan decided it was time to have the whole business aired and had made plans to fly to Montreal.

"If you could meet us at the airport, the four of us could spend Sunday afternoon together," Isabelle reasons to her mother.

She has bought a new outfit and decides to wear it on this trip, to show her parents how her sophistication and fashion knowledge has blossomed. Aglow with her maturity, Isabelle walks into the airport terminal all smiles and poise as she tries to be nonchalant in her modish pale grey organdie ensemble. The blouse buttons conservatively up the front to a round lace collar at the neck, has long voile sleeves, and miniature pleats have been stitched in place along the length of the bodice. The fully gathered skirt is fashionably short, stopping an inch above her knees. Pilgrim-style black patent shoes, with chunky heels and large gold buckles sitting high on the square toes, complete the costume.

"Jesus!" says Jake to his wife when he spies his daughter coming towards them in the arrivals deck. "She looks ridiculous. What's the matter with that girl?"

The trip to the living room in Wakeham from Dorval airport is cold and icy that summer day in June '68. Nothing is accomplished as far as Dan and Isabelle can see. Jake and Verda Carberry are still adamantly opposed to the living conditions, even more vehement about Isabelle not considering their wishes in deciding to live with Dan. They misunderstand the purpose of the young people's visit, thinking they have come to offer an apology for their foolishness and to say they have made other more appropriate living arrangements. For their part, Dan and Isabelle want to explain how they feel about each other, that they are going to live together no matter what, and that the social consequences of such behaviour are nil.

"Well, I guess that's that."

"Yes, it is," says Isabelle to her father in an unexpected waft of courage.

"Are you going to get married then?"

Isabelle, wide-eyed, the idea hasn't occurred to her before this, looks at Dan, and Dan looks down into the drink he is holding on his knee. "We haven't thought about it," says Isabelle with a timid smile.

"Ungrateful little bitch," Jake Carberry mutters loud enough to be heard. "We thought we brought you up properly." He gets up and goes to the kitchen to fix himself another drink.

Mr. Carberry returns and presents a list of will-not-attend's in a display of anger that Isabelle hasn't seen before. He refuses to attend her upcoming graduation and refuses to come to their wedding, should they have one. An impasse has been reached and it is time to leave for another frigid ride back to the airport. This time Anna and her friend Claire are in the backseat of the car with Dan, his long legs folded so that his knees reach chin level. Isabelle climbs into the center of the front seat, straddling the hump in the middle of the floor with her feet, leaving the more comfortable window position to her mother who is slightly on the plump side. Anna and Claire are on Dan and Isabelle's side, Anna enjoying the fact that her older sister is defying the girls' parents' wishes. The stifled sounds coming from the backseat are unintelligible to those riding up front, except to Isabelle, who knows the gist of the conversations without hearing the words.

The apartment in Toronto seems welcome that night, a quiet refuge from the storm. Louisa and Jim are also living in Toronto this summer and are expecting their baby around the end of June. Parental traumatisms are fresh in their memories and they commiserate with Dan and Isabelle. Jim thinks, if given enough time, the Carberry's will gradually calm down, everything will be fine, and life will roll along smoothly again. But oh the bumps along the road! The potholes appear to be out of all proportion with the rest of the journey.

Dan and Isabelle think seriously of marriage. One weekend, they drive to Niagara Falls to escape the Toronto atmosphere and to perhaps see a different aspect to life. Largely to appease Isabelle's parents, they do decide to get married. There is also an income tax advantage, Dan muses, although he keeps this thought to himself. The following weekend, Isabelle goes to graduation sporting a white gold ring with a large diamond that Dan made a good deal on in a Toronto pawnshop. Mr. Carberry is there with his Polaroid taking enough photos to fill an album. The wedding day will be August the 31st, just a little over two months away. A new flurried hurry takes over, wedding plans are at the top of the agenda, and Isabelle makes another flight from Toronto to Montreal to discuss the arrangements with her mother.

Tired of arguing, the young duo thinks it best to keep the wedding traditional in order to avoid any more confrontations. They would have preferred to write their own vows, leaving out the honour and obey promises, or to have a small civil ceremony in front of a justice of the peace. Visiting the minister is put off until the week before the day of the marriage. Neither Dan nor Isabelle believe in God, both having been disenchanted with the church, and they don't care to hear what Reverend Paulson will have to tell them.

The morning of the wedding, Isabelle sleeps in. Jake stands at the doorway to her bedroom calling her name several times before she stirs from a deep sleep. It takes a little time to reorient herself from that filmy region outside of reason, thinking the 'Isabelle, Isabelle' she hears is coming from inside a dream. Jake reminds her of the day's import. "It's getting late, Isabelle, you'd better get up now. Your mother has lots for you to do... You're getting married today, you know."

The present dawns on Isabelle's face with a disquieting murmur and she rolls over to get comfortable again under the covers. Jake sees behind the face and wonders what will become of his headstrong daughter. She has grown away from him in the past years. He hardly recognizes the small self with the dark eyes like his own who used to play games with him and laugh and screech when he tossed her in the air or swirled her around in a circle by one arm and one foot. "Again, Daddy! Again! Swing me some more!" Her thoughts are indecipherable now. The designs taking form in his mind serpentine by sheet like and membranous, and hold a troubling uneasiness. He wants to pick her up, hold her as he used to when she was his little girl, carry her far away, elope with her to someplace where he can look after her, save and protect her from a hard and unforgiving world.

The ceremony is simple, the sunny day is magnificent, and the wedding party is colourful. Jake swears up and down he isn't going to wear no white dinner jacket with a purple whatchamacallit flower pinned on the lapel and a black bow tie around his neck like a monkey's uncle. "No goddamned way. No sirree bob. Hell will freeze over and burn up all over again before you catch me in that sort of a getup."

"But Dad, you have to. Just this once. It won't hurt that much. Dan and the best man and the ushers are wearing the same outfit and it has to match the bridesmaids' dresses."

"Hogwash."

But Jake gives in to Isabelle with a little persuasive help from Verda and he looks dapper in spite of himself. When the first triumphant notes of *The Wedding March* herald the purpose of the day, Jake gives his arm to his daughter and leads her down the aisle to where Dan, Reverend Paulson, and the wedding party are waiting at the front of the church. Loudly proclaiming the exultation of new beginnings, the organ strains trumpet throughout the place of worship, sonorous and solemn, abject and sublime, gathering volume, pass through the open doors and windows, and bleed into the summer day beyond for all to hear. What seem to be heavenly flocks bursting into hallelujah choruses resound in Isabelle's ears. But perhaps the singing is not praising but warning. Perhaps the noise contains a different note, unintelligible to Isabelle on this red-letter day, yet equally capable of inducing high spirits or triggering a rash of goosebumps on your arm. We do hear what we want. Whether or not Dan hears leagues of divine creatures singing songs of love, dear Reader, and whether or not they cause a fluttering in his soul also, are questions never posed.

"Does anyone have any just cause why this man and this woman should not be united in holy matrimony?" Reverend Paulson asks the congregation that fills all the pews in the building. Several of Isabelle's high school chums are sitting in the audience. In the seconds that follow the Reverend's question they look around in their seats, half expecting Cordell, Isabelle's high school boyfriend, to come swinging down on a long rope from the upstairs balcony at the back of the church shouting, "I do, Rev, I do!" The seconds pass, no one interferes, and Verda's friend, Phoebe, sings a solo while the bride and groom are in the vestry signing the register. The next day, Dan and Isabelle leave for the Bahamas for a week. There was only one hitch in the plans– Isabelle's wedding gown didn't arrive on time.

Mrs. Carberry flew to Toronto one day to help her daughter choose a dress. They found a beautiful one. Long and elegant in creamy white satin, the skirt was topped with a fitted bodice of sculpted lace. There were alterations to be done, so the shop was going to mail the dress to Wakeham when the seamstress had completed the work. Once the package had been duly sent from the wedding boutique, Isabelle and her mother watched the mail every day but a parcel notice was never sitting in the postbox. Finally, with the big day nearing and the dress not arriving, Isabelle tried on a girlfriend's sister's wedding dress to see how it would fit, just in case the worst would happen. The morning of the wedding, Isabelle was at the hairdressing salon when Mrs. Carberry telephoned.

"Hello, Madeleine. I hope I'm not calling at a bad time. It's Verda Carberry. Can I speak to Isabelle for a second?"

"Sure, Verda. Got some last minute arranging to do?"

"God love ya, dear. If I live through this I'll be good to a hundred."

"Isabelle's under the hair dryer, Verda. Give me a second to turn it off and pass the phone to her."

"Thanks, Madeleine."

"Hi. Is that you Mum?"

"It is, dear. The Toronto shop just called."

"Don't tell me."

"The dress was returned to them by the Post Office."

"Hell's bells. What a pile of ...."

"What dear?"

"Nothing."

"Whoever prepared the parcel for mailing wrote the address as Wakeham, Ontario instead of Wakeham, Quebec and the parcel traveled around Ontario before being delivered back to the sender, 'Address Unknown'."

"I had a feeling all along that it wouldn't arrive on time."

"I guess I did too, dear, but I didn't want to shatter any hope you might have had."

"Thanks, Mum."

So Isabelle was married in someone else's dress.

A Nugget of Sunshine

A romp in the spring rain. Young cheetahs in the wild. An amusement park with free admission before too much sweet and sticky cotton candy turns to glutinous porridge. Married life is a shining jewel for the first six months, carefree and high-spirited, like the euphoria preceding a demise.

The newlyweds rent an apartment in Kingston, Ontario so Dan can finish his studies at the university. They love to distraction. Intoxicated with the newness of being husband and wife, they flaunt their status as a student married couple until the weight of the non-exceptional brings another reality. When it comes down to the nuts 'n bolts of the matter, Dan doesn't like being beholden to one person, resents the matrimonial arrangement, and becomes more and more elusive. Isabelle does nothing to help the burgeoning troubles. Feeling Dan's aloofness, she distances herself from the estrangement, sets her course in another orbit, as a pilot would adjust a flight plan to avoid stormy weather. A job working at the university library occupies her days, but most of the time it is just a step above boredom. She is elated when asked to work on special projects that require researching in the underground levels of stacks of old books where she is able to browse unobserved through the cool labyrinth of bulging shelves. One week, the psychology section, notably the annals of the British Psychical Society of the early 1900's, receive a good perusal. Shrouded shapes in a dim séance room illuminated only by flickering wall candles sit about a round table, playing cards promenade over the tabletop to spell out names and words, chairs rise into the air, spoons fly off in all directions, phantom lights hurl themselves at the wall and ceiling, women shriek and faint. The following week, classic literature is the main interest. So that's who Thomas Mann is! Amazing! Then the old boys of ancient philosophy are resurrected from their tombs, their voices echoing through the ages, still eloquent and wise. What a panoply of thoughts lie in those pages! What power to fascinate! Words make her real. They create a mooring that keeps her from drifting off into uncharted territory where a language beyond words vibrates in unspoken tomes that blame and injure.

Isabelle can tag along with Dan to his many activities if that catches her fancy; if she doesn't care to follow, that doesn't matter either. There's little they dare talk about, being unable to find the right words or finding that when the real sentiment does come it is too late, arriving out of context, and the mood has past. There was a time in the beginning, albeit of short duration, when their words to each other touched a chord inside that inspired one and uplifted the other. But they can't reach each other anymore, two hayseeds in

47

the wind. Discussion and communication are limited to the preparation of the grocery list, or how many times did your mother call this week, Dan? A suffering silence hangs heavy in the marital atmosphere.

"I need to see you, Louisa."

One day in early April 1970, Isabelle calls the only person to whom she feels close. Louisa and Jim and their twenty-month old daughter, Sarah, who is already tall and has her mother's distinction, are still living in Toronto. Jim works for an engineering firm. They have moved into the basement apartment of an older house in a residential section of the city. Tall straight maples and elms, their wide boughs interlocking overhead and forming a shady canopy, grow along an avenue of quaint and cared-for family homes. A set of swings, a peaked-roof doghouse with a name affixed over the front door–Rover, Skippy, Poncho, Bowser, Max–and a sandbox well-furnished with toys stand in the back yard of each, a low picket fence keeping the area snug and secure. Painted white gingerbread trims the gables on the ridged roofs of the red brick dwellings that line both sides of the street. Small dormer windows looking out of musty attics keep a vigilant watch on the friends and neighbours who live up and down the lane. It's an intimate and unsophisticated city scape that Harold Town would choose for a painting.

A short vacation with Louisa is what is uppermost in Isabelle's mind, a few weeks to hear laughter and be silly and reminisce. She and Jim were unable to attend the wedding in Wakeham at the end of that fateful summer and Isabelle misses Louisa.

Dan drives her to Toronto. Perhaps being someplace that is free of tension will soothe and heal the small sores that have erupted over the past year. Surely these are minor irritations, comparable to those of a housekeeping nature, like cleaning out the cupboard under the sink or scrubbing the floor. Unpleasant and time-consuming but do-able. They are never ugly to each other, not down and out ugly. This is nothing that a fresh perspective can't change. Won't it be healthy to be away from each other for a time? A kind of deep breathing exercise to invigorate and renew. They are young, dear knows, merely twenty-two. They can be forgiven for immaturity, for lust, for impatience, for young hearts that aren't quite sure of where they want to be. Theirs are passionate hearts, tender young hearts, hearts that deserve an interlude if that's what is required to begin afresh.

Spring arrives early in Toronto. The mild breezes and warm showers are cleansing not only for the earth. Isabelle feels a new lease on life, drinks in the air like a bud thirsty for water, feels the gauge on the pressure cooker adjusting downward. The atmosphere is electric with tense promises. Yonge Street teems with young people sensing the coming of another outdoor season. Louisa and Isabelle talk, walk, shop, and sit in the outdoor cafés of The Village relishing fresh coffee and bagels and the glorious afternoon sun. Sarah accompanies them everywhere.

Into the first week, Louisa makes an appointment for Isabelle with her own gynecologist because her menses are still irregular, on a few months, off a few. Isabelle's doctor in Kingston is baffled. There doesn't seem to be any reason for her erratic system. He performed a 'D and C', a cleaning out of her uterus, a few months previous thinking that might help to regulate the flow, but it still prefers its own disorderliness, being out of regular service and unmappable.

"Four months?" Isabelle isn't sure she hears what this new doctor is saying, or that he means what she hears. "A baby?"

"Are you surprised?"

"Well, yes. I don't see how that's possible."

"No? You're very pregnant, my dear."

"But I thought you were supposed to have morning sickness and food cravings and dizzy spells. And I haven't gained a lot of weight, at least I don't think I have. Don't pregnant people gain weight?"

"Not always. Pregnancies vary. By the size of what I can feel, I would say the baby is due around August."

"August."

"That's right. 'Round about that time. Do you have someone with you, Miss?"

"With me?"

"Do you have a boyfriend?"

"Of course, I do." Isabelle moves her hand to where he can see the ring on her finger and throws the words at him, "My husband!" She doesn't like this doctor's attitude and his manner of standing too close to her at the examination table.

"I'll open a file for you, dear. You'll need another appointment in a week's time. There are more tests I'd like to do."

"Oh, thanks, but I'll not be staying here," she says, climbing off the table and covering herself with the short blue examination gown as she goes to find the clothes she left on the hook behind a folding screen. She dresses and leaves as quickly as possible, whispering to herself as she walks out of the doctor's office. The baby. The baby. He said, The baby.

"What? You're pregnant? In August? Oh, Isabelle, dear sweet Isabelle." Louisa can't help being theatric. "What will you do? This morning you were leaving Dan, yesterday you were ready to start a new career. You enrolled in design classes…. Well, I guess you never know what's around the corner, do you? … What are you going to do?"

"I'm calling Dan."

Isabelle telephones Dan late that evening. He has just come in the door when the phone rings.

"Dan, it's me." He sounds tired. "Are you okay?"

"Sure."

"I went to see Louisa's doctor this afternoon and we're going to have a baby." There's no point in beating around the bush with Dan.

The other end of the line is silent for a few seconds and a flash thought occurs to her that he probably knew anyway, then, "I thought so."

"You thought so? How?"

"I don't know."

"But why did you think that?"

"I just knew." Dan always surprises her.

"Why didn't you say something?"

"There was nothing to say."

"Well, I don't know how you knew, I didn't have a clue. Crazy, eh?"

"It is."

"Can you come to Louisa's, Dan? I'd like to be at home now."

Dan drives to Toronto the next day. He, Isabelle, Louisa, and Jim laze on the floor cushions in the living room, chatting and reminding each other of life's surprises. "Expect what you don't expect, Dan. ... You *are* married, you know. That's part of the deal. ... I'm not sure I could handle a little Dan, Dan. Better hope for a girl. She and Sarah could be best friends, but you know... if it's a boy... the in-law thing? Better be a girl if you want my opinion...Go on. Get outa here." Only half listening to the others talking, Isabelle quietly enters the world of her mind, her mindspace, to feel her own precious happiness. The little person inside gives her a new purpose, a new meaning. Even if Dan is absent, her place is with him, and she will create a perfect home for their new baby.

Pregnancy is a special time. Isabelle has never felt better. She cooks and cleans, sews dresses for her new shape, buys tiny cotton shirts and fleecy sleepers, hangs wallpaper, and decorates the baby's room to romance her dreams. A hooded wicker bassinet, which comes dusty and broken from Callah's attic, is transformed with yards of pale blue dotted muslin and soft white jersey sheeting into the centerpiece of the nursery.

Dan goes about his own affairs, attending classes, studying at the library, playing either golf or bridge or poker. He's a good bridge player, remembers all the bids, and figures out who holds which cards. He chuckles and giggles to himself out of sheer pleasure when he executes a Tasmanian finesse on his opponents and the cards fall exactly the way he has tagged them. In self-defense, Isabelle learns to play contract bridge and accompanies Dan to a few tournaments, but isn't prepared for the seriousness of the concentrated silence during the play when even a cough receives a raised eyebrow. How can anyone enjoy a game when they know they will be raked over the coals and given an on-the-spot lesson in Goren's game rules if they make a mistake? Isabelle finds it nerve wracking, too punishing, and eventually Dan collects his American Contract Bridge League master points by himself.

The poker boys have a language all their own–ten twenty, twenty forty, seven-card stud, high low, Texas draw, Chicago, no limit hold 'em, spit in the ocean. Life is a taut zinger for the duration of a poker game, everything else inconsequential. "You play the man, not the game," Dan tells her. He watches the cards as they're dealt, discretely studying the players' faces and telling himself who has made what combination. Raise or hang up, fold or hang tough, time out, all in, a flush draw, a full house, overhand run up, the double duke, the wheel–card shark talk. To rile his opponents, Dan enthusiastically over bets the pot, making it look like he has a sure thing, increasing his chances to win on a bluff. Or he hesitates, ponders, and fidgets with his earlobe, rolling up the flap, pulling on it, flipping it back and forth, when he wants the guys to think his holding is shaky, making them add to the pot in the center of the table. Then he'll go all in and win with his trump cards. The boys call him 'Mad Dog.' He loves the rush from a good gamble.

Dan teaches Isabelle the game of golf so she can come with him to the club. The meticulous landscaping is noble and fine. The damp odour of green permeates the air as she searches for her ball in the cushiony blankets of pine needles lying on the floor of each small wood along the course. The vigour and quiet of the outdoors make her breathe deeply in the freshness, savouring the clean pungent aroma that cools the inside of her lungs, but she can't muster much enthusiasm over hitting the ball and chasing after it for hours. The more pregnant she becomes, the better her excuse not to play.

The summer is hot and sultry. At the beginning of August Isabelle's time is approaching but the baby is not in a rush to make a statement and, by mid-August, Dan is fed up hanging around Kingston to be near the hospital. Some friends, Tom and Arlene, have a summer cottage on a lake near Verona, about fifteen miles north of the city. Dan has docked his boat on their wharf and when the day is nice they spend it at the lake. The first blush of morning on the thirteenth of August is stifling with haze and heat. The windless air hangs low and heavy like an opiate drunk with its own sweetness. Throngs of cicadas begin their high-pitched summer buzz long before noon, the one-note screech confirming the outdoor temperature. After packing a lunch, Dan and Isabelle head to the lake. The usual gang of friends, having had the same notion, has already arrived to wallow in the hot laziness of the unexpected dog days in the ripening summer. Some are sitting in the shade out of the scorching sun, others are in the lake, cooling off. Arlene barbecues steak and hamburgers on the grill, while Tom rigs the boat for anyone who wants to water-ski.

Lingering on past suppertime, Dan and Isabelle are reluctant to leave. An evening by the lake is beautiful when the stillness descends and the orange sun ripples across the water like vermilion music, silvery-red notes sinking below the surface reflections to the painted sand on the bottom, a summer rendering of what is perfect. It's too hot to be in a stuffy city apartment. Another couple, Meg and Jer, have rented a cabin on the other side of the lake, so Dan, Isabelle, Tom, and Arlene decide to pay them a visit. Driving into the camp from the highway is difficult, the road being not much better than a cow path, so all four go in the motor boat. Dan drives, and speedily, as is his wont. At the first sharp blows of the prow of the boat slapping the water, Isabelle gasps and holds tight, bracing herself a few inches above the seat to cushion the strikes. Her belly puffs up like a blowfish, swells like the sea after a storm, turning and churning with waves that don't break but build into crescendos, rising, recoiling, rising, recoiling, readying to burst but then choosing otherwise.

"Slow down!" Arlene yells to Dan, but he doesn't hear a sound over the din of the motor and the wail of the wind that clamours in his ears. The boat is half way across the lake before Dan looks around to see Isabelle's discomfort and Arlene motioning to him to cut back the speed.

The assault quiets during the last quarter mile. Hidden amongst the trees as it is, the cabin is hard to spot from the water, but Meg and Jer see the boat heading towards them and wave from the shore. The guys feel like a bridge game and Meg joins in to make a foursome. Arlene and Isabelle make themselves comfortable in another corner of the living room and chat about men.

"Dan pick up his clothes?"

"No way. His mother ran around after him like a personal servant."

"Tom doesn't either. I get so mad at him. He'll rush in the apartment late from a card game, bang the door shut like it never occurred to him I might be sleeping, drop his clothes in a pile on the bedroom floor right where he takes them off, leave them turned inside-out, jump into bed, and expect me to be in a good mood."

"Exactly. The only things they're concerned about, as far as I can make out, is winning and sex."

"Watch out when one or the other isn't going their way."

"Do you notice how all of a sudden they've got a pile of schoolwork when there's work to be done around the house?"

"And how."

"Then they'll be so cute that you can't help laughing and loving them."

It's close to ten o'clock when Isabelle levers herself up off the couch, kneads her stiffened back muscles with her fingers, and ambles to the washroom. She intends to sit on the loo for just a minute then return to Arlene in the front room, but the water won't stop. It floods out in a wet gush like a plugged drain set free and she can't turn it off. Arlene goes to investigate when Isabelle takes longer than expected and knows immediately what's coming. When the water slows, she finds a pillow for Isabelle to hold between her legs and they go back to watch the bridge game in progress. Isabelle feels fine, just a little damp, and stretches out on the sofa, reclining her back against the arm and keeping the pillow in position. Soon a muscle pulls together. It draws itself into a fist and then another hardens. And another. Arlene starts to get excited.

"Come on guys! There's going to be a baby here!"

"Wait a minute, Lenie. This is important."

"Guys! Don't leave me alone!"

"I'm here, hon," answers Tom.

"Meg, where's the telephone?"

"There isn't any."

"No telephone? Swell."

"This is our getaway space, remember?"

"Well, that's just hunky-dory, Meg."

"What now?"

"Tom, you and Dan have to go back across the lake to our cottage and phone Isabelle's doctor."

"Right now?"

"Yes, right now!"

"You're not kidding, are you?"

"Not for a sec."

"What do we say to the doctor?"

"Ask him what to do? Jeez, Tom."

"No way."

"I'll talk to him, Tom."

"Right, Dan. Tell him the water has burst. And guys, make sure you've got enough gas with you in the boat."

"Will do. We're on our way. C'mon Dan."

Shortly, Dan is talking to Dr. Nicholson at his home. "Bring her to the hospital, Dan. I can't be there, but the intern who has been working with me is there tonight. He knows Isabelle and there shouldn't be any complications."

The road into the cabin is rough but passable. Dan jumps in his car and takes the highway that winds around the lake. Tom goes back across the water in the boat to report to Isabelle, Arlene, Meg, and Jer. The contractions are pretty regular now, several minutes apart, but Isabelle is doing well, even amused at all the fuss. It's near midnight when Dan arrives back to the cabin. Obviously shaken, he hardly speaks, just waits for Arlene to tell him what to do. Tom guides Isabelle out to the car between cramping and helps her into the front seat of Dan's yellow convertible. Sitting won't do and Dan is already behind the wheel ready to take off, so Isabelle arranges herself on her back, rests her head on Dan's thigh, and extends her legs out the window, holding the pillow between. Arlene gives Dan an elastic band, which he wraps around his finger, just in case, and they're off.

The car inches along at a snail's pace, twitching and jerking spasmodically around the rocks and boulders that contort the path from the camp out to the highway, the second rough ride of the evening bringing on more contractions. As soon as Dan reaches the paved surface of the road, the speedometer needle shakes and wavers on the far right of the dial. Had it been daytime, the blur of noise on the highway would have been a streak of yellow sunlight. Entering the city limits of Kingston they speed through the intersections without stopping. A police car, the siren wailing and approaching the realm of non-hearing, red flashers accusing, chases after Dan and forces him to pull over to the side of the street. Within seconds, two young uniformed cops are at the side of the flagrant vehicle beaming a spotlight into Dan's face and lighting up Isabelle's belly, her legs sticking out the window, the pillow between, the rounded bulbous body and long thin legs of an upturned spider.

"Jesus Murphy," mutters one of the policemen.

"What's the elastic for?" the other asks Dan.

"Darned if I know."

"Which hospital are you headed for?" continues the first officer.

"Hotel Dieu."

"Fast, obviously."

"Come on, guys!" Isabelle is scrunching up her face. "My wife's in labour!"

"Yes, sir. Follow us."

The law enforcement rushes back to the patrol car. The sirens reach a sustained shriek, spinning lights set the night sky on fire once more, the loudly official vehicle pulls in front of Dan, and escorts the pregnant convertible in a reverse order high speed chase through the city streets to the hospital. Two attendants are ready and waiting when the combo speeds into the emergency entrance.

The hospital staff takes over and the panic abates. There's plenty of time for a barrage of tests and Isabelle waits another hour before Alex is born. She waits alone. Dan couldn't stand the wait and left the maternity ward to go to the golf club.

"Do you have a husband, dear? Would you like to call someone?" the recovery room nurse asks Isabelle.

"Yes, if you don't mind."

"I'll bring you a telephone."

"Thanks."

Isabelle dials the Cataraqui Golf and Country Club and asks for Dan.

"Sure, he's here. Hold on a minute. He's in the middle of a bridge hand." She waits.

"What is it?" asks Dan when he answers the phone.

"A boy. You have a son."

"Is he all right?"

"Of course, he's all right. You should see his hair. So cute. It sticks straight up on his head like he's had a fright. Perfect little fingers and toes. He's beautiful."

"I hope he has your looks and my brains."

"Are you coming to see him?"

"It's nearly two o'clock. I'm going home to get some sleep."

"He's coming in the morning," Isabelle tells the nurse as she replaces the receiver.

Jake Carberry drives his wife to Kingston the day Dan brings Isabelle home from the hospital. She is afraid that Alex will catch cold in the open convertible, but Dan rolls his eyes up into his head and gives her an old woman look, so she holds a blanket over Alex's one-week-old face to protect him from the wind and enjoys the sunshine after the stay in the Hotel Dieu baby unit. An old-fashioned floor cradle on curved rockers is sitting in the middle of the kitchen, built by Jake for his new grandson. The rough surface of the cherry wood has been planed and polished by Jake's own hand to a patina finish as smooth as satin. He and Verda are waiting in the Elmsley Street apartment when Dan escorts Isabelle and young Alex through the door. Jake is as pleased as punch. "Well, I'll be damned. Would ya look at the wee laddie? I bet he's got a good set of lungs." Smiling profusely, he pulls a fat cigar tied with a blue ribbon out of his pocket and, with a stylish gesture elaborate for Jake, presents it to his son-in-law.

Verda Carberry has brought her suitcase, prepared to stay an unstated amount of time to help Isabelle look after little Alex. Jake returns that evening to be ready for work the next morning. Dan is gone most of the time, summer courses and exams having finished, but there is golf on fair days and bridge or poker on rainy days. He can't let the boys down; they count on him. Verda cooks real meals with mashed potatoes and gravy and bakes mouthwatering pies with fresh blueberries, so he always manages to come home for supper when he charms and flatters Mrs. Carberry until she blushes.

"Now, I think it's time my favourite mother-in-law had a wee drinky before we sit down to dinner. Don't you think so, Isabelle?"

"Why not?"

"How about it, Mrs. C., just a wee one?"

"Nothing for me, thanks, Dan."

"Oh my nasal nodes! What *is* that odour? They're picking up the sweet smell of baking. What *have* you been up to?"

"It's just a pie." Hee hee, squeal.

"C'mon now, Mrs. C. You must have slaved over a hot oven all afternoon."

"Oh, I wouldn't say that I worked very hard."

"A pretty young lady like yourself needs a little pick-me-up every once in a while."

"Well, if you insist. Tee hee. When you put it like that…"

"At-a-girl, Mrs. C. What'll it be?"

"A little scotch on the rocks would do nicely."

"Whoa! Scotch for a pink lady like you?"

"Oh, Dan, cut it out. Just ignore him, Mum."

"A Singapore Sling. That's a more ladylike drink for you, Mrs. C."

"Have a scotch if you want one, Mum."

"I might even have a wee umbrella to stick in it."

"Tee hee. Just like a fancy drink."

"Then we can sit and have nice chat, just the two of us. What do you think? Eh, Mrs. C.?"

"Oh, all right Dan. Whatever you say. I'll have that slingy thing with the umbrella."

Isabelle appreciates her mother's help during the first few days since she doesn't know how to arrange a diaper. The first dirty one sends her agog. She looks at the runny yellow brown mess holding her breath so not to inhale any more of the smell than necessary, then lets her mother take over. But, after a week of Mrs. Carberry setting the schedule and giving instructions, she has had enough. Up early one day, she completes the morning chores before her mother gets organized. Mrs. Carberry gets the message and the next morning, as the two are eating their breakfast of toast and jam, Dan has left early to play golf, she announces, "I guess I'm of no use here any more."

"It's not that you didn't help me, Mum. I don't know what I'd have done on my own."

"That's what mothers are for."

"I'd like to look after Alex myself now."

"Well, if you think you can manage…."

"Yes, I'll be fine. Just fine. I'm looking forward to it."

"Well, okay, dear."

"I can always call you if I'm in trouble."

"True, there's always the telephone."

"Thanks for staying with me for a week. I appreciate it. Really, I do."

"All right, then. I'll give Jake a call."

Jake arrives to take Verda back to Wakeham that afternoon.

Alex is a good baby. It isn't long before he's sleeping straight through the night. During his first months, he awakens hungry around two in the morning, stirring about making baby noises, but if the cooing and gurgling turn louder, Dan yells, "Shut that baby up! I need my sleep," before Isabelle has time to reach Alex and comfort him with a breast. All the while, unbeknownst to Isabelle, Dan is planning a Christmas holiday in the Caribbean. He convinces her to wean Alex onto the bottle and asks his mother, Callah, to look after Alex while they are away over Christmas.

Dan has decided this life is not for him but in case there is a remedy hiding in the offing, he plans a two-week vacation in Barbados to give a solution a chance to appear, if there is one. The trip is for himself and Isabelle only. Alex isn't invited. Isabelle goes along with the plans, as is her nature, not objecting, fearing disagreements. It's a tender and fickle world that plays with you, that gives then takes away when you least expect it, a world all the more fickle for the absence of a nugget of sunshine at the center of your being. When it isn't there to light your way, you work hard with logistics, balancing advantages and disadvantages, like a marketing exam.

If Dan wants to discuss their non-relationship, Isabelle is not aware of it, nor would she raise the topic for discussion. The subject of relationship has no tab in Dan's index to living and is listed under 'T' for 'trepidation' in Isabelle's. That was one cask best not pierced. The southern island is a favourite sunspot vacation away from the Canadian winter. Besides, Louisa and Jim are now living in Barbados. They both have teaching positions with CUSO, the Canadian University Services Overseas organization. It'll be fun to visit them, thinks Isabelle, and she knows Dan's need to challenge the day to day, to surprise the ordinary flow of happenings. There's something gorgeous about him. He has a romantic sleight of heart, a sensitivity coupled with a galloping readiness for the promises of life, a marriage of opposites with which Figaro would be pleased. He's daring, inventive, unpredictable, and everything turns into an exciting adventure with Dan. That's what she likes about him, that and his impressive stature and good looks. She tries not to think of Alex. Putting hurtful things away somewhere and not allowing life to sabotage her heart is something at which she is very good. She can make that tender spot into an unfeeling place where whatever is contained within remains a mystery. It's a deathly habit, a survival mechanism learned a long time ago.

For two weeks they live at the ocean-side Sunset Crest Villa. The days are splendiferous with choice–sightseeing around the island in a canopied mini-moke, golfing for Dan, shopping for Isabelle, snorkeling, swimming, tanning, reading, eating gourmet dinners of the day's fresh catch from the sea. In the evenings, waist coated waiters on the beach parade about with an assortment of cool liquids balanced on a round tray at the end of their fingertips while the sweet piercing sounds of native steel drums claim the Caribbean nights as their own. They are rich and privileged twenty-three year-olds: Dan, a student, a husband, and a father with a wife and child who disturb him; Isabelle, the disturbing wife and mother, without her child. Isabelle isn't sure of the exact source of the money. Perhaps Dan asked his mother. Callah can never deny anything to her only child upon whom the sun rises and sets.

One evening, a steel band is playing by the ocean. Dan and Isabelle have a few drinks as usual after dinner and join the night crowd on the beach. The resounding beat of the drums, their echoing tones and melancholy timbre reach a counterpart in Isabelle, hollow on hollow. The haunting notes touch a haunted heart and she feels like singing. She feels like releasing a mournful, yet beautiful, little spirit into the sky so it can sprout wings and fly off on its own. Slowly, she makes her way to the tent stage on the sand, farther away from the thronging chatter. The melodies are familiar Beatle tunes. *Yesterday, all my troubles seemed so far away! Now it looks as though they're here to stay, Oh, I believe in yesterday. ... Listen, Do you want to know a secret, Do you promise not to tell, Whoa oh, oh, Closer, let me whisper in your ear...* She joins in, timidly at first, then in full voice. One of the band members invites her to come closer and sing with a microphone. Low and inarticulate sounds, like a distant humming, are barely audible until she lets herself go, then a foreign unfamiliar voice surprises her with its clear intensity. She isn't aware of the crowd listening. When she does look outwards, there is Dan, off to the corner, standing apart from the others, staring at his incomprehensible wife, an insulted and angry look freezing his features, in short, he's had an overdose of humiliation. She watches him leave.

Isabelle doesn't care. She feels triumphant. When the song is over she joins in on another one then walks back to the villa to take whatever disdain is coming. Dan is in bed when she arrives. She quietly undresses, slides in beside him expecting a long string of recriminations to start in at any second, but Dan just rolls over, turning his back to her, and, without saying a word, goes off to sleep.

Back from the holiday, they travel out to the farm at Willow River.

Isabelle thinks Alex doesn't recognize her. Changed somehow, he looks much older than he did when she left him two long weeks ago. Callah has arranged a play mattress on the dining room table and Alex is having the time of his life. Lying on his stomach, he is curved upwards like a little tugboat in high seas, head in the air, arms and legs flailing and kicking. Is that my baby? Isabelle watches the intent gleam on his face. He is proving something. Look at me! Look at me! Look see what I can do! Before picking him up to hold him close to her, Isabelle hesitates a moment. He doesn't seem to belong to her any longer. What if he doesn't react to her, as if he's forgotten who she is? A sacred covenant has been severed, an enormous crime committed, and she is the perpetrator.

Holidays are supposed to make you feel better, take you away from the ordinary spin of events and rejuvenate your spirits. Isabelle doesn't feel any better. She feels worse, torn apart, guilty, and cruel. She tries to make it up to Alex, never leaving him for a minute. Dan is arriving at his own conclusions, privately interpreting his future, and won't hold his son. Nothing will rectify the union. It had been given a chance to redeem itself and had revealed itself for the way it was, hopeless, a tiresome relative who has worn out her welcome. No point in trying to revive the old tart. Just checking in to eat and sleep, Dan spends as little time as he can at the apartment. The ideal family of which Isabelle has dreamed turns into a dreary landscape of housekeeping, cooking, and diapers on her own.

Controlled by forces that start to knot inside, Isabelle begins to feel trapped in a hostile terrain, a warring world of disparate elements without a pillar to hold onto. She craves for nourishment, for discussion, for the inspiration of the theatre and music and books, she yearns for love.

During the winter, a school friend, Tony, invites her to attend a play with him in Toronto. Three go for the weekend–Tony, Isabelle, and little Alex. Tony succeeds in getting her to talk about what she is feeling and suggests it would be a good thing if she could cry at least a little. Isabelle does let go of the crushing hurt that is suffocating her and is forced to face a marriage in rack and ruin. A wolf has been lurking at the door for months, if not years, and there was no point in keeping it at bay any longer. Her life with Dan has to come to an end; she has to get on her own with her baby. More of an idealist than a pragmatist, she doesn't know how she will manage alone with her young son but the details are of far less importance than being free of a relationship where inside there is nothing.

Isabelle and Alex arrive back to the Kingston apartment on Sunday afternoon. When Dan arrives later that evening, she breaks the news that she has to leave. Dan isn't surprised, saying, "I knew that day would come." For one last time, she feels his old hypnotism exercise its power over her senses, his superiority that always knew of things that she didn't, his arrogance floating in layers of truth upon truth, or deception upon deception. The anarchy is entangled with love in the moonlight and foreign cut-off places to which she has no access. They agree to separate at the end of May, after the year-end examinations. And so it happened, sensitivities giving way with minimal drama, that two hopeful young people quit one another's company after only two years and eight months of marriage. Alex is nine months old when Isabelle brings him with her to Ottawa.

Spiderwebs

Like a broken watch without an energy cell, which leaves one no longer able to keep track of time, the next six years in Ottawa are dark and shapeless. A day, or sometimes the whole week, appears to shrink to dimensions other than its normal duration, a minute becoming a second and an hour becoming a minute. Time whizzes by so fast it conforms to no ordinary calibration or is so unnoticeable it seems to desist altogether. But then other days, or an entire month, will take on ponderous never-ending proportions and proceed at a snail's pace when even her mental faculties seem to shilly-shally, the slightest decision taking her an eternity to make. A confusing state, or rather, it is the state of confusion that skews our experience of time, as a gravitational field will warp the space around it manifesting the most bizarre effects where the reality of our five senses is no longer trustworthy. It is much like a curious dream in which time is relieved of all principles from the earthly realm and undergoes either surreal diminutions or vast expansions as simple to navigate as a child's balloon. One can fly through a dream space at an astronomical rate, passing over rivers and continents and ages as if they and time have been miniaturized and compressed by a movie director into an abridged version for the theatre screen. One can also play a game of fast and competitive tennis where you are lunging at the speeding ball for match point and suddenly time has been curtailed, slowed down so that you and the ball are in slow motion, in complete harmony with each other's intentions, and you make the perfect impossible connection between your outstretched racket and the ball, winning the game. The irony is that fast is slow and slow is fast depending on where you're at, a conundrum so wearying to assimilate into one or two lines of reasoned thought that one gives up trying to understand the chaos and just accepts what is. So, although Isabelle finds it difficult to tell exactly how long an interval lasts by relying on her common sense, she replaces the expired wall calendar six times during her stay in the nation's capital.

It's spring of 1971. She rents a small apartment in the east end of the city. A job in a university library, which she finds not long after arriving, is an hour's bus ride away and pays her a salary just large enough to cover the rent, food, and other necessities. The babysitter, Dora, who is not yet twenty, lives in the same building, which is convenient for taking Alex to her in the early morning and picking him up at night, but not an ideal arrangement. She looks after several youngsters who are older and more rambunctious than Alex who possesses a quiet disposition. A day at Dora's is a free-for-all–playing, laughing, teasing, arguing, fighting, screaming. Isabelle supposes that the

61

income pays her rent since Dora is alone. A year later, the university starts a daycare service for the personnel on the staff and she brings Alex with her on the daily bus ride across the city. As part of the program, she spends five hours a week with the children and pulls herself out of bed at five every weekday morning. That allows enough time to eat breakfast with Alex and get themselves ready before leaving the building at six-thirty. At the daycare by eight, she plays with Alex and his young companions for an hour, then works at the library from nine to five. It is often six-thirty in the evening or later before arriving back to her modest but clean little abode in AltaVista. The traveling routine, the long waits for city buses, and the constant noise and activity of daycare are irritants to be suffered as best one can. Isabelle is positive that they hurt Alex's gentle nature, but there isn't an alternative in sight.

One day, Isabelle thinks she has lost her child. A monitor from the daycare telephones the library to say Alex is sick. "He's vomiting up everything we give him, Ms. Carberry. I think he has a touch of the flu," she says. Apprehensive, Isabelle leaves work to take him home. Soon she's on the phone talking to Dan's mother, Callah, in Willow River, thirty miles outside the city. A lengthy conversation ensues after which Isabelle slowly replaces the receiver in its cradle on the telephone that sits on the counter top between the kitchen and the living room, sensing that something large and not exactly good-natured has just taken place. Her mother-in-law has talked her into letting Alex stay with her at the farm during the workweek.

She takes the bus to see Alex on weekends. On occasion, Robinson and Callah will drive into the city with their grandson late Friday afternoon, arriving just after she's home from work, and will return on Sunday night to bring him back to the Willow River farm. During the week Isabelle pulls a veneer over herself. Everything's okay, I'm just fine. Nothing's the matter. How she loves to see Alex's little face on the weekends, but her heart breaks every time she has to leave him.

An old pattern resurfaces. When her emotions are too intense, she feels a tightness, a craziness inside, except now it is more severe. Even the smallest amount of food won't stay in her stomach. She has to get rid of it otherwise it crawls around inside her body, an alive and gruesome sludge, a fleshy affair of slimy portent that makes her innards squirm. It becomes more and more of an obsession, this bizarre need to purge, to empty, to cleanse and make clean. We have Latin medical names for the behaviour–bulimia nervosa and bulimarexia–we blame it on societal pressures to conform to fashion's wicked standard of thinness for women and give the condition a scientific label from the original Greek *boulimia,* the hunger of an ox–*bous* meaning ox and *limos* meaning hunger. But is not the hunger actually a mad craving for love? The ox all decked out in a masterful costume worthy of the lead actor or prima donna in a grand opera? And the beast must be fed. Is not bulimia an agonized and insatiable desire for that primal emotion that has somehow gone awry? Food is merely a guileless player, a shabby surrogate for the real thing. Of all our God-given instincts, love is the most unstable and vulnerable, the one most susceptible to perversion. When we pin down our real thoughts on the matter, our illusive honest ones that delve to the core and shake our sensibilities, doesn't each form of illness have its roots in love? Or the lack of it? Aren't all of our sicknesses simply manifestations of love in another state?

But Isabelle is unaware of the eerie mutations of love. She walks in a daze, living and breathing on another plateau, trifling with the dangerous side of untended melancholy, putting on a show. *Hey! Look at me! I'm lively and fun, can eat like a horse and don't gain an ounce!* Whatever enters her head is what she does. Should she feel like going for lunch at the university center, she does so, eats heartily, laughs, and discusses animatedly with co-workers. Her opinions and ability to argue at length give her a reputation as outspoken and standing up for her rights, but she will throw up in the washroom on her way back to work.

She is appointed library representative on the university staff association. A large group of office assistants and technical personnel work on the campus and the national union, CUPE, is trying to make an entrance into this pool of employees. Isabelle is opposed to unions. The idealism of the individualistic and money-oriented society in the writings of Ayn Rand have convinced her of the might and right of this philosophy. The Randian world is godless, but so is hers. She fights the union as if defending a personal affront to her own self and becomes one of the key players in foisting the union's attempt to gain a foothold at the university. She talks to whoever will listen about the 'evils' of unionism, how it robs the human spirit of its individuality, how you would become a pawn in their network if you joined. She writes up flyers, distributes them, and shows up unexpectedly at their unpublicized meetings, voicing dissent over misrepresentation, questionable tactics, and psychology. She's passionate. She's angry.

And she's hurting inside. Isabelle is being consumed by a monster who is stronger than she is. She lives in only a small part of her brain, a fluffy unthinking portion, a lightweight section up front just behind her forehead. The rest is in a chaos so dark she is afraid to enter that space for all the evils lingering in the shadows. So she tries to behave as if nothing is wrong, braving the weather, so to speak, in a valiant attempt to ignore the gnawing.

Ariff, a student at the university, spends many hours researching in the library. He seems never to tire of working on one project or another and his conversation fascinates Isabelle. Raised in the Muslim tradition of deep respect for mystics and spiritual practices, he takes to heart the prophecy of an old Arab who read the lines on his palm and told Ariff he had only three more years to live. His latest project is to produce a radio show, a cultural presentation on Asia and he asks Isabelle to join this venture with him.

The Asian Embassies and High Commissions in Ottawa welcome the publicity from this new interest in their countries. They give Ariff and Isabelle music and literature indigenous to the lands they represent, which is then assembled into a half-hour documentary. Each of several nations is provided with a spotlight: India, Burma, Pakistan, Thailand, Malaysia, the Philippines, Indonesia, Brunei, Sri Lanka, Tibet, and Afghanistan. In the radio studio, Ariff and Isabelle talk back and forth to each other about the country they have chosen for that particular program, interspersing their dialogue with local music. Once word of the exposure passes from one diplomat to another, they are invited to many receptions and extravagant parties peopled by the diplomatic entourage. Elite society flaunts an enticing picture of exotic wealth, glitter, and rich pleasures. Young and good-looking, Isabelle can talk about anything from art to politics, can ask the right questions to flatter and please, and fits easily into their fast lifestyle of glamour and notoriety. It's an exciting way to live. In the beginning.

Another friend, Ollie, teaches university courses on the technical aspects of staging drama and television performances. Ollie also produces educational videos for classroom use. He invites Isabelle to act as the host in several of his documentaries. Work in the cataloguing department is humdrum and routine compared to this other world she inhabits. Nevertheless, if she considers her library job an unpleasant duty, it is a necessary one, since it provides the only income she has.

The staff association becomes more active after the threat of unionization. Isabelle is appointed Vice-Chair. The post involves some traveling around the province to meet other university staff associations and she finds the demands becoming stressful instead of challenging. She has jumped at every opportunity to be involved, to forget herself, and some weekends she misses getting out to Willow River to see her son. Recently, however, she has been torn inside over spending time at the farm, but too many weekend activities, late-night parties, and morning-after hangovers keep her in the city anyway. Thinking of the farm raises ambivalent feelings. She is trapped in a dilemma of conflicting loyalties; she wants terribly to see her son but Robinson has fantasized a desire for her and thinks that looking after her son entitles him to be rewarded in some fashion. Trying to avoid him in his own home is a sour game. She tries to make light of his obvious interest in her, of his eyes that follow her every movement, of his offers to visit his Montreal haberdasher who can accommodate his style to tailored women's wear, of his pleas to escape to Toronto for a weekend. But the deceit, the guilt! She is tied to him because he has her son and repulsed by him because he wants her too. One weekend, after a few drinks too many, he waits for her in the hallway. A group of friends have gathered to visit in the thirty-foot long farmhouse living room. Isabelle is coming from the kitchen, through the hallway, to join them. Robinson blocks her path, pushes her against the wall, lays his hands on her breasts, and laughs, "What's the matter? Don't you think I can get it up any more?"

The world becomes an ugly place. The simple act of living is overwhelming. Each event attacks, wounds, yet she is unable to say to anyone, not even to herself, that everything is not all right. She has to keep that stiff upper lip, hold her head high, and plow on. *Shove it under the rug and work harder.* That's what you're supposed to do if anything is troubling you. Whatever the worrisome thing is, it's supposed to go away if you ignore it.

She searches for doctors to help her with sleeplessness, presenting the problem as overwrought nerves brought on by work pressures. She would like to feel a bond, an understanding with the treating physician, secretly hoping that he or she would care enough to ask a bit more about herself, hoping for a connection, hoping, yes, yet not knowing how she would respond if ever invited to elaborate. But each suggests another barbiturate, another sedative to calm and soothe a frazzled temperament. And, for sure, Isabelle is not about to proffer any unasked for information. So no one penetrates through the verbal trappings to the discontent swelling and bubbling in the undertow, to the cry of outraged protest buried at the bottom of a scrapheap, until Dr. Jelinek.

Here is someone different, she thinks, *someone who knows the nature of the beast.* But Dr. Jelinek is just as disturbed as she is.

She leaves his apartment one night in shock. They had spent the evening wining, dining, and dancing at a popular downtown nightclub. Quite a bit older than she, he's in his fifties, but tall, good-looking, and very gallant, playing the part to a fault. They go back to his apartment in the early hours of the morning. The airy one-room flat is sparsely furnished since Dr. Jelinek is in the throws of a marriage dispute and his wife has thrown him out of their house. "This is temporary," he explains, apologizing for the disorder as he bends over to straighten a stack of books that is sitting in the middle of the floor. "I'm rarely here. When I am, I study these medical diagnoses. As you can see the place hardly looks lived in. I spend most of my time at the office. It's my ... what do you young people call it nowadays? ... bachelor pad, it's my bachelor pad until my wife comes around. And she will, come around that is. This isn't the first time. ... I miss my children. ... But there's no harm in entertaining oneself a little in the meantime, is there? Harm in loving? None whatsoever. What's a man to do? Spend his days moping? Life is about living, my love, my precious! It's beautiful like you. Every drop is to be drunk and savoured like a fine wine," says her paramour, kissing the tips of his fingers and releasing the kiss into the air in a lavish gesture. So Dr. Jelinek sits on the floor, resting his back against the wall, and invites Isabelle to sit beside him. She prefers to remain standing. He begins to undo his tie, talking all the while about how much he likes her, how he enjoys her company, how he would oh so love to touch her in the way he would a ruby red cherry he has just plucked from a branch. "I would hold the stem delicately in my fingers and roll the little fruit over and over on my lips, caressing every pore of its smooth skin." The doctor's eyes close as he goes through the motions. "Then I'd stroke the silky flesh with my tongue, up and down, back and forth, before nibbling it off the stem to let the lovely thing fall and tumble inside my mouth. Then I would gently bite the exquisite jewel, very gently, in an invitation to the succulent juice inside to come to me, to adorn me, to tantalize me with its charms. Ah! Oh! Can you imagine with me, Isabelle? Can you imagine the titillation? Can you feel it? How delightful! How perfect! How sweet! How sweet the anticipation!" And would she allow him to caress her? Would she? "Please, Isabelle?"

Not receiving an answer, he raises his hand to his head, resting his long fingers on the top of his forehead for just a second or two, then pulls off a toupee, exposing a bald head. Isabelle is even more horrified than she was a moment earlier. Dr. Jelinek now looks seventy years old and his love is readying to leave. He begs her to stay, pleading over and over to let him touch her, and if she won't let him touch her, then will she let him look at her, please, please? Oh, please, Isabelle? But she runs out and finds a taxi home.

Thoughts are confused, wound around themselves, caught in a tangled web. She starts to panic, feels lost, and afraid. No place is safe. A dark cloud, noxious and angry, gathers inside her head when she is alone in her apartment. It becomes darker and blacker and plunges her into an empty hole where her body and mind ache and cry out, cry into a lonely space where there is no one to hear, or to listen, no one to calm a frightening presence that is threatening to take over, to wipe her out of existence as if she was nothing. There is no reason to live, no reason to be in this life. Inside is a void, a black hole and Isabelle cries out and grasps her head because the hurt is crushing. It whirls in a space where there is nothing to stop it from spinning faster and faster, sucking her into the center, and collapsing her to nothing. The ache torments with a fear of something unknown, a dark nothing that rapes her senses and defeats utterly.

And it won't go away. The hole inside grows emptier. One night, after finishing a bottle of scotch that was sitting in the kitchen cupboard, Isabelle walks into the bathroom and opens the door of the medicine chest. The containers of prescription pills are in the corner of the cabinet. She takes them out and places them on the counter, one beside the other, harmless little cylinders of clear plastic. She reads the labels. *Valium. Dilantin. Phenobarbital. Diazepam.* But there's no need for her to check the names, she knows what they are. She's not checking, she's biding time. She's giving fate a chance to declare itself in the interim, allowing providence to intervene in the space she's allotted, to drop a bomb or to send a police car shrieking down the street. A sign she could recognize, perhaps even react to. Subtle occurrences of unapparent intent aren't likely to make an impression at this point. And that's the way it should be. All's naught if not a truth of some sort.

The night sounds of the city, a traffic mosaic of horns bleating and tires squealing on pavement, are far in the background of her particular landscape. The moon and stars are invisible this night what with the brightness of the city lights and the late September cloud cover, thin, greying, and perverse. Someone in the downstairs apartment has just opened a faucet sending a gush of water surging through the pipes. The only other sounds are that of her own breath rising and falling and the periodic whirring of the refrigerator in the kitchen. She empties the remainder of each bottle onto the palm of her hand. A dolly mixture. Dollies with the ability to take one away, to cancel the show, to render the pain insensible, to remove its power to hurt and injure. She glances at the various shapes and colours, flat, round, oblong, yellow, blue, white, but no more than a slanted glare, a quick survey of the jumbled heap. She knows not to meddle with waiting and pondering. Idling has destroyed many an impulse, nipped it in the bud, quenching forever the initial flame. Strike while the iron is hot. A longer look might change her mind, might raise doubts, and doubt isn't what she wants to feel. Doubt raises suspicion, questions the validity of what one is doing, usurps one's desire. To hesitate, to consider, may allow the farce to continue. That's not an option. She wants an end, a conclusion, or an act that will lead to one. She throws the handful of pills in her mouth and tries to flush them down her throat with a drink of water. *Aaahwk!* She'll choke before she can swallow, dear God, putting a nix on it all, wasting all of this precious emotion. She spits out several onto the counter and one or two clatter to the floor. *Oh no!* More hurry less speed. Where did they go? *Get down on your knees, Isabelle!* I think I'd better get down on my knees. *Look! Find them before the ones in your mouth get to you and make you dopey.* They're already starting to soften! *Hooter! Bazooker! Nellie! Miranda! Hurry, Isy! You need those on the floor.* I need those on the floor. I do. Maybe the mouthful won't do the job. *Then what, Isy? Then what, honey?* More of the same. *That's right, back to where you were.* Good God! Is there no mercy? There's one! *'Ata girl, Isy. You got it, hon!* Now where's the other? Two fell, if not three. *I heard them rattle across the linoleum as well as you did. Nina, Pinta, and Santa Maria! Over there, honey! I see it! Do you see it, Isy? A little more to the left. Okay girl, forget about the third. Don't waste your time. You've enough now.* Okay, I've enough now. There might not even be a third.

She splashes some water into her mouth and gulps down the soggy paste of pills on her tongue. The others are scattered over the counter. She gathers them up and shoves them into her mouth. Another gulp of water. There's no turning back now. The candies are gone. The mighty elixir is being ingested. The deed is done. Doubt has been rendered a vain notion, a thing of human invention to swindle the soul, a cheat, an annoying oddity if ever there be one. Deceptive doubt. It allows one to think one has a choice when one doesn't. There are things one must do. There are contracts to keep.

Then she goes about cleaning the kitchen. She gathers up old letters and writings, words she doesn't want anyone to read, puts everything into a green plastic garbage bag, carries the bundle outside, and places it by the curb to be picked up next garbage day. It's the middle of the night. There are no tears and she is calm. Back inside, she lies down on the bed and waits for something to happen. Nothing. At five in the morning, she picks up the telephone to call an ambulance, expecting an emergency receptionist to answer at the other end of the line with a barrage of questions. Instead, the sleepy 'hello' that answers her call is Jake's voice. The Carberry's have moved to Ottawa and are living in an apartment in the southeast end about half an hour away. It's still dark outside when Jake arrives and, without saying a word, he drives Isabelle across the city to his apartment where she lies down in her parents' bedroom.

Later that morning, Isabelle has a strange dream. An antique dresser made of bird's eye maple in a natural finish stands beside the bed where she is lying on her side. The wood spiral in the center of the top dresser drawer forms the face of a clock. The sinuous lines of the maple grain draw all of her strength into the interior of the wavy circles where the tense center of the spiral appears to collapse in on itself and spin inwards toward an unknown fate. When the hands of the timepiece reach twelve, her father is going to kill her. It's ten minutes before twelve. Aware that this is a dream and that she should wake before the appointed time, she is unable to unlock the fixated gaze that holds her eyes on the surely advancing minute hand. Frightened, she watches as the seconds go by. Each short passage of time, each tiny interval of non-decision holds a life in suspension, a memory in lapse. Each 'tick' begins a decline to another state, one of impossibility, of disbelief, of careless error.

Then as the hands of the clock come together with a last 'tock' at exactly twelve, the wall in the bedroom comes smashing down and her father emerges out of the dust and rubble. He's coming to get her.

Isabelle screams at the top of her lungs. Mrs. Carberry, startled by the cry, runs into the room and tries to hold onto her daughter as she thrashes around in an attempt to escape. Daylight takes on an eerie tone, the room begins to fill with darkness, and hollow sounds haunt the space as she passes out.

The next three weeks are spent in the Ottawa Psychiatric Hospital. She dozes for the first few days. There's little to differentiate the dreaming world from the waking world. Mired in a muddy bog, she sinks in the wet soft earthy matter, suffocating with the heaviness. Her eyes are closed but she can see through the swampy stew. She can see in front of her. She can see bubbles of air rising to the surface and she can breathe, like a mudfish in its element. Then she is diving, going deeper and deeper. She passes a straggly weed, then others slither by, ribbonlike fronds in green and brown, willowy marine algae. They're waving in the mud. She knows their names and feels their touch, their slime, their greed, kelp, sargasso, dulse. They're all there, thriving in this muddy sea. The sinewy leaves are coiling and pointing, they're motioning to her, calling to her to follow their directions, inviting her to come down, down, to plunge to an even greater depth still farther away from the surface. Then she is sitting upright in the hospital bed and her hand reaches up to touch her temple, to wipe away the mud and the blood that she is sure is trickling over her face. She expects her fingers to be sticky with brownish red matter when she brings her hand down to look at it.

"So, how come you're in here?" her roommate asks one day after they have begun to say a few words to each other. A tall strong redheaded girl in her twenties, she reminds Isabelle of Louisa. Marie, one of the other patients on the floor, calls her Big Red.

"I tried to kill myself."

"Yeah? You're lucky you don't get the shock treatment. I did."

"What shock treatment?"

"They give the shocks to Marie too. Didn't you know?"

"No. I don't know anything about shocks."

"You will."

Marie has multiple sclerosis that is ravaging her frail body, trimming the flesh from around the bones, and leaving a meagre frame that can scarcely support her weight, slight as it is. Isabelle's eyes are inevitably drawn to Marie's fingers, artistic fingers, long and delicate like a piano player's, and still perfectly formed. The disease that is attacking the rest of Marie's body hasn't touched her beautiful hands. When she feels good, Marie is lively and animated, smiling at her own quick mind, and looking out for the others.

"Lucy, dear. Listen to me a minute. Move your glass of juice, sweetie. You're going to spill it all over yourself. Big Red, honey, will you give Lucy a hand?"

Big Red is always by her side. She cares for Marie, combs her dark hair, which is streaked with silvery threads, into her favourite style, dabs her face with a cool cloth when she's too warm, brings her cups of tea and biscuits with jam, and takes her for short walks when she's able. Then something will go terribly wrong in Marie's brain and a vehement and unkempt mass of anger will spew from that tiny woman with the lovely fingers and the fine intelligence. Perhaps it's a sad intelligence, but the genie is unmistakably there. Isabelle sees it in Marie's eyes. This other Marie yells and screeches and fights with the hospital staff who, used to her by now, answers the cry with a white straitjacket. Marie is tied to a geriatric chair and confined to her room until she quiets down. For the next few days, she sits in the hallway with a blank stare on her face. Big Red tells Isabelle it's the shocks. "The bastards tried to kill her again with the shocks."

Near the end of September, Marie is anxiously waiting for the most solemn of Jewish festivals. The period of penitence began ten days earlier with Rosh Hashanah. On the day of Yom Kippur, she spends the holiday fasting, meditating, and anticipating some greetings from her family who she thinks might arrive with a warm round raisin challah. Sadly, no one comes, and Marie's mind plays tricks on her again. She begins to shout and curse and kick and the nurses and orderlies come running with the straitjacket. Marie disappears for a while and Big Red and Isabelle know she is gone to the white windowless room at the end of the corridor. They don't speak until Marie returns. When the nurse brings her back she is quiet again.

It begins to rain one morning and it rains without letting up for three days. Isabelle knows then that she will be all right. The rain is washing away the mud and dirt and spider webs and the dripping on her face has stopped. It's okay now, she thinks, I can live again. It isn't hard to figure out how to behave in a mental ward, so Isabelle is a good patient, obedient and polite, reading quietly in her room, scribbling a few words in a notebook now and then, disturbing no one. One day, the chief psychiatrist, Dr. Baird, thinks she is no longer a menace to herself.

"Well, Isabelle, I don't think it's necessary to give you a shock treatment. Your EEG, the electro encephalogram we gave you again, is normal now."

"Gee, thanks. That's great, Dr. Baird."

"Today, I'd like you to look at these pictures and tell me what you see."

He holds six cards in front of her, one at a time, while she gives each a cursory examination.

"They don't look like anything at all, Dr. Baird. They're just inky spats and splashes."

"I see. They don't remind you of anything?"

"Vaginas," she blurts out, because Dr. Baird wants an answer.

"I beg your pardon?"

"Vaginas.... And spiders. They look like vaginas and spiders."

That doesn't seem as dangerous a thing to say to him as bringing up empty holes and things that he doesn't know anything about. Inkblots are easier to handle than shocks. Anyway, how do you see a dark nothing in a Rorschach Test? And who knows what Dr. Baird might do with a black void? So to be on the safe side, she keeps her inner world to herself.

"Nothing else?"

"No, Dr. Baird. It's like I said."

"Can you tell me why they seem like vaginas and spiders?"

"I don't think so. I've no idea why. They just do."

"You know, it's all right to touch yourself."

"What?"

"To touch yourself. To play with yourself. There's nothing wrong with that."

"I don't know if it's right or wrong but I wouldn't dream of it."

"Why not?"

"What if dead people are watching?"

"I don't think it would matter even if they were."

"No? My Grandpa Davidson? He'd be scandalized, shocked beyond belief. He never said anything stronger than 'boo' to anyone in his life. Not for me. Oh God, no. Not with Grandpa watching. I think I'd die of embarrassment."

Dr. Baird classifies the unfortunate occurrence as a nervous breakdown that can be followed up with regular visits as an outpatient and gives Isabelle a discharge from the institution. Work resumes at the library the next day.

A year later, there is a similar incident. This time Isabelle doesn't tell her father she is going to the hospital, but he finds her anyway. He stands in the doorway to her room one afternoon, holding his cap in front of him and fingering the brim as he speaks. Isabelle isn't very alert but Jake's words register in her mind nonetheless.

"Don't tell your mother I came to see you in here. She'll be mad as hell at me. I came to tell you that you're my daughter and whatever you do is all right with me. I don't think any father and daughter could be any closer than you and I."

Isabelle doesn't know what to reply. But she doesn't have to think long because Jake has already left. It's the first time she can remember her father saying something tender to her. That's the only thing that strikes Isabelle from the phantom visit, the unexpected tenderness and the dampness in his eyes. At least, she thinks she saw a moistening in his eyes, but perhaps that's her imagination. Not until years later, after Jake Carberry is dead, does Isabelle ask herself what he meant by the uncharacteristic pronouncement. Jake isn't given to closeness.

Isabelle leaves the hospital on her own a week later. Her father has been the only one to visit. No one else knew she was there, except Mrs. Carberry, and Isabelle is just as glad her mother didn't come to see her. Walking out of the building onto Carling Avenue, she crosses the street to wait for the city bus that will take her back to her apartment in the south end. All is quiet once more.

Not long after, Mr. Carberry convinces Isabelle to leave Ottawa and live at home with him and Mother for a while. The Carberry's have moved again and are now living in a small cottage they have bought for their retirement years in Fall Creek, Quebec, just south of Wakeham. Isabelle visits with her son by telephone as she doesn't have a car, neither does she have any money.

For an entire year, she spends the days walking along miles and miles of country roads, noticing the grand perfection of the stately trees in the woods, listening to the clear water trickle over the stones in the creek as it wanders toward the valley, admiring the fieldstone fences that someone built rock by rock years ago, and wondering at the clear blue skies, the peace, and the stillness.

Sketching with a pencil, she copies drawings done by the old European masters, idyllic sketches of medieval landscapes–animals grazing in open pastures, cowherds idling along worn paths with their staves, quaint villages in the midst of a forest, church spires and castle towers off in the distance. A special dimension of complete concentration where time doesn't exist opens its doors to her, unveiling a sweet reality, a reality that harbours a satisfaction and a calmness that she didn't know was possible. Those demons who had terrified and threatened her still have not been touched, but a burden has been lifted somehow. Life isn't so painful, without any hope of change, which, not long ago, made it seem less painful to die rather than go on living.

Part Two

The Spinning of Atropos

"All the world's a stage,
And all the men and women merely players:
They have their exits and their entrances
And one man in his time plays many parts,
His acts being seven ages."

William Shakespeare,
As You Like It

A Holy Order

God has many faces in Wakeham. There's a United One, a Presbyterian One, a Catholic One, an Anglican One, a Nazarene One, a Jehovah Witness One. Still other religious scenes, notably the Church of Mormon, send missionaries from south of the border to make door to door solicitations in the hope of bringing a few wandering sheep into their fold. The rural churches never step out of line. The presbytery and the synod councils jealously rule their territories like giant corporations guarding their market share with sanctimonious disclaimers against each other.

The churches think little people ought to have rules to follow since the priest or the preacher is the only one who can communicate with God. Rules help you to resist temptation and do right. The devil wants your soul and when you have a rule to follow you're protected from Satan's false promises, you're sheltered from a fearsome, jealous, and vengeful God who whispers lies in your ear clouding the truth and confusing your devout judgment. A good rule can save your soul, so it can.

It's important to go to church every week and receive a formal release from guilt-trips over past behaviour or unperformed actions. Whatever your sin, you want to clear your conscience of misdeed in case you die. But should you be in need of an ecclesiastical declaration of forgiveness and can't manage to get to church, the holy man will come to your house. And if you declare yourself a sinner, he will absolve you of your sins and grievances right then and there on the spot before you meet your maker at the pearly gates. You don't want sin on your soul or God might not accept you into heaven, then you might end up thrashing about in a burning lake like the rebel

75

angels in Milton's *Paradise Lost*. Or worse still, if you happen to be a Catholic you might go to purgatory with unbaptized babies and Protestants and flounder forever in limboland. For sure, you wouldn't be allowed a burial in the cemetery next to a good Christian.

Wakeham villagers take note of those who attend church and those who don't. They know the rules and they know not to upset the apple cart. Those who do will suffer the consequences of ostracism and dismissal by popular vote without due process or the right of appeal.

Thus, Dugan Begley is a pious and good God-fearing person. He goes to church faithfully, not to hear what the priest has to say, but to make his appearance at a social event, to be a part of the community. A timid backbencher, he does his part in the congregation and pays his dues, but if asked to speak out he is possessed with a demon who confuses his words and makes him speak in a tongue no one can understand. And never in this world would Dugan contemplate going against the wishes of an aging gentleman dying of cancer, wishes that Isabelle's second husband, Gaspard, confers on him in one of his last days.

On a winter afternoon at the beginning of 1990, Dugan is walking along the country road towards the brick Victorian house just outside of the village of Wakeham where Isabelle and Gaspard live. He's going to pay a respectful visit to his ailing next-door neighbour. Isabelle greets him at the door, invites him into the entrance, and asks him to wait while she attends to Gaspard. A hospital bed has been set up for him in the living room. She helps him to sit, surrounding him with pillows to keep him from leaning over to one side, then brings Dugan into the room. She leaves the two alone to chat to themselves.

"Good afternoon. How do you do, Sir?"

"Well, well. Nice to see you, Dugan."

"You look in fine shape, Monsieur d'Urville, for a man in your condition."

"It's Gaspard, Dugan. Call me Gaspard. We've known each other long enough for that."

"So we have, haven't we. Good. So tell me Gaspard, how are you getting along?"

"Oh, I'll not last much longer, Dugan."

"Now, now. Don't say that. One never knows what's in store."

"Well, I know this one."

"I don't know what to say."

"You don't have to say anything, Dugan. In fact, I'm glad you stopped in this afternoon."

"Oh? Thanks."

"There has been something on my mind lately, something I'd like you to do for me."

"Anything, Gaspard. You've been a fine neighbour and a good friend to me for these past... how long has it been?"

"It's almost two years since we moved into this house."

"It doesn't seem possible."

"Two years in July, that is. But I'll not see that day."

"Gaspard."

"You can say 'Oh shit' if you want."

"Not a chance. But whatever it is you'd like me to do for you, just name it. I'll do my best to help you out."

"Dugan, it's my wish that you look after Isabelle when I'm gone."

"I beg your pardon?"

"Isabelle."

"Your wife?"

"In a manner of speaking. I've seen you look at her."

"You must be mistaken, Monsieur d'Urville."

"I don't think so, Dugan. An old dog doesn't learn many new tricks."

"Today's the first time I've met her."

"Inconsequential, Dugan. A high wall doesn't separate our properties. We catch a glimpse of one another from time to time."

"Aye. True enough. But I'll not object to your wishes, Sir. ... Gaspard."

"Good. I don't think you'll regret it."

"No, Monsieur d'Urville. Not I."

"She might not agree at first, but she'll come round. She loves this old house and the land. With your six or seven acres right next door, if she consents, by golly, you'll have a mighty nice little piece of property between the two of you."

Isabelle cared for Gaspard during the beginnings of his illness, before it became too serious for her to manage alone. He had to be driven to the Montreal General Hospital to receive radiation treatments for fourteen consecutive days every three months. The week following the radiotherapy, he felt bad enough to prefer death to the cure he knew wouldn't restore his health but was merely a palliative measure. The wallowing sickness of that initial week turned the living room, where Gaspard passed these unpleasant days, into a vomitory. Overactive glands would suddenly squirt sour water into his mouth making him grab for the dishpan at his side, or dribble into a towel while his tired stomach wrenched with dry heaves. His state did improve afterwards and he felt fair enough until the cancer began again to burn and twist and tear as if boiling water was searing the flesh from the inside. Then the internal fire raged and ate at him like a hungry rodent until it was time for the next treatment. As the cancer progressed, it spread from a spot between his shoulder blades lower and lower down his spine, paralyzing his legs. The local center for community services now helps out as well as Gaspard's sister, Henriette, and her husband, Armand. A few times a week, Henriette and Armand come to the house at four in the afternoon while Isabelle drives into Montreal to attend evening classes at university. Most days, it is past ten o'clock before she returns and either Henriette or Armand will spend the night downstairs with Gaspard so Isabelle can get some sleep. Eventually, the doses of morphine that Gaspard can receive at home aren't strong enough to control the pain. Death is settling in on him. Gaspard has wanted to spend his dying days at home, but one morning, when the pain is insupportable, he tells his doctor that it's time to go to the hospital. Then he calls his children and asks them to bring his grandchildren to the house. He wants to see them one last time.

Merely touching Gaspard's decaying torso and limbs starts off a paroxysm of agony. Torrents of abuse fly at the nurses whenever they try to change his position to avoid the onset of bedsores. But his tough body is not easily calmed. Nor is his heart easily bruised; it beats on strongly and unheard of amounts of morphine are required to still the desperate hallucinations that plague him. He is convinced that his hospital bed is plugged into the wall socket and that whoever touches the stainless steel sidebar will be electrocuted on the spot.

"Unplug the bed! Pour l'amour de Dieu, unplug the bed! For Christ's sake, Isabelle, stay away from me! I'm okay. I don't touch the sides. See? I've enough room, but don't you come near me!"

Isabelle is as frightened as he is, not of being fried alive with high voltage but of the tormented and nightmarish miasma into which he has fallen, and rings for the nurse to bring an extra shot of morphine so he can have some peace. At five o'clock in the morning five days later, Isabelle is sitting in an armchair beside him, reading, when the night nurse makes her rounds. She comes into the room to check on the machine that is administering the drug automatically into his system. "Monsieur d'Urville doesn't look comfortable," she says, lifting his head to remove the pillow and fluff it up. As she is adjusting it back under his head, Gaspard's eyes open.

"Gaspard! It's me. I'm right here." But the eyes are sightless, brown staring glass eyes beyond responding. "Do you think he can hear me?" Isabelle asks the nurse.

"Perhaps," she replies, shrugging her shoulders.

"I love you," says a quiet voice.

Gaspard's head moves to one side and the eyes close. He takes several shallow breaths in quick succession and then a longer one that gurgles and shivers with ragged and fluttery clots of fluid as it passes by his throat and enters more deeply into his lungs. Then the rattle stops. "Is that…?" Isabelle looks at the nurse who nods her head and leaves to report the death.

Isabelle holds Gaspard's lifeless hand and cries quietly to herself for several long minutes. It's a sad end to an industrious life to die paralyzed with morphine in a lonely hospital bed. She gathers herself together, goes to the payphone in the hall, and calls Henriette to tell her it's over.

The funeral service is held a few days later in the Catholic Church at Wakeham. Isabelle can't stop her arms and shoulders from trembling like a new puppy. A dialogue is taking place in her head and she finds it difficult to listen to the eulogies that are coming from the pulpit. Too many other words are chattering and distracting her with muddled thoughts and images from an earlier time.

She can scarcely remember the way it was in the beginning, the excitement of new love, the pride and security she felt being with her young at heart but older mate. He's thirty-one years older than she is when they first meet. She's thirty-three at the time. Gaspard is in good health, a dashing and distinguished looking gentleman with an attractive charm and a relaxed easy manner about him. When Gaspard dresses up in a stylish suit and tie, a debonair version of Cary Grant with silvery hair stands by Isabelle's side. No, any memories of the first happy months aren't strong enough to make a lasting impression. Gaspard has a temper that he hides from Isabelle before they live together. It comes out at the silliest things—when she holds the wallpaper the wrong way when they're redecorating their new home, or when the noon-time meal isn't going on the table at the moment he walks in the front door after working at his lumberyard all morning, or when he doesn't see any evidence that Isabelle has been cleaning the house, or doing something useful while he is away. Isabelle has brought out her drawing pens and brushes again and has begun to experiment with watercolours. She'll lose herself for hours at a time in a summery scene of friendly passersby in an imaginary village square, bright red flowers spilling out of window boxes, or in a wintry scene of a lone cross-country skier in a snowy wilderness of peace and quiet. The daily escape into her own private world, away from Gaspard's jealousy and mounting criticisms, saves her sanity. The time spent on drawing or painting is invaluable to her, even though she knows she isn't good at either one. She can copy whatever she looks at, can render a decent likeness of a scene someone else has committed to paper, but she can't release her own spirit onto the paper in a flush of creativity.

About four years into the live-in relationship with Gaspard, Isabelle applies for a job on a pilot project to develop a car pooling service for several rural counties in the region. Starting up a new program that will help those without transportation find a job, cut down on traffic into Montreal, and reduce environmental pollution is both challenging and rewarding. God knows, the region needs all the help it can get to stop the flow of young people away from the area. Gaspard doesn't see the point to helping some lazy sons-a-bitches get a drive somewhere and becomes more jealous than ever of Isabelle's new friends. A year and a half later, at a regional economic summit, Isabelle and her team ask the Quebec Minister of Transportation to get involved in the program. He refuses. The ministry is not ready to integrate such a para-public form of transportation into the traditional service. After that disappointment and without funds to continue, the project comes to a halt. Isabelle feels a pressing urge to return to school, to study for a business degree, thinking she might have more credibility if she has a different title behind her name. A Bachelor of Arts doesn't carry much weight in the mostly male enclaves of the rural municipal administrations.

The week that Isabelle enters a Financial Accounting course at McGill University, is the same week that Gaspard receives the news from his doctor that he has a cancer in his prostate gland.

"Gaspard, I don't know how to tell you this. Eighty percent of those who get this type of cancer recover. Most never hear from it again. The cancer you have is advanced enough to be alarming. You must have had some indication that all was not well with your waterworks long before you came to see me."

"Well, yes, as a matter of fact I did."

"I thought so."

"Isabelle is so young. I knew it would mean the end of our relations, if you know what I mean, so I put it off."

"You ol' bugger, Gaspard."

"Bad, eh?"

"You've really done it this time, my friend."

"Just tell me, Turner. No sniveling or beating around the bush. I want it straight."

"Gaspard, my guess is that you have six months to two years left to live."

Gaspard's temperament mellows during his illness.

"You know, Isabelle, I don't mind if you want to go out with someone else."

"You don't?"

"You must have lots of boyfriends at the university."

"I have a lot of friends, nothing serious."

"You're young and I can't be a man for you any more, so if you'd like to be with a young fellow… go ahead. You have my permission."

"Gaspard, you surprise me."

"Well?"

"That's very generous of you."

"When you do go, I'd like to know, that's all."

"I'm touched, really I am, but I have no interest at all in being with someone else."

The last few months have been exhausting. Gaspard can't be left alone. Washing his surprisingly firm body daily with a sponge while he is prone in bed, helping him to change positions from sitting to lying when he isn't comfortable, administering enemas when the cancer paralyzes the lower part of his back, injecting a needle into his thigh or his arm every three hours—these are nursing duties to which Isabelle is not all accustomed. In fact, disease and the care of the sick are areas which she has avoided, unable, until now, to calm a disconcerting aversion to, even a fear of, badly disturbed bodily functions. Caring for Gaspard takes its toll on her stamina as well. Lack of sleep puts black circles under her eyes. She has thought of nothing except what is at hand, whatever is demanding her attention at that moment and giving her a direction. Should there be complicated and messy ideas lying underneath the surface, that's where they remain.

Two years of radiation treatments and months of morphine drugs haven't emaciated Gaspard's body or confused his mind as has happened to many. Every morning, he sits at the side of the bed propped up with pillows at his back and sides, a footstool under his feet, a hospital swing table and tray in front of him while he eats his breakfast. Afterwards, he looks through La Presse.

"Isabelle, do you know what I feel like eating today?"

"What's that, Gaspard?"

"I feel like a good beef bouilli, the way my mother used to make it."

"Do you really?"

"Lots of juice and pasta bows. Maman went easy on the cabbage, but she added lots of carrots and onions. I can taste it already."

"You know it's wonderful how you never lost your appetite. At least, you can still enjoy your food."

"Yep. I think that would be the real thing."

"I'll call Henriette and get your mother's recipe."

Only once does a tear escape and roll down Gaspard's cheek.

"What is it, Gaspard? Do you want some morphine? It's not quite time, but if the pain is too much I'll give you another shot. You shouldn't have to suffer so much."

"No, it's not the pain."

"It's not?"

"No."

"I understand if you want to cry. I think you should, but I didn't think you could."

"I'm not crying."

"Then, what's that on your face?"

"Nothing. Just a few tears."

"Gaspard, say whatever you want to, whatever comes to mind. I'll sit here and listen."

He hesitates. This is a rare moment for a man who has spent a lifetime being in control. He mortgaged everything he owned and built up his business from nothing to a several million-dollar enterprise. Why a man so brave in thought and deed, so revered in the community, should be so timid in regard to showing his feelings seems a disappointment, a deception, and a pity. Such a moment is difficult for Gaspard, it's one of weakness when the disguise fails to hold forth, and it's not a comfortable place. He's not at all sure that he wants to speak, then, as if he has made a decision, "I won't see my grandchildren grow up."

"Is that it?" His words are not what Isabelle expects. Gaspard has a way of speaking directly to the point, of not mincing words, and this comment seems to fall short of what the situation demands. He's dying. Doesn't he have something more to say? Or perhaps it merely does not correspond to what Isabelle hopes to hear. She wishes he would tell her why he liked her so much in those first happy months. Was it because she was young and nubile? Just that? Because she made him feel young? Her own reasons are none the less suspect, security with big 'S' flashing loudly in front of the others. But I loved him! I truly did! And so she did. Love has long been confused with lesser imitators of desire. Perhaps it's best this way, to just let it be, to let him keep his thoughts to himself without confirming what she knows already. Gaspard has a knack for being right and if he refuses to say what's on his mind at this point then it's probably for the best. She doesn't want to hear that love was foiled again, not really. "They'll remember you, Gaspard. You're somebody special to each of them. Even little Sébastien will remember his Grandpapa."

Isabelle doesn't count lost loves any more. She can close that place in her heart and lock the door leaving behind a small core of herself each time she turns the key. Gaspard's quick tongue has injured many times, but she blames herself for the hurt, believing she has made another big mistake in choosing a partner.

"She's just waiting for me to die," Gaspard tells his children one day when they're visiting. Isabelle has gone into the kitchen so Gaspard can have some time alone with them, but he is speaking so loudly that she listens. He is saying it for her to hear. It sounds like an apology to his family for divorcing their stern-looking mother eight years earlier. At the time, it was the scandal of the village, the hottest piece of gossip in years, and all the well-married women in the village took note.

"If Gaspard d'Urville leaves his wife at sixty-four years of age, what about our husbands?" Irma said to her friend, Dorothy. "Earl and Jack could leave us! Know what I mean, Dottie? It makes me uneasy. All those guys in the club look up to Gaspard and look what he's gone and done."

"How could he?! The most respected man in town and he runs off with a loose woman half his age."

"She's Jake Carberry's girl. Something's wrong with that woman."

"Only half there most of the time, I'd say. Stunned look on her face like she's not seeing what she's lookin' at. Don't know what Gaspard sees in her, 'cept looks, and what does he think he can do to keep her at his age?"

"Can't make head nor tail out of him leaving that nice home of his where he could have anything he set his mind to havin' for the rest of his days."

"Rumour has it she spent time in a loony bin and left her son. At least, she must have left him, or lost him. Where is he anyhow?"

"Heaven help us! Not someone I'd want for a friend if you know what I mean."

"I don't care what they say," Gaspard had told Isabelle. "Even if I've got only a few more years to live, I want to live them being happy. The way it is now, I've already lived my life and it doesn't make the slightest difference to me whether I'm alive or dead."

The bells in the belfry toll in a slow and regular rhythm as the funeral procession leaves the church. At the head walks an altar boy in his loose linen surplice, holding a large golden cross high with both hands. A second robed religious clerk carries the incense vessel. A third follows with the aspergillum. Softly chanting phrases in Latin and muttering prayers beneath his breath, the priest, in his long white celebrant's vestment embroidered with gold brocade, leads the six pallbearers who carry the coffin. They pass through the great wooden doors of the church, which creak as they sway open on oversized iron hinges in need of an oiling, and enter the grounds of the dead at the rear of the building. Gaspard repented before dying. Living with a woman in an unlawful arrangement is lamentable to the Catholic church, which refused to recognize his divorce, and he confessed to his sinful behaviour when the good priest came to the house the day before he entered the hospital. Gaspard's soul received further priestly dispensation when he told Father Malachi that the union with Isabelle was not being consummated, had not been for two years, and his funeral is accorded all the pomp and ceremony due to a prominent Catholic.

The rotund religious man leans over the mound of dirt that was excavated from the grave, gathers up a handful of earth, and scatters it over a corner of the oak chest that isn't covered with floral tributes.

"Ashes to ashes, dust to dust."

An altar boy hands the Father the holy-water sprinkler. He shakes it several times in the direction of the corpse, then, taking the incense burner, he swings it several times back and forth across the coffin.

"Requiescat in pace," he murmurs, making the sign of the cross. "In the name of the Father, the Son, and the Holy Ghost."

"Amen," softly chorus those about the grave side, crossing themselves also.

Entirely befitting a burial, the day has been dull and now it is drizzling with rain as family members and friends pay their last respects to the dead. Henriette notices that Isabelle's shoulders are trembling and moves to stand close beside her, tucking Isabelle's arm into her own, giving her some of her warmth, and they walk away from the cemetery together. The April chill in the air is as unpleasant as is the frigid reality in Isabelle's emotions. Her feelings are scrambled, tossed about like goose feathers. She feels relief to be free again and guilt at not feeling grieved, both deliverance and condemnation vying for her attention at one and the same time.

And so it was that Dugan Begley was ordained with a holy order.

Not long after Gaspard's death, Dugan telephones next-door. "Hello, Isabelle. It's your neighbour, Dugan. I called to inquire about your health. I hope you're well."

"Yes, I'm just fine Dugan. Yourself?"

"Never better, thanks. I wondered if you needed help with anything around the house or the yard. I'm at work during the day, but I could stop in on an evening or during the weekend if you need help with anything."

"Thanks for offering, but Ernie is happy to give me hand anytime."

"So, Ernie's doing your work for you, is he?"

"He is. He was our handyman for the last few years, ever since Gaspard was unable to take care of things himself."

"I see."

"He's a good fellow. He talks away a mile a minute about who's doing what in town, but he's okay."

"Yeah. I know Ernie."

"I called him just last week to ask him to take off the storm windows and install the screens. I'm anxious to get some fresh spring air into the house."

"Now's the time all right. I've changed mine already."

"But that was considerate of you to call and ask."

"Perhaps you'd like to go out to dinner sometime, just to change your routine."

"Not really, thanks. I'm tied up with studying for some pretty demanding courses right now."

"That's fine, Isabelle. I didn't mean to put any pressure on you. But life goes on after death, you know. I'll call you sometime later just to see how you're doing. Take care now."

Isabelle busies herself with schoolwork. She hopes to set up a small office of her own in the country house to provide financial services to the local farms and small businesses. It isn't until two years later that she consents to go to dinner with Dugan. He has helped out many times with the garden, the windows, the yard, the trees, and the hedges, usually without being asked. It's only polite to accompany him to dinner at least once, since he lives alone and seems to like her company. Dugan's awkward shyness and his inability to listen for any length of time are a little irritating, perhaps he's nervous, but he chats away amiably about events in the village, and her every desire is Dugan's command.

"Do you know what I'd like to do sometime, Dugan?"

"What's that?"

"Skydiving. I'd like to go for a skydive."

"You're kidding."

"No, I'm not. I'd like to jump out of a plane with a parachute."

"Yeah?"

"I've wanted to do a parachute jump for as long as I can remember. It looks so wonderful to float down through the air. I'd like to know what it really feels like."

"I'd like that too."

"You would?"

"Sure."

"You don't strike me as someone who would like that sort of adventure."

"No? Why not?"

"Confronting the devils and demons of fear and mistrust, forsaking comfort, plunging into the unknown… all those things."

"That's me. Bending the barriers."

"I think it would be exciting."

"So do I."

"Well, let's do it then."

"But summer's almost over. We're well into August."

"The weather is still nice in September. I know a small airport near Embrun, Ontario that has a skydiving club. It's only a two-hour or so drive from here. Instructors give you lessons in the morning and then you jump in the afternoon."

"That's fast work."

"I'll call and book a time for us."

One day at the beginning of September of 1992, Dugan and Isabelle go through six hours of ground and simulated aerial training in preparation for a parachute jump. By concentrating completely on the routine, Isabelle can visualize herself getting into a small plane on the runway, rising a few thousand feet, positioning herself under the wing, and arching back gracefully into space whenever the jump master gives the 'go'." Twelve students listen intently to five instructors. In mid-afternoon, they watch their parachutes being folded by trained parachutists who have jumped hundreds of times. The friendliness of the trainers and their responsible and knowledgeable characters make the class comfortable. The aspiring jumpers trust them and the equipment. They're familiar with the location of the safety cord for the back-up parachute on their gear, minimizing any fear that will creep in if an opening be left for it. The atmosphere is jovial and upbeat. Isabelle shares the group emotions of confidence, of being in control, and of keen anticipation of the coming jump. She has her doubts, however, about how Dugan is feeling. He doesn't eat at lunch and seems distracted.

Five go up in the plane each time–the pilot, the jumpmaster, and three jumpers. Each is equipped with a radio and is in contact with the ground instructor, Andy, who guides each one down through the air during their first jump. Isabelle's turn comes and she walks across the runway to the plane, the maneuvres already going through her head. Dugan stays on the ground to watch.

The plane rises to three thousand feet and begins to circle over the fields surrounding the airport. "Okay, guys," says Luke, the jumpmaster, "if anyone has a last minute change of heart, now's the time to speak out. ... No one? ... Super. So who's first? ... Isabelle, you're the closest, so let's go. Remember, when Andy talks to you over your radio, he'll call you Jumper Number One."

The door of the aeroplane is opening. Isabelle talks to herself, Concentrate. Concentrate. Live those mental images. She extends an arm outside the plane, grasps the support bar of the horizontal structure, and begins to position herself in the wind under the wing of the Cessna. She shouts the steps out loudly, "Left hand! Right hand! Left foot! Right foot!" the sound of her voice strong and confident.

"Go!" yells the jumpmaster.

She releases her hold, stretching her arms out wide to either side, and steps back into space.

All her senses swoon. Such exquisite ecstasy! An airy carousel of fabulous unicorns prancing on cloven hooves transports her swiftly towards unknown horizons. Whirls and whirls of a delicious allure and thousands and thousands of faint sparkles of light fall through space without a care, each one as free as a spirit in a cloud. The sweetness is almost painful. There's a tug and then her parachute is above her–a huge red and white rectangle billowing and flapping in the wind. Reality creeps back. She checks the parachute strings above her to see that they aren't tangled and reaches up to grasp the toggles. As she floats down through the air, her nerves still hum with a feeling of delight. She is simply intoxicated. She has done it. She has won out over those devils. The rapture escorts her to the domain of the unspeakable.

Soon the ground is coming up to meet her. From a height, the tall grassy hayfield looks like a neatly manicured lawn. She pulls both toggles down as far as she can when Andy gives the order and the brakes work quickly. The grass rushes up to touch her feet, she lands and stumbles a few steps to regain her balance, and then she is standing in the meadow with the parachute lying limp beside her. Dugan comes running. "How was it? How was it?"

"Wonderful! Just wonderful! It takes your breath away."

"I think I'd like to keep my breath. Would you do it again?"

"You bet. I'd like to go back up there right now."

Dugan helps Isabelle to smooth out and fold the parachute, then they walk back to the hangar to await Dugan's turn.

Near the end of the afternoon, about six o'clock, Dugan dons a helmet and walks over to the runway. The last three jumpers of the day are on board. The motor revs up, the propeller whirrs, the plane takes off, rising again to three thousand feet, and begins to circle above the airport hangar and the group of spectators standing on the grass. Jumper Number One springs from the small white craft on the first tour and those on the ground count the seconds before the large parachute opens, "One, two, three, four, five, six. Cheerio!" Jumper Number Two emerges from the open door in the middle of the Cessna on the second round. Likewise, his parachute opens in six seconds. On the third circle above the field, a body falls into space and begins a free-fall. The nine onlookers, their heads craning backwards and gazing up to the sky, count the seconds, "One, two, three, four, five, six, seven, eight, nine, ten,…. Hey! What's up? The parachute should be open by now…. Who is that anyway?"

"It's my friend, Dugan Begley!"

Andy is in the middle of the field a hundred yards away, guiding down the first two jumpers and talking to the jumpmaster over the remote radio. "Jesus, Luke, what's the matter with Number Three?"

"He fell out in a ball, Andy, headfirst. I swear, he just tipped right out the door. I didn't have time to grab the pilot chute and throw it out after him."

"Goddamn! So, where is it?"

"It must be under him. He must have fallen on top of it. Hell, I don't know where it is!"

"Hold on. I have to look after Number Two for a minute. …… Number Two, pull on the left toggle. Bring it half way down and hold it there a second. … Good. Release it. Now for the right one. Do the same thing. …

That's it. … Okay, you still there, Luke?"

"I'm here, Andy. You know, I think Number Three is unconscious."

"Good God!"

"I think he passed out just as I was beginning to give him instructions."

"Poor bugger, he must have been scared shitless."

"Fifty, fifty-one, fifty-two." A few spectators are still counting the seconds. Dugan's chute is not opening. At sixty seconds, a small dark shape flies into the air. Soon after, a larger apparatus begins billowing out to an umbrella shape and Dugan's body swings back and forth until it stabilizes in the wind.

"Number Three, Number Three! Listen to me. Reach up and grab onto the toggles just above your head. … Good stuff, Number Three. That's the way, boy! You just do what I say, now, and I'll guide you down."

Jumper Number One has landed, Number Two is on his way down, and now Number Three, Dugan, is closer to the ground than Number Two. Andy is turning this way and that to talk to one and then the other. Dugan lands safely quite a distance from the hangar and a few seconds later Number Two lands fifty yards to one side. Dugan has a big grin on his face when Andy reaches him with Luke running not far behind.

"I did it!"

"Jeez, you did, man, but you gave us one helluva scare," says Andy.

"What happened up there?" asks Luke.

"I'm not too sure."

"That's not surprising."

"I remember falling through the air bent over and holding onto myself and this hard thing was under me, right here against my chest."

"That was the pilot chute."

"I didn't know what it was, so I threw it out to get rid of it. Tossed it away like a small fish."

"You're lucky you're not a dead one. That hard thing was what opened up the main parachute," answers Luke.

"You kidding me?"

"Talk about a wake-up call."

"I don't know how you can smile about it, Dugan… that's your name isn't it?" asks Andy.

"Yea. It's Irish."

"That was a close one," he continues, "but I bet we won't be seeing you back here again for a while."

"Perhaps not. But no hard feelings, eh guys?"

"No, no. None at all. We're just a little shook up, that's all. Right Luke?"

"Hot damn! I'm going home to have a good shot of whiskey."

"Just sign my certificate that I did a parachute jump and everybody's happy."

Andy and Luke help a slightly shaky Dugan to release the parachute from his bodygear, gather it up, and then they walk with him towards the hangar. The waiting group of fellow jumpers cheers and applauds.

"Dugan, you could have been killed! Are you all right?"

"I'm fine, Isabelle, just fine. I did it!"

One night in March 1993, Isabelle awakens from a strange and vivid dream:

Several people have been summoned together in a room, a large bathroom. The atmosphere is still and quiet, heavy with thought, few words are spoken. Should a movement be made, the gesture is conducted in such a manner so as not to disturb. The light that enters the vault-like chamber is diffused and obscure, like the solemn and suggestive half-tones of a cloud-covered sky in November, the sun barely illuminating the haze. Everything in the room is a dim aqueous white, except for the heads of those standing about and the colour of their skin. An antique porcelain bathtub on curved iron legs sits at an angle in the middle of the floor. Three individuals clad in long hooded white robes have gathered around the tub; a fourth, Isabelle, is in ordinary street clothes–a sweater and slacks–but all in white. All four are watching Isabelle's mother who is sitting in the bathtub, naked and untroubled, her eyes looking down into the water. Her skin has a tanned look to it and she doesn't appear eighty years old, she looks to be in her mid-forties, closer to Isabelle's age, and her hair falls loosely about her face and neck in the same shoulder-length style. There are five to six inches of water in the bottom of the tub and Isabelle's mother has just had a baby. The newborn is lying naked under the water. Isabelle, who stands at one end of the bathtub, is afraid the little body can't breathe. The robed figure on her right, who seems to be in charge of this ceremonial grouping, lifts the infant out of the water to show her it is indeed alive. He holds it up effortlessly with one hand as if it weighed ounces not pounds, and presses his finger into the left side of the small neck making a gaping hole that passes through the virgin flesh straight into the esophagus. The child doesn't struggle with this rude intrusion into its person or make a sound or open its eyes. Nor does it appear wet after just being taken from the water. The hooded character replaces the tiny form under the water where it lays on its back, undisturbed and sleepy, beside the mother.

Two months later, one evening in May, Isabelle feels a blunt and insistent pull begin to tighten the muscles in her abdomen. It's going to be another difficult menses so she puts away the assignment she's working on, heads upstairs to make herself comfortable on the bed, and awaits the onslaught. The urgent throes work in muddled waves, in shapeless forms of gnawing pain that wrench her bowels and send a cool stream of liquid fire down each thigh to her knees. The madness has come back again but with a new fury. It's elusive pain, organic pain without a name, divine pain speaking its agony, demanding attention, wanting a form, wanting freedom, wanting to escape her body. The deadening thickness rises slowly to her head, paralyzing her chin, blurring her vision. The light in the room grows faint and blackness approaches from the inside. Then the creature recedes into dullness and the tired flesh relaxes into an exhausted quiet, a welcome reprieve until the next renting ache begins the cycle over again.

Early the next morning, after a dark night, Isabelle telephones Elaine, the girl who helps her with the housecleaning.

"Elaine, it's Isabelle. I'm sorry to be calling so early…"

"No problem. I've been up since four-thirty getting breakfast for the men. What's wrong?"

"I'm not well. My period has really been overactive this time and I've lost a lot of blood."

"You sound terrible."

"I'm not that bad. Are you coming to the village today?"

"I hadn't planned on it, but I could stop in to see you around nine o'clock, if that would suit."

"Would you please, Elaine?"

"Sure. I can pick up a few groceries at the same time."

"Let yourself in the front door with your key, if you will. I don't think I can make it down the stairs to open it for you."

"Are you sure you're not that bad?"

"I'm pretty weak. And Elaine, would you bring some orange juice when you come?"

"Okay, I'll be along as soon as I can."

"Thanks."

Elaine opens the door and walks across the entrance hall. She quietly climbs the stairs to the second floor, one after the other, not wanting to wake Isabelle if she happens to be sleeping. Elaine is a big soft dimpled girl with a kind heart and not inclined to move quickly. When she reaches the top of the staircase she sees a bloody trail of blackened dried-up patches and bright wet splashes of a livid colour that cross the floor from the bedroom to the bathroom.

"Precious Almighty."

Elaine follows the trail into the master bedroom, where Isabelle is lying on top of the bedcovers, her nightdress and the bedclothes stained with bloodshed. A pile of soaked cloths lie in a heap on the floor beside the bed.

"Elaine. I'm so glad to see you. I didn't know who to call."

"Isabelle, this isn't normal, you must be hemorrhaging. You've got to get to a doctor."

"I don't think I can get out of bed."

"I'll help you."

"Did you bring some orange juice?"

"I did. Here you go. Drink as much as you can. I'll find some clean clothes for you to put on."

"Thanks, Elaine."

"Put your arms around my neck and try to pull yourself up with me when I stand."

Elaine helps Isabelle down the stairs, out of the house, into her car that is parked by the front door, and drives straight to the emergency entrance at the village hospital. Isabelle walks in on her own while Elaine parks the car. The nurse at the reception desk looks once at her pallid face and quickly ushers her through the double doors to the doctors' station. Once inside the treatment room, she collapses in a heap and a trickle of blood makes its way along the floor as another wet viscous clot exits her body.

The attending physician's diagnosis is 'miscarriage'.

Divine Madness
August, 1993.

I'm a professional accountant! This isn't the career that Isabelle would have chosen twenty years ago, but circumstances had a hand in guiding her along. Having completed the required courses at McGill, she wrote the last of the national accounting examinations in June. I think I see her now walking along the lane. Yes, there she is. She's just left the roadside mailbox to go back to the house. Look along with me. She's reading a letter that has just arrived. I can see over her shoulder. It's telling her that she has not only passed the exams but has done so with honours in the auditing section, ranking among the top in Quebec and in Canada. She quickens her pace as she arrives at the end of the message–"et nous souhaitons que ce succès se perpétue tout au long de votre carrière"–thinking she ought to scream *Yahoo! I did it!* at the top of her lungs, but she doesn't indulge the notion. She keeps the yell inside because she doesn't want to raise the neighbours' curiosity. Instead, on entering the house, she goes straight to the kitchen table, sits down in a chair, and begins to reread the words she has just finished reading a minute ago. Then a rumpled noise breaks into a half-suppressed giggle, the titter of a schoolgirl, her shoulders start to vibrate in rhythm, and she laughs until her ribcage strains against her sides in short empty spasms, tears blurring her eyes.

She opens a tiny office in the house that Gaspard has left to her, placing her shingle on the front porch so it is visible from the road. 'Financial Services' the sign reads. The workweek is divided between local clients and the financial consulting firm on Peel Street in downtown Montreal where she works as a trainee. Advertisements in the local newspaper along with word of mouth bring plenty of work and she approaches prospective clients with financial plans for their small businesses.

"It's getting close to income tax time," she says to Ned Nolan who owns a service station in the village. "Mind if I ask if you pay a lot in taxes, Ned?"

"Too much. Too much. I hate to even think about it. Like a bad dream."

"What do you say to letting me look at your books for an afternoon–no charge–and see what kind of ideas I can come up with to save you some money?"

"Not a bad idea, that."

"Couldn't hurt anyway. Maybe I could help you out with your bookkeeping too. This is such a busy place, I don't know how you have time for those things. I live just around the corner, easy for you to drop off your purchases and sales slips and cancelled cheques once a month."

"Oh, don't worry about that, my wife looks after all that stuff."

"Does she? Good for her. Does she handle your payroll too? That can be a complicated affair. You have the two governments to deal with and all the calculations for the deductions at source. And, of course, they have to be remitted to each revenue minister on time, along with your share as an employer, or you're up for stiff penalties. No point that I can see in sending the tax department any more money than you need to just because you didn't get your forms in the mail at the right time."

"Hell, no!"

"But doing the numbers is easy to follow when it's set up properly."

"Matter of fact, she does that too. Pa had been doing it for years so I just kept on with the system he used."

"I'm sure there've been a lot of changes since Nelson's day, but that's fine, Ned, I just want you to be worry free. You've got plenty to occupy your days without having to worry about the accounting end of things."

"Thanks for thinking of me, Isabelle, but you wouldn't be trying to drum up a little bit of new business, now would you?"

"Well, maybe. But just talking friend to friend, maybe there are a few things I could help you with, like an evaluation of your business–interesting to have–or some good practical suggestions."

"Such as?"

"Such as maybe you keep too much inventory on hand and some parts become obsolete. I could look at your pattern of sales, suggest a safety stock level and recommend that you buy when the stock reaches a certain level. You may be missing out on price fluctuations to get bargains. Or your receivables–I could have a look at them to see how old they are. Do you have trouble collecting? Maybe you need a tighter credit policy. Any bad cheques? May need a customer profile before accepting cheques."

"A customer profile? That would go over like a lead balloon here in Wakeham. No, I don't have that problem on account of I know everyone around here and I'm not one with pretty words. Don't know of anyone who'd dare give me a rubber cheque. But those other things are interesting, Isabelle. Tell you what. I'll talk to my wife, that's her baby, the books and the payroll, and I'll ask her what she thinks. Our accountant lives ten miles from here and it would be handier if the office was closer to home."

Near the end of August, a real estate agent presents her with an opportunity to buy a private seniors' home in the nearby town of LaViolette, the Ovila Street Residence. The idea of being in active business appeals to Isabelle more than the strict discipline of accounting facts, which places her squarely outside the real challenges of daily entrepreneurial life. Thus, in the following autumn, in mid-October, she signs the deed of sale purchasing the home and the business that is already operating inside the building. The owner of the property, Eva Pilcher, is a nurse and continues to look after the health of the residents until other arrangements can be found.

Twelve elderly men and women and one orange tabby cat named McIver, Mac, for short, make the Ovila Street Residence their home. Each has their own room, their favourite things about them, come and go as they please, and are well looked after. The staff cleans, launders, and prepares tasty meals that are finished off with homemade pies and desserts–blueberry cobbler, apple betty, raspberry crisp, strawberry preserves, pumpkin cheesecake, pies according to the season, upside down cakes, pudding *chomeur*, and sugarless lemon sponges and mousses for the diabetics. Isabelle redecorates the halls with paisley wallpaper, sews flounces into new curtains for the windows, hangs paintings of pleasant landscapes on the walls, scenes with dabs and dashes of colour, blends of austerity and frivolity, buys new dining room furniture, an automatic dishwasher for the staff, fluffy towels, and matching sheets and pillow cases. It's a bustling and happy place in which to live.

Eva and Isabelle become friends, sharing stories about themselves, recipes, favourite books, sweaters, and offer each other advice. Both are independent by nature, not afraid of new demands or responding to a call, and one idea leads to another, and another that magnifies with time into a major concern like a small town rumour mill. In January of 1994, the two women begin to make serious plans and, by the end of June, they have purchased an old hotel in LaViolette that was in difficulty.

The building had been neglected as of late. During the past several years it had turned into a den for drugs and prostitution, but in 1929, the year it was built, and in the years following, it had become a well-known landmark in the area. Visitors from far and wide were attracted to the classic architecture of this state-of-the-art hotel, the foundation of which had been scoured out by hand by men from LaViolette, crews of workers loading shovelful after shovelful of compacted clay ground onto open wagons that were hauled away from the work site by teams of draft horses, their hooves slipping and sucking through the mud. A fireplace nook was nestled in the corner of the grand high-ceilinged lobby with cathedral windows. The hardwood floors and oak trimming in the offices and stairwells were polished to a shine. On weekends, in the 1930's and '40's, a ballroom orchestra entertained with the big band sounds of Guy Lombardo, Duke Ellington, and Glenn Miller, the lead singer crooning the words of *Cheek to Cheek* and *Blue Moon* in fine style to an appreciative crowd. The partygoers might well have thought themselves at the Roosevelt Hotel in New York City swinging to the jazz rhythms of the

Royal Canadians or Benny Goodman's clarinet or Satchmo's trumpet. *Georgia On My Mind. 'Ol Man River.* Other tunes from *Show Boat.* Even the oh-so-polite waiters in short tuxedo jackets hummed along to the beat of *That Old Black Magic* and *Chattanooga Choo-Choo* or *They asked me how I knew, my true love was true.* The elegant dining room boasted a stained-glass crest in the center of each large handcrafted window made of smaller leaded panes. The tennis courts on the back lawn were alive with dapper young men and ladies in starched whites and the grass and hedges were trimmed with immaculate care. The Manoir had a character all its own.

Eva and Isabelle plan to renovate the entire structure. They want to give it a new vocation as a seniors' complex that would accommodate seventy-two people, a Manoir, a modern facility with two levels of care, exercise rooms, a chapel, boutiques, a bank center, a pharmacy outlet, a café, an entertainment center for concerts and theatre–all in keeping with the particular cachet of the structure.

Dugan, swept up in the thrill of the moment, wants to be included in Isabelle's new undertaking and decides to help out financially. He invests eighty thousand dollars in the venture, even though the relationship with Isabelle is anything but steady, on for a month, off for three months, on for two weeks, off for four months.

Isabelle plows headlong into developing the project, like a cocky matador first entering the arena, confident and poised for an ordeal, his strength intact. The preparation of the business plan and the search for financing partners are stimulating, demanding, and time-consuming. Soon she is torn between the Manoir project, accounting duties, and the Ovila Street Residence. One of the girls on the staff, Agnes, had worked at Eva's home for six years and is familiar with the residents' needs and the routine. Gradually, Isabelle gives Agnes more and more responsibilities in managing the daily operations at the Residence to free herself for more work on the complex.

Neither logic nor reason can explain the blind force that makes the LaViolette Manoir a part of Isabelle and instils in her a fierce desire to restore it to its former glory. Desiring makes you innocent and vulnerable, leaves you wide open to the vagaries of those who would criticize or wound or not respond to your needs. It's dangerous to desire, like Icarus flying too close to the sun. Desire is laced with fear and threatens your sense of self, but the lure and pull of possible fulfilment is a powerful lodestone of many attributes, capable of seducing all humankind. The appetite for joy intoxicates. You reach out to grasp its outstretched hand and, in so doing, to perhaps fall into the great empty bowels of the earth, but despite the risk and the potential failure, Isabelle knows that is where she has to be.

Plans don't work as they wish and after a year of struggling to find financing for their three million-dollar renovation project, Eva and Isabelle have to give up. The entanglement of stress and money is a heavy burden to bear and Eva suffers from burnout. She wants out. Unable to sell her fifty-percent ownership in the destitute structure to anyone else, Eva sells her share to Isabelle who becomes the sole owner of the LaViolette Manoir as well as the owner of the accumulated debts and the attached headaches.

Dreams match the state in which you are living. When Isabelle enters this nighttime domain she encounters a grey space, dark and light muting themselves into a smeared world with little definition. Sometimes a splash of colour will appear at the end of a dream sequence, a swatch of blue-green, the colour of a peacock's tail feathers, on the sweater of a friend who arrives with a bit of moral support. The brightness is startling against the muddy tones and changes the mood from oppressive or nightmarish to calm, alert, and expectant. But most are struggling dreams—her lungs are pressed to extremes to maintain a breast-stroke over the surface of a deep calm sea, while beneath her, in the transparent and cool liquid darkness, is an odd feast of swimmers, lithe and muscular bodies all moving in one direction like summer moths, outwards into the greater depths of the sea; she pushes her way with a great deal of difficulty through waist high snow, slowly climbs the icy path to the top of a snowy mountain, then slides down the other side; she maneuvres a car, inch by inch, in a tedious attempt to turn the clumsy automobile around inside a small garage; she squeezes through a narrow door below ground level at the back of a building just as the stairwell passage is filling up with water; she wades across turbulent rapids almost being swept away in the swift current, then scrambles across a pebbly beach and up a steep embankment before reaching a grassy plain on the other side.

One night, Morpheus, riding on the wings of a butterfly, heralds in a dream that is different from the others and Isabelle looks at herself in another body. A high narrow platform bed is sitting at eye level along one wall in a small rectangular room, clean but unadorned, like a barren prison cell. On entering, Isabelle stands stock-still and stares intensely at the scene in front of her, for lying stretched out on the bed is herself. One arm is bent at the elbow, her head resting on her hand. The horizontal Isabelle is pensive, quiet, attentive; her eyes are downcast. The standing Isabelle knows she is looking at herself and says to her other self, "Look at me straight in the eyes," testing to see if this silent actor will react to her. The second Isabelle does as she's told and the two Isabelle's look at each other for some time before the dream fades.

On the outside, for everyone to see, Isabelle maintains an appearance of unwavering control and confidence in the ultimate success of the latest project on which she is working. On the inside, the gloomy spectres of fear and doubt, attached like cankers to each new risk, jostle like sparring partners–fear of another rejection, fear of another failure, with doubt undermining the little successes along the way. Tossed into the fray and batted about as well, these small triumphs initially manage to cast a shining allure that beguiles with sincerity, but which will soon be tarnished with illusion. The Manoir eats up every penny she earns from accounting clients and from the Old Folks Home.

Dugan puts some stability in her life, not stability in the harmonizing sense of the word, but in a protective and caring sense, a close runner-up to feeling sane and normal for a time. Dugan gives her the warmth one human being can give to another by a simple physical presence. Isabelle calls on him when she wants to get away from her world, when she is weakened, depressed, stressed, lonely, when the madness creeps in and pushes. But then Dugan feeds her wine, then whiskey, and the days run together in a Dionysian Odyssey, a wild uncontrollable journey into the shadows, into a comfortable and not comfortable place of forgetting but remembering, into a liquid world of melding, of hatred, of fear, of not wanting to care, of submission, of great fatigue. And during those forgettable and unforgettable times, the spider has his insect. His web has trapped his prey and he loves and hates it at the same time. He loves its beauty, hates its strength. It fights him, refuses to yield, threatens his image, and cracks the fragile mirror where Narcissus looks back at himself.

One afternoon at the beginning of July 1995, a girlfriend, Colette, calls to invite Isabelle to the presentation of a new business venture being given at a conference center north of Montreal. Colette happens to meet an old school buddy during the evening session whom she hasn't seen in years. They want to stay on a while longer, have a drink in the bar, and catch up on each other's news, so Colette arranges for a friend, who lives in the same area, to drive Isabelle home. His name is Vincent Nyles and he and Isabelle chat away easily during the hour and a half drive back to Wakeham. As the car is turning into Isabelle's driveway off the country road, they are discussing houses, styles and renovations, so she invites Vincent to step into the spacious entrance hall of her own home. She wants to show him the painstaking work that went into restoring the hundred-year old dwelling. The young couple who owned it before Isabelle and Gaspard moved in, bought it for a meagre sum from an eighty-year old spinster and had renovated the entire house themselves. As in many vintage homes, the wood floors, window frames, baseboards, and stairs had been covered many times over with generous coats of drab dark brown paint. Today, in the front hall, the soft gradations in the woodwork attest to the meticulous work that went into bringing back the artistry of the first craftsman. Double rounds on the mouldings, which frame two tall windows stretching up to the high ceiling, glow with a warm blonde richness that has deepened with age. A satiny smooth banister on the wooden staircase curves around the corner to lead upstairs; the handcrafted upright balusters have been recreated to match the first lathe turns in the pine newel post at the bottom step, the finish polished to a golden gloss. Wide-plank Douglas fir floors have been sanded down to the original and high carved baseboards around the walls match the skilled handiwork of the rest of the room. It is a beautiful home, heavy with ancestry and old-fashioned charm.

Vincent lingers just a minute to take in the ambiance of the room, then leans closer to Isabelle to say goodnight. Instead of the customary handshake and a kiss on each cheek, he gives her a quick peck on the mouth, then leaves.

Another meeting is scheduled for the following week. This time, Isabelle meets Vincent after work at his business in Ashvale and they drive together into Montreal in Vincent's car. After the assembly and back in front of Vincent's office, he asks Isabelle to step inside for a few minutes before leaving for the drive home. "It's well arranged and nicely decorated," he assures her. I'd like you to see it. Why don't you take a few minutes to relax? We can talk over this new marketing scheme. I'd like to know what you think about it."

They install themselves in front of his desk, in two armchairs facing each other, and talk more about themselves than about the new venture. Vincent is speaking in questions, looking for an invitation, testing the field for a nuance of acceptance like a cat feeling the size of an opening with his whiskers before passing through.

"Do you like living alone? What kind of music do you like? I'm partial to the piano myself. Would you like a drink? I have some twelve-year-old scotch here in the cupboard that I keep for special clients. Do you cook meals for yourself? It's important to eat properly, you know. Especially when you live alone. I make a great spaghetti sauce. I like to cook every once in a while but I have to eat out a good deal of the time. Business, you know. Gets to be boring. Which restaurants do you like? Do you like to eat out?"

The devil's most devilish when respectable.

Guarding her reactions, she is non-committal about her likes and dislikes, revealing as little as she can about herself, but she is more and more taken with his manner. In spite of his transparent probing he does have a calmness about him and a quiet sense of humour, and he gives her his full attention.

Vincent moves his chair closer to Isabelle's so that he's sitting directly in front of her. *Take a deep breath, Isy.* He leans forward, approaching her slowly, his eyes in her eyes, and reaches out with both arms to touch her hands. *Oh, help!* He feels them, turns them, studies them, holds them. *The music soars within the little lark.* Taking her left hand in his, Vincent pushes the sleeve of her jacket higher to expose the inside of her arm and Isabelle feels a weight like lead begin to drag the bottom of her stomach down to her knees. He rubs the soft naked skin, skin as velvety as the sac-like belly of an old Bruce Crossing toad, with the plushy underside of the fingers of his right hand. *And the lark soars.* His face is asking for hers, his whole body is entreating hers to meet his, dense wrested thoughts tumbling together like a tuna casserole. A thousand Furies bearing fiery torches respond to the occasion and she is already there, meeting him mid-way, lips half parted, when Vincent kisses her, a kiss so long and sweet it makes Isabelle's dreams spin. She feels the rapture, the bliss, and the excitement of her love-world returning.

Isabelle swims in joy. Vincent is in her spirit, her mind, her heart, indeed, her heart seems a new organ, plump with coursing blood and woolly with feral oscillations. After so many years, she feels again the dizziness, the giddiness of love. It fills her with a golden light, energy that makes her expand beyond the boundaries of her body as if she was pure space and larger than life, love energy that makes ludicrous every other kind of energy in the world. She wants to set new goals, remember old challenges, plan for the future. The world is hers once more. She's bursting with emotion, with longing, but doesn't know if the sensation is extreme joy or extreme sadness. The joy she can almost touch is so sweet that it's painful and tragic because it still eludes her. Vincent isn't with her. She longs to feel his presence, see his smiling eyes look into her own, touch the febrile skin on the back of his neck, but he leads another life with his wife.

Isabelle has spent many hours working on another project for the Manoir— a center with specialized antique shops and dealers, art boutiques and galleries, music rooms, a piano tuner, a library, a bar and restaurant, and meeting rooms. Waiting for decisions from potential investors makes her nervous and agitated like a gazelle sensing the approach of a lion. Within the next few weeks the answer arrives, another refusal, which only increases the tension of uncertainty and dampens the newly found joy, tainted as it is.

On a Saturday morning at the end of July, Isabelle sits outside under a cloudless blue sky enjoying the sunshine of a bright summer day, a wanton morning rife with the promise of more heat. The air is warm and perfumed with the scent of hydrangea blossoms the size of cannonballs yet poised as lightly as dollops of sea foam, and sensual hordes of oriental lilies like little pink and white birds in flight, floating delicately above the flower beds as if reflections in a mirror. A fragrant zephyr rushes by with a soft whirring noise, a whiffle, as if carried on the rapidly beating wings of myriad tiny insects, causing the leaves to flutter on the grand old trees and to sashay in the vagrant air as would a silken Indian sari. The far-off horizon's unconcerned allure appears to ridicule her own earthly matters, exposing them as counterfeit exchange, laying bare the inadequacies, making no distinction whatsoever between the near and the far or the now and the then, and speaks of infinities not weeks or days or hours. Grace flows freely from the green acres, touching her battered soul and realigning the weight of the universe. The warm vibrations from the sun soothe and heal and her mind wanders to a telephone call that came out of the blue on the previous Monday evening.

"Hello, I'd like to speak to Isabelle Carberry, if I may."

"Yes, go ahead."

"You don't know me, but my name is Judy Rosen. I'm calling from Montreal. Are you the owner of the Manoir in LaViolette?"

"I am. Where did you get my name?"

"At the Town Hall in LaViolette. This past month I've been looking at a lot of properties in the area and that awesome building in the center of the town takes my eye every time I pass by. I tried to go inside but the doors were locked so I went to the Town Hall to get some information. The secretary gave me your name and telephone number."

"I see. The Manoir has been closed for some time now."

"What are you going to do with it?"

"Right now, I'm working on an Arts Center for music and theatre presentations."

"In the country?"

"Very much so. Like the Piggery at North Hatley in the Eastern Townships. There are a lot of musicians and artists in this area who would love a space to call their home."

"That's a neat idea, all right."

"But I don't know if it will fly. It's hard to get funding for the arts."

"Are you open to other projects? I have one I think would suit well in that building."

"Sure. I'm ready to listen. What's it all about?"

"I've been involved in an association of Country Inns that are mostly in the New England area. Each one is unique and special. But I'd really like to talk to you first before getting into a lot of details."

"A country inn sounds interesting. But I want to warn you, this building needs a lot of repair work and people around here aren't interested in investing in it. The financing would have to come from outside the area."

"Financing isn't my problem. Finding the right partner is. Also, I'd like to see through the place."

"Well then, can we meet sometime this week? We could talk awhile, then take a tour through the building. How about coming to my house in

Wakeham?"

"Let me look at my agenda a minute... I'm tied up until the weekend. Does next Saturday afternoon suit you?"

"That's fine with me. Saturday it is. I'm looking forward to meeting you, Judy."

"Same here. See you then. I'll call you before I leave for directions."

Judy doesn't show up for the Saturday meeting, arriving on Sunday afternoon instead. She's a special lady, effervescing with ideas and energy and old family money and great enormous breasts like round smooth melons. Her wealthy brothers have a preference for the way money should be spent and lives should be lived and Judy has never met their expectations or stood in their good graces, the rebel angel in the family. She has gone on a buying spree around LaViolette and has purchased two farms. One comes complete with horses and machinery and hired help, the other, she intends to live on herself, grow organic vegetables and fruit, and open a school to teach children the ways of the earth. Isabelle is a little overwhelmed by the Judy dynamo, but thinks the possibilities enormous if they could manage to put both their energies together. They plan a trip to Boston in September to get to know each other better and to look at country inns.

During the week after Judy's visit, Isabelle receives a telephone call from Colette. Colette is aware of the difficulties at the Manoir since Isabelle confided her troubles to her. She wants to introduce her to her brother, Paul, who has just returned to Quebec after twenty-six years in South America and Puerto Rico where he was responsible for the artistic vein of several large projects. Colette has made him curious about the Manoir.

She lives in a century-old stone farmhouse that she has renovated into an exclusive country retreat, a prime candidate for a special issue of Better Homes and Gardens. The farm borders the picturesque riverside not far past the limits of the town of LaViolette. After hanging up the telephone, Isabelle drives the twelve miles to Colette's where she and Paul spend several hours becoming acquainted. Later that same afternoon, they drive into LaViolette and Isabelle shows Paul through the building that is beginning to show signs of neglect–floors that need a good cleaning, musty smells, a broken window pane, beeping smoke detectors–but no one can ignore the classic style of the architecture.

Within a week, Paul calls and wants to see Isabelle the next day, so they arrange to meet at the Manoir at eleven o'clock on the following morning. He wants another tour of the four floors, the roof as well, and as they make their way through the cavernous basement, the grandiose lobby, vast dining room, kitchen, entertainment area, up to the guestrooms on the second and third storeys, then out onto the roof, he tells her of his plans. Paul is one of many brothers and sisters who have their roots in Quebec, most of whom are still living in the vicinity. Paul thinks his family ought to buy the Manoir. They could live there themselves and would be able to look after each other in their old age.

"We're all at that time where we have to think of such things," says Paul. "You don't know my family, except for Colette. We're a talented bunch. Together, we could operate an upscale family-owned hotel."

"I don't doubt it for an instant."

"It would be something unique, very special for this area. The work to be done is extensive. No question there. The building will have to be gutted to replace the plumbing and rewire the electricity. And those thin old windowpanes and worn out frames? They'll have to be changed. I want to keep the old look but you might as well be trying to heat the outdoors with those relics. They're finished."

"You're right, Paul. I asked an architect to survey every inch of each level and make a plan of the work to be done. He says the same thing, but the structure is still as solid as a rock. You'll end up with a new building."

"It'll cost a considerable sum of money. Here's my plan. I'd like you to sell my place in Brazil for me."

"Are you serious?"

"My equity is tied up in that piece of land. We could buy the Manoir but I'll need that money to do the renovations."

"I wouldn't know where to begin selling real estate!"

"You know a lot of people. I'm new here and you seem to have a talent for dealing with people. … A one-hundred thousand dollar commission will be yours. I'll be able to rebuild the hotel with the balance."

Selling the building and moving on to other endeavours is beginning to sound appealing, like the appearance of a blowhole in a coastal cliff allowing jets of seawater to spew into the air depressurizing the massive force below the surface. Isabelle heads for home, Paul's proposition of selling his Brazil property circulating in her head during the ten minute drive back to Wakeham. Exotic trips, ocean air, sun and sand, new people to meet are making her imagination soar. The land covers about five acres, part of it a mangrove forest, right on the Atlantic Ocean south of Rio de Janeiro. Over the years he had owned it, Paul had built up a small tourist resort with individual thatched roof cottages, a restaurant and bar, and wooden footpaths leading to the beach through the mangroves. A sunny paradise is what comes to mind when you wander through it in a video Paul filmed himself. He thinks the Canadian government ought to buy the property as a tourist and public relations enterprise between North and South and somehow he thinks Isabelle is the one to sell it. A designer at heart, not a businessman, Paul is ill at ease in the world of wheeling and dealing in facts and figures, preferring instead the decorative and creative end of commerce. However, if she sells to Paul she will have to take a big loss and feels less than certain about flying off on a new adventure selling property. Still, she could speak to a few people she knows who might be interested and should the land happen to sell, well, the commission will come in handy.

This same day, a meeting has been scheduled with Billy Hallaway at four-thirty in the afternoon and Isabelle returns to the Manoir to meet Mr. Hallaway. Billy has big plans also and wants to know what is in store for the building because he needs a functioning hotel to realize his dream of a boxing gymnasium. "Boxing is a discipline," Billy repeats as often as anyone will listen. "I'll offer instruction and fitness training for amateurs at all levels, boys and girls both. Girls need physical discipline as well as boys! Hey, hey! C'mon! The girls love it. Keeps them in good shape." Billy grew up in a notorious Montreal boxing family and arrived the hard way at his own conclusions about the importance of a drug and alcohol free existence, as well as the importance of early training for a young person–ideals that he wants to incorporate into his gymnasium. Professional fighters would also be brought to the Manoir for periods of a month at a time during which they would live on the premises and eat a planned and healthy diet while in training at Billy's boxing resort. The basement would have a new life as a fitness theatre and Billy would look after the repairs and renovations himself. Visions of big-time boxing exhibitions and crowds arriving in LaViolette that would put the town on the map dance in Billy's head, but he needs an operating hotel to be in business. So does Isabelle.

"Will here. Hello there."

Early one Monday morning in August, Isabelle telephones Will Dennison, a fellow she knows in Toronto who has made himself wealthy by buying out or taking over businesses in trouble. Isabelle contacted him last spring before she and Eva called off the seniors' complex, Will being the last straw she had to pull at that time. Sympathetic to her project, he thought it a good investment but he himself didn't invest in any business that had less than twenty million in capital.

"But, Isabelle," he had said to her, "if you want to talk about structuring the ownership of the corporation so you and your partner can keep control yourselves, I can help you out there. I'm in Montreal on business about twice a month, so give me a call whenever you'd like to meet. I'd like to see you again and we could talk over dinner."

This August morning, Isabelle has reached Will in his car as he makes his way into downtown Toronto in the rush hour traffic. Will is apparently curious about who is calling on his personal cellular, that number being reserved for emergencies. (Alex had given it to her, Will being a cousin of Alex's father.)

"Isabelle! Surprise! I don't hear from you for years, now I'm talking to you every month."

"Well not quite, Will. The last time I called you was in May."

"Is that right? How's your project coming along?

"We couldn't get the financing so we called it off."

"Too bad. It sounded like a good idea. Would have been good for the area too. What's up this morning?"

"This is an odd one, but you're pretty impulsive so I thought I'd ask. Are you interested in a piece of property in Brazil?"

"Go on."

"A fellow I know asked me to sell it for him. He's from around here in Quebec but has spent the last twenty-some years in South America. Now he wants to move back home and would like to be rid of the property. It's really something, Will. It's like a paradise in the sun with palm trees and a sandy beach on the ocean."

"It's too far away, Isabelle. He should ask the municipal government in the area to sell it for him. Whereabouts is it?"

"About two hundred miles south of Rio on the Atlantic Ocean."

"Nice spot."

"Beautiful. Paul tells me the country is planning a five hundredth year celebration in the year 2000 and they expect to have about a million visitors."

"I think I've heard of that. Doesn't it have something to do with a sailor named Cabral? ... Pedro Cabral?"

"Right on. Terrific memory there, Will."

"Portuguese, if my guess is right."

"You got it. I'm impressed. He was the discoverer of Brazil and landed his ship not far from where Paul's property is located. The main celebrations are to take place nearby and they're supposed to continue throughout the year. Tourist accommodations are needed, so there's a good opportunity for someone who wants to be in the business."

"There must already be a string of resorts along the waterfront."

"Not really. The beaches in that area are just beginning to be cleaned up, so as yet there are only a few small hotels by the ocean."

"Need a good sized investment to develop it. What does he want for it?"

"Two million dollars, U.S."

"Well, I doubt if he'll get his price, but it's not for me. I've got my feet firmly planted in Canada. But if I meet anyone who might be interested in it, I'll give you a call."

Judy and Isabelle get together twice during August. Several days before they are to go to Boston to tour Country Inn establishments, Judy calls to say she isn't feeling well. She is going to Boston anyway, but to the hospital since her doctor has discovered a cancer that needs a special treatment. Isabelle doesn't hear of her again until late September. The real estate agent who sold Judy the LaViolette properties tells Isabelle that Judy is dead. One of her brothers contacted the agent because the family wanted an annulment on the sales since the proceedings had never been finalized. Judy was thirty-eight. She left her money to charitable causes, the angel part of the rebel having the last say.

Isabelle goes back to her work. When there's a lull in the Manoir activities, there's catching up to do at the Residence and accounting clients to look after. Her thoughts drift to Vincent as easily as her nose turns to a vanilla scented candle flame. The attraction between them has intensified over the summer, a fanciful mind being easily encouraged by the warm ferments of the season. Isabelle is obsessed with the passion, the rush of happiness, and the tumult of emotion that every encounter brings. It's impossible to escape such a possession. *Is there a like place in heaven? Just drop me off in this breathless world. I could wander here forever.* She finds it difficult to settle into financial paperwork so she writes in her journal, puts her head back to think awhile, goes outside into the fresh air, walks around in the back yard, rips out some high flowering weeds that are growing near the steps, and begins to cut back the perennials that have come to the end of their blossoming season. Around four o'clock in the afternoon, Dugan appears in front of her in an old pair of corduroy jeans softened from numerous washings, and a body-revealing sleeveless neckless jersey like a weightlifter would wear, biceps rippling, and holding a chainsaw at the end of his arm.

"I saw you out wandering around, Isabelle. Thought you might want some of those Manitoba maples trimmed."

"Oh! Hello, Dugan. You startled me," she says, noticing that his physique is more like that of a twenty-fiver than a fifty-three year old.

"Those trees grow wild if you let them."

"Do they? I kind of like the way the branches lean over and touch the ground. It reminds me of a weeping willow outside the factory where my father worked when I was little. The long trailing vines formed a curtain around the outside of the tree. I felt like an actress entering a different world whenever I swept aside the green veil and stepped into the center of that leafy dome. I'd spend hours just imagining in that magical place. I loved being inside that tree."

"I guess that's all right if the branches stay put in the yard but the trees on the edge will break your neighbour's fence."

"How's that?"

"The limbs grow fast and fall over. They'll be a lot more trouble later once they're big. Better to fix them now."

"Well, okay, go ahead and cut those branches that are hanging over if you like. I don't want to get into repairing fences, but leave the others the way they are."

Dugan works for an hour with his chainsaw, gathers the cuttings into a pile on the lawn, then returns to where Isabelle is cleaning a flowerbed.

"I didn't know you were around, Dugan," she says, her eyes straying to the dark patch sweating through the front of his shirt and the wet skin glistening on his face, neck, and arms.

"I'm on holidays for two more weeks."

"Nice."

"What's new?"

"Nothing so far. Two people are interested in the Manoir now, so I hope something comes from one or the other."

"Would you like to go out for dinner tonight? You keep cutting me off, Isabelle, and you know I would do anything for you. You know I love you. What more do you want?"

Isabelle accepts his invitation, wanting to test for some spark in him she may have ignored that would allow her to like him more. Over dinner, Dugan makes a plea on his behalf that he's the perfect complement for her–he is the practical and reliable side; she is the idealist, the dreamer. When Dugan gives her a kiss goodnight at the front door, the vapours of achingly sweet forbidden fruit sticky with desire and Vincent overtake Isabelle, and she can't bear Dugan's touch.

Love twists itself into strange shapes and winds unexpectedly through unknown passages. Isabelle yearns to move beyond the borders of the commonplace and everyday, past the emotional and tender, to the aesthetic and divine. A wondrously elusive place summons her with its enchantment, but her love is a lonely one, burdened with secrecy and sullied by the illicit. Still, love demands a stage on which to play out its anguish, its desires, and its madness. Love dares and challenges you to descend to the very depths of soul where treasures of the spirit frolic in seemingly wild and dangerous abandon while they wait and long for discovery. The gods are known to be suggestive when they're in a seductive mood, disguising themselves in forms that are irresistible to mere mortals. So it is with Isabelle's love that refuses to be compromised, making her live the extremes of agony and ecstasy, swirling her into the great hungry cavern of love's melancholy, and consuming her with the rush of its passion until it runs its course.

J anuary is frigid.

Vincent should be back any day now. Isabelle has been watching the calendar, anticipating the end of his month-long vacation. The telephone rings early one morning during the second week of the new year. "Isabelle. It's Vincent," the words smooth and caressing. "I got back a few days ago, but there was so much work waiting for me at the office I didn't have time to call." She would have liked to ask him if he missed her or if he had thought about her while he was away, but she was afraid of his reaction. He might think her sentimental, a goose, indulging in drivel. Or he might say he didn't have time to think about her, or give some other plausible reason she didn't want to hear, something having to do with his wife. During his absence, she managed to bury her feelings–out of sight, out of mind. Alas, the feeble-minded thought was of short duration. And here he is, her lover, Vincent, very much alive, his quiet voice tugging at the very roots of her soul. She forgets her resolve to keep her feet on the ground and feels herself rising through the air to another space, soft and resistless, like a divinity passing through a thought. *How do I love thee? Let me count the ways.* Oh, do let me count them again! Perhaps I can think of another.

"**I** never knew such a woman as you."

"Why don't I believe that?"

"There is no other woman as strong in the whole area."

"Come on, Monsieur Jeanneau."

"And you work hard. You know how to work and you work well," he says to Isabelle in his hesitant English that accents the last syllable. French applied to English with charming results.

"You flatter me."

It is an afternoon in mid-month and Isabelle had walked across Wakeham to Monsieur Jeanneau's house. The cold winter air was as high and dry as a strained note on a piccolo, as sharp as a snakebite. Underfoot, the snow creaked and crunched, each step landing on a bed of crystal shards, leaving behind a trail of shadowed white on pure white. She calls him her 'éminence grise'. Monsieur Jeanneau is approaching eighty years of age, has made millions in his lifetime, and holds the first mortgage on the Manoir. He knows of the struggles she has been through in the many attempts to get a project going in that building. Usually, he shakes his head and reminds her she has paid too much for it, but this afternoon he is full of compliments.

"Everything today is hard," he continues. "It's not like the old days. You're too nice to work so hard. You don't need to work that hard to live."

"That sounds all right to me." Isabelle laughs a wistful disbelieving-but-wanting-to-believe laugh.

"That's the way it should be. Work less, love more."

"So how do I get this building out of my life?"

Monsieur Jeanneau offers to teach Isabelle his business. "You could be a partner with me." It was half a question, half a statement.

"But I don't have any money to buy a partnership in your business!"

"Doesn't matter, that." He gesticulates grandly in the air in his nonchalant manner, extravagant arms welcoming a host of symphonies, large open palms embracing the world. He's at home in his high-backed swivel armchair, enjoying the moment, a shy smile on his face. Inquisitive eyes are looking directly at Isabelle, searching the lay of the land to see what they will encounter. One is never too sure of what is going on in Monsieur Jeanneau's thinking. Cool as a cucumber. Always. "We can make an arrangement," he tells her. "You do all the work, I provide the money."

Isabelle listens in partial disbelief. Many times she has sat in this cushioned chair with uncomfortable wooden armrests across from Monsieur Jeanneau's desk and marveled at his remarkable stories of business dealings, which sound like a John Grisham novel. *How did he manage to do all he did? Had to be a good portion of luck involved.* Half a million in income taxes is what he has sent to the government each year for the past twenty years. "You know, we had no money when we were young. I never owned a pair of skates and I never went past grade three."

"Don't tell me that!" says Isabelle, thinking of her own eighteen years of schooling, which all of a sudden seem as useful to her as a bent nail does to a carpenter. Where had they got her? Except here in front of Monsieur Jeanneau considering a business proposal from a man whom her parents spoke of with foreboding. Perhaps it was the money they feared not the man. "Three years of school? I guess schooling and success don't necessarily go together."

"University's a good place to keep smart people out of the way where they can't do any harm."

Isabelle smiles at this comment. "That's one way of looking at it."

"My father said that if a man's word wasn't as good as his handshake, then he was worth nothing. I always remembered that. 'Respect each other and honour your commitments,' he told me and my brothers. Excuse me, but he didn't talk to my sisters the same way. No intention to harm. None at all. That's just the way it was. But, you know, somebody who want, they can.

And I happened to be in the right place at the right time."

"A success story."

"Not everyone will agree. Qu'est-ce que tu veux que je fasse? But what can I do?" throwing out his long arms, hands upturned, questioning a perplexing thing out of his control. "But now I keep several million around in spare money. ... Just in case I want to buy something," he adds as an afterthought, chuckling at her astonishment. Isabelle considers his proposition. *But a moneylender?* Monsieur Jeanneau finances those who are unable to get money through normal avenues at a rate of interest higher than the banks. And he has a reputation around town. Tough. *Don't get yourself messed up with Jeanneau,* is the local maxim. Perhaps he has mellowed with age. Still, she is skeptical.

The end of February brings no new developments. Nothing is moving, the entire pond is frozen, even the fish at the bottom. Isabelle is ready to sell everything–the Manoir, her house in Wakeham, the Old Folks' Home in LaViolette–and start over again if that's what it takes. *Oh, to do just that! To buy or not to buy. To have that decision to make all over again!* What she wouldn't give for a retake. She's at a loss for what to do, unfastened, buffeted back and forth by shore waves, scattered, puzzled, shunted. She desperately wants a focus, an eye peering at her from a thicket, a light in the distance, no matter how far, just so long as she can see it well enough to locate it. What does it take to loosen whatever strings are holding tight? To slacken this dogged determination to remain unfinished? To hit on the right mix of ingredients that will open the door? This morning, as has become her habit for the past few years, she sits at her desk to write in her journal. A curious dream of two years ago seeps into her thinking, stealthily, like spilt milk spreading across the floor, just as it has often done when she is quiet a few moments and lost in thought. She flips back through her notebooks to find the entry and reread what she has written:

February 22nd, 1994.

Last night, I dreamt I was traveling alone in Egypt. I was about to embark on a journey up the Nile River on an open barge made of rough logs fastened tightly together. Two young men sat at the front of this raft that they steered with a long wooden pole attached to a rudder underneath the flat bottom. They didn't know where to find the place I was looking for; their job was to keep the boat afloat. Not far ahead, the water was murky and apparently treacherous where it flowed out of the darkness of a primeval looking jungle. Long creeping vines coiled themselves around ancient trees and hung from thick overhead foliage that obscured the sunlight. Tall straight reeds reached high out of the river.

111

I wondered how I would ever make it through the dangerous scene in front of me. Then a woman about my own age appeared on the boat. She had a smooth brownish complexion and was wearing a peasant dress in red batik that reached to the floor of the raft. Her long dark hair fell softly over her shoulders in loose natural curls and a noticeably calm and peaceful expression was on her pretty face. She looked directly at me and said, "I will guide you."

Some months after the Egypt dream, Isabelle had awakened to idle thoughts of the dream lady who was going to guide her. Was she the girlfriend of one of the men at the front of the boat? Or was she, perhaps, their mistress? Or was this an Egyptian custom of which she was unaware? The woman wasn't there when the journey began. How did she appear so abruptly? Or was she an apparition? That's it. Of course, she was. It was a dream. Then was she an apparition in a dream? A ghostly affair? That's ridiculous. She was as real as I was, except I wasn't really real either. I was my dream self. But I was real. Sure I was. I don't stop being real just because I'm in my dream. I'm real here and I'm real there. Those are my feelings I feel. If it wasn't me, if I was an apparition, how could I feel my feelings? Why shouldn't the lady be as real as I am, in the same way that I'm here and also there? What's to prevent her from being in two worlds at the same time? I am. It reminds me of Coleridge's poem about dreaming you picked a flower in a garden and woke up with the flower in your hand. I wonder if she has a name.

'Name' had scarcely been thought when "Winona!" reverberated in her head, clearly and without a moment's hesitation. The voice that said, "Winona," was her mind's voice, the usual voice that talked and doubted and questioned and speculated. It made her think she had imagined the name herself, because the voice that spoke was not an unfamiliar one. She was quite impressed and began to talk to the dream lady.

"Please excuse me for calling you 'Winona' if that's not your name, but I really feel it is, otherwise I don't know where it came from. I didn't have time to think."

Isabelle hadn't thought much about Winona since that time. The past two years had been stressful and demanding, the Manoir having been an unknown entity for so long that the enthusiasm of the challenge had long ago turned into an expensive and distressing burden, an unwanted child. Last December, another negative reply to a funding proposal was received. During the fall, she completed work on a prospectus for the Rural Center for the Arts and submitted it to Monsieur Péladeau, an arts philanthropist, a resident of the town of Ste. Adèle, a community situated north of Montreal in the foothills of the Laurentian Mountains. He was an icon of Québecois culture, a business tycoon and an ardent admirer of Beethoven's music. His answer was returned just before Christmas. An assistant conveyed the message that Monsieur Péladeau already funded many arts societies and, regrettably, wasn't able to take on others at that time.

The holidays. Decorating the tree and the house. Sliding in the park with Anna and the kids. Eating extravagant meals with equally extravagant proportions of wine and drink. Watching movies. Wrapping presents. Opening presents. Even the bustle of the Christmas season didn't bring much relief. Alex, Anna, her husband, and the two children visited during the break. The interlude of non-stop activity was welcome, but the torment was still there, unresolved and festering. A double necessity made Isabelle live a charade for the others while trying to ignore the agonizing state of her inner life, but the pus, smelling foul, was beginning to trickle out of the sore into the open.

Not-knowing has always turned Isabelle inside out. She hovers in a no man's land that is surely like a Protestant hell or the limboland of the Catholics right here on earth, a nebulous region, more pathetic than violent, oozing of rot and spoilage, of deeds undone, of greyish glutinous matter, smelling of sluggish vomit and sour wine. Now and then, a frantic exasperation takes over and refuses to loosen its discomfiting hold, keeping her on edge day and night. A delicate balance between acceptance and rejection, between yes, she is all right, and no, she isn't, sways back and forth leaning too easily toward inadequacy and emptiness. Failure is invading her life like a plague in the process of blurring everything about it, an insupportable concept in the scheme of living, a cause for which one could die. Mercifully, there are moments of joy and happiness when the scale tips over to hope and feeling wonderfully alive and all is right and beautiful once more.

But it is a tiny core in the center of her being that gathers all her attention when she is calm enough to look inside. It seems to be at the very root of her, a singular authority immune to criticism or control, a wee nugget of something or other that glues all the pieces together. What a mystery it is, this irrational item, this unearthly little nib of a thing that seems to have a claim on her life, that reappears again and again in the same places in her body with the same demanding feelings of urgency and need.

"Are you a guide or aren't you? I'm not enjoying this at all. Can't you do any better than that?"

There have been so many leads, refusals, and setbacks that Isabelle, in spite of her wonderment at the dreamy phenomenon, finds it difficult to believe she is being guided. What kind of a guide would allow you to struggle and fight and despair so? Shouldn't she be receiving a few hints on what to do to make things work? This morning, at the end of February, as she sits at her desk, Isabelle talks to Winona admonishing her for not doing her job.

"How much more of this can I take? How much? You've put a lot of obstacles in front of me, Winona. Isn't it time to give me a break, arrange things in my favour for a change? There's a limit to my endurance, you know. You may be more familiar with the world I met you in, but here is where I'm living right now and I know it better than you do, so it seems. You are testing me, aren't you? Well, I'm tough to break. I'm trusting you to help me work things out, but I'll balk one of these times, then I don't know what will happen. Stop playing games with me, Winona. I'll get mad at you if you throw many more punches at me!"

*"Take your hands off the steering wheel. Be
able to say to the Universe, 'Thy will be
done,' and to know it with your intentions.
Spend time in this thought. ... The final piece
of reaching for authentic power is releasing
your own to a higher form of wisdom."*

Gary Zukav,
The Seat of the Soul

The end is at hand. When the tree appears in front of her, silent and unyielding, she lets go of the steering wheel. The instant she feels the tire touch the gravel at the side of the road she knows what's coming. Her eyes are wide open when the car hits the tree trunk, as if to observe a drama from afar, anxious to see the sequence of events in the last act, the surreal episode having taken on all of the elements of reality.

It's a Friday morning in mid-March and Isabelle is preparing to go to Brockville, Ontario for a weekend orientation for incoming Presidents of the Rotary Clubs in the district. She irons clothes, packs her bags, and tidies the house so it will be clean and neat when she returns on Sunday. Ought to be a good encounter, she thinks. Stimulating. Energizing. She's looking forward to it. Her club is going to sponsor a clean water project in Guatemala and she arranges a file to take with her. Robert Graham, of the World Community Service District Committee, is supposed to be at the training session and she wants to check a few points with him. If anyone knows how to submit these projects, it's Bob. He's the one to talk to. After the papers are in order, she spends the better part of an hour on the telephone trying to reach Mr. Antoine Villeneuve. Another busy signal. How many is that? Doesn't he ever get off the phone? Mr. Villeneuve owns a seniors' Residence called La Villa Pomerleau in Ste. Thérèse, north of Montreal, and is looking for other locations in which to expand. Norman Brennan, the mayor of LaViolette, has referred her to him, thinking the Manoir might be what Mr. Villeneuve is looking for. A secretary finally answers, "Est-ce que je peux vous aider?" takes her name and telephone number and says she will convey a message to her boss to return the call whenever he is free. Isabelle writes a company cheque to herself to cash at the bank and begins to load the car. A heavy-duty covered cardboard box of accounting papers is on the back seat that weighs about eighty pounds. She tries to maneuvre it out of the automobile, wanting to leave it behind in the house, but the clumsy bulk is too awkward to handle alone, so the case remains where it is, on the seat directly behind the driver.

Two o'clock in the afternoon. She stops at the bank to cash the cheque and takes the highway that leads north out of the village, glad to be on her way. The afternoon is clear, a pleasant day for a drive, the fresh March air a harbinger of nicer days to come, and there is no need to rush. She has plenty of time to travel the hundred and twenty miles to Brockville before the registration period opens at five o'clock. She begins to run through her list of things to do, checking to see that nothing has been forgotten: project file, summary of club plans, stopped at bank, cleaned house, called Mother, doors are locked, windows down, enough food and water and litter for Toulouse, ironed suit, didn't forget toothbrush, … and then begins wondering about Antoine Villeneuve, the person who might be interested in the Manoir. I wonder how Norman knows about him. Maybe he advertised in the Montreal papers. I didn't see anything in *The Reaper*. Maybe Norman met him at a meeting of municipal mayors. Or maybe he has relatives here. It would be easier to convince him if he already knows the area. A good presentation that would sell the quiet country location, the distinctiveness of the building, and the large aging population should arouse his interest. Those three points are a good combination for someone in the business of housing seniors. Isabelle begins mentally preparing her delivery.

Suddenly, a noise and a thump. The right front tire grates onto the stony shoulder of the road blasting a spray of grey shale into the air and sending the crows flapping and screeching with sharp irritated cries above the muddy March fields. The shock snaps her out of her reverie and, startled, she jerks the steering wheel to the left. Oh no! The car veers crazily across the highway like a shaman's quartz crystal on an attack route. Winona! What are you doing? She pulls the wheel to the right with all her strength and just before flying off the road into the ditch, the car swerves back across the highway. Whew! Now it's headed for the drainage channel on the other side. Not again! *Don't touch the brakes, Isy! You'll lose control.* I'd better not touch the brakes. I might lose control. Once more, the chassis of the station wagon hovers over a steep grade and turns back just in time. Thank you. Thank you. Thank you. Again, Isabelle tightens her grip on the wheel and tries to guide the runaway vehicle back in the right lane but she doesn't have enough strength. I'm going to die. I should pray now, she thinks. I should try to pray. The old Buick wagon of eighteen hundred pounds holds too much momentum and she is powerless to stop the insane zigzagging. Too late to pray. Idiot. What were you thinking? Something serious is about to happen. Dear God.

It's the middle of the afternoon, has been a bright and sunny spring-like day, however, it now seems to be nighttime and the car is still hurtling across the highway. It is hurtling across the highway in everyone else's time zone, but, for Isabelle, time has slowed down. The space between seconds has expanded into dimensions without measurement. She speaks to Winona, "Am I going to die here? Is this how I die, Winona?" But whatever is in store doesn't seem to matter anymore. Her life is out of her hands. That much is certain. And somehow it will turn out all right. It will. She doesn't know how, but it will. She prepares to take whatever is coming, and it is coming in leaps and bounds because the dice have been cast, and she relaxes her hold on the steering wheel. Let's get it over with. It can't be that bad. This is not the way I'm going to die. Then, not far ahead and to the left of the highway, a driveway appears. *Get off the highway, Isy!* I've got to get off the highway. She gathers her strength once more and pulls the wheel to the right, aiming the car back on the road. Turn! Turn! The loose cannon follows her intention and straightens itself out. Surprise! Now the driveway. Pull hard to the left and hold on. *Harder, Isy! Harder! I'm cheering for you, honey! Go, Isy!* The car speeds into the driveway where a solitary tree stands to the right, a small white house is not far behind, and a middle-aged balding man, his feet braced apart on the ground, is standing near the side door of the home, his hands waving madly in the air. The wild ride is coming to a close and the tree looms in front of the windshield, a dark obelisk signaling the end of the journey. Isabelle watches spellbound as eighteen hundred pounds of metal and glass crash head-on into the trunk. The violence of the impact throws her head against the steering wheel knocking her unconscious. I'm going home. *Are you really, Isy?* There's something I have to do first. *Yes, there is, dear.* If I could just see through this smoke. Then I'd know. *Sing me a song of a gal that is gone.* Where's it coming from anyhow? No smoke without fire. *Say, could that gal be I?* If it would just clear away. If I could just see some blue sky. *Merry of soul she sailed on a day.* I'd know what it is I have to do if I could see. *Over the sea to Skye.* Just give me minute. Just a minute to gather myself. *Take all the time you need, Isy, you'll come around when you're ready, child.* The force of the collision reverses itself when it comes to a dead end, propelling the old Buick backwards. It spins dizzily around, the tail end smashing into the tree and bouncing off before coming to a full stop, its dilapidated body headed in the opposite direction to that in which it entered the driveway. At the same time, eighty pounds of accounting papers speed like a projectile into the back of the front seat.

Isabelle reaches for a tissue to wipe her face. There are tears in her eyes, not because of the pain or why me questions or self-recriminations, but because her guide is beside her. The tears are releasing a slush of tension, like the outwash tossed aside by a meltwater, a calm purity replacing a detritus of anxiety. She is lying quietly in a hospital bed about one week after the accident. Nothing else holds any importance at this moment. If she were to slip into death, into *the land of Nod, on the east of Eden,* the last expression on her face would be one of peace and happiness. Everything is just perfect. The whole bizarre wild drama of her life is okay; the strange tale has a reason to it; each person, each event has a meaning. That comforting presence moves in Isabelle and she weeps knowing that a higher force, a guardian power, is watching over her. If her body isn't alive and well, her inner spirit is, and she will never be alone again.

Isabelle is scarcely able to move. There's a broken bone in her spine. A tube is taped to her nose with white adhesive; it leads through the nasal passage and her throat into the stomach. A clear solution drips into her veins from a plastic bag that hangs on a steel tree above her head. A catheter hangs below the bed to take away the yellow drip. A major concussion makes a puffy lump on her forehead in front of the left brain. Her nose was broken when her face hit the steering wheel and there are bloody stitches along the cut where the end was split open. Her abdomen is swollen to the size of a seventh-month pregnancy–in its struggle to hold her in place, the lower portion of the seatbelt crushed her internal organs and, as a result, they can accept neither food nor water and have ballooned with air and liquid debris from injured tissues. Black and blue and red bruises cover her body and wild pains shoot at will up and down her left leg, which has no feeling above the knee.

Many hours are spent staring off into space, allowing thoughts and images to come and go, settling into a stillness, a recognition of that formless energy beside her, and surrendering her own will to that of another. And Isabelle allows herself to feel cared for.

Words run into each other and meanings don't connect. Conversation is difficult, nigh on impossible. The friends who gather around the bed talk back and forth to each other, updating each other on the latest morsels of gossip, who's getting divorced, who's kids are in trouble, who's visiting who, who's spending too much money, who's sick at home, and who's in the hospital, the recent happenings.

"What do you think, Isabelle?"

"About what?"

"Oh, it's okay. We thought you were listening."

"I was."

Why do they speak so fast? Although nothing in their manner appears to have changed, the words are coming at her too quickly to register. Skittery and slick. When she does manage a reply, she changes the subject so as not to reveal that she hasn't caught the gist of the conversation. But then her voice lets her down. It turns into husky gravel after a few sentences are spoken and gradually fades away into a whisper. Or, a particular thought will be in her mind, she knows what she wants to say, the sounds are right there on the tip of her tongue, but she can't figure out how to say it. The moment she tries to verbalize the thought, she can't make the connection between her brain and her speech muscles, as if the connection were not hers to make anymore, or as if the amplifiers to a stereo system had been turned on but the tapes in the tape deck weren't registering a thing. The words just won't form and she wonders how they got there in the first place. A thought or an idea seems as ethereal as a spirit and as non-local to our fleshy bodily equipment as radio waves are to a radio. Wolfgang Amadeus Mozart is not inside the radio. The likewise is too difficult to contemplate. Maybe she'll try again later when the act of thinking isn't so tiring. When the quiet returns after visiting hours and she tries to playback the time, to re-enjoy the company, she isn't sure who has been there or what they have told her. She can't remember. Trying to remember is worse, like trying to catch a drop of mercury, elusive mercury. Tiring. Annoying. Impossible. A glimpse of a memory will tease and beckon with an invitation to come closer, but will slip away under the weight of further scrutiny. It's much more pleasant to give her own thoughts space to roam where they wish and simply watch their gentle flow as intentionless as sheep in a pasture or clouds.

Alex travels from Ontario when he can get away for a day. He is twenty-five now and looks after his grandmother, Callah, on the three hundred acre farm by the lake, part of which has been converted to a summer camping ground for tents and trailers. Isabelle hasn't seen Callah for some time since she doesn't travel anymore—she's afraid of falling in unfamiliar surroundings—and soon idle thoughts of her ex-mother-in-law are filling her head.

Eccentric and independent all her life, Callah was the spark in the engine who spurred everyone on to greater heights, the fly in the buttermilk who ranted and raved when something was amiss, but she is losing herself now. Alex has his hands full. At eighty, his Nana is stooped and walks gingerly, favouring her right ankle. For the past few years she has worn two pairs of eyeglasses to read and two pairs of pants to keep her warm in winter. Her usual prescription glasses aren't strong enough, she says, so she balances a second pair, which belonged to her father, on top of the first. And, on cold days, she pulls on a larger pair of brown polyester pants over the first pair, fastening the oversized waist with a horse-blanket pin.

Everyone in the county knows Callah. Some don't like her, thinking

119

Callah too smart, too ornery and contrary, too comfortable with her differentness, just too much of everything. Many have had disagreements with her but one is hard put to find a person who doesn't respect her, not even Alex's young and boisterous friends, who at first argue with a diminutive seemingly frail old woman. However, they soon find their places with Callah. On occasion, when she's in the right mood, she'll join the boys outside around the picnic table under a lawn tree and have a beer with them, listening to their tall yarns, exaggerated intentionally to get a rise out of Callah who will laugh wholeheartedly at their antics. "Oh, go on, you don't mean that!" The fellas call her by her first name.

"Anything we can do for you today, Callah?"

"Why, thank you, boys. Well now, yes, there is something. Could you carry in some firewood for me? Just put it in the box by the cookstove. Some mornings are terribly cool when I get up and I like to start a small fire just to take the chill off the air. Not a big one, mind you, it only lasts for half a hour, but that's enough to do the trick."

"Sure thing, Callah."

Boomer and Digger chat to each other as they work at the woodpile.

"Wha' d' ya think, Boomer? One hell of an ol' gal, that Callah, eh?"

"You got that right, Dig."

"She'll bite your head off one minute if you don't do somethin' right, then turn around, pull out a chair for ya to sit on, plunk herself right down beside ya, look ya right in the eye and ask ya to talk out whatever's botherin' ya," says Digger, adding another block of wood to his armload.

"Yeah, man. I know what ya mean. Sometimes she gives me the heebie jeebies, but then she'll go and make me smile."

"Boy, I tell ya! They don't make 'em like that anymore."

"But, jeez, I don't know about her clothes, man," adds Boomer. "Bitchy rich and she dresses like a bag lady."

"Threw away the mould after Callah came along, Boom."

"Ha ha. I guess that's what happened all right."

Callah has been driving the pick-up instead of the car since Robinson died. She can see better, she says. The stoop on her back reduces her to four feet and so many inches, not enough to make her five feet tall, so to drive the truck she has to look between the rim of the steering wheel and the top of the dashboard to see the road in front of her. A baseball cap, the peak pulled so low on her forehead that it covers her eyebrows, keeps the sun out of her eyes. They're sensitive to sunlight. Alex wonders how she can see out the window at all and laughs when he drives down Willow Park Road to the farm and an old green pick-up with no driver is inching its way towards him. Callah on her way to town.

Callah has attended to the business of the family all her life and the older she is the longer it takes her to get organized. The drive from the farm into Willow River takes only ten minutes, but Callah ponders and reponders her schedule many times over before she is ready to make the trip. "Gather round guys," Digger says to his friends, "Callah's goin' to town. Come see this." The running board under the truck door is high, so Callah leaves a kitchen pot, a long cord fastened onto the end of the handle, turned upside down in the yard near the driver's side. She picks up the pot, scrutinizing it for any sign of disturbance, and replaces it on the ground in the proper position. Then, holding the string tightly in her left hand, she opens the truck door, steps on top of the pot, grabs onto the steering wheel, reaches the step with her left foot, brings up her sore right foot, climbs onto the seat, then pulls the pot up behind her into the truck. Anyone who passes the farmhouse knows about Callah's pot sitting in the yard, or sitting on the front seat when the truck's in town, and tells the story.

Isabelle smiles when she thinks of Callah, of her unabashed honesty.

Dugan arrives quietly in the room one afternoon during visiting hours and settles into a chair beside the bed. Isabelle has given him a key to her house so he can feed Toulouse the cat while she is away and he often comes to sit and tell her the news. A few minutes later, Vincent walks in with a bouquet of fresh flowers, plants a kiss in the middle of Isabelle's forehead, nods a hello to Dugan, and begins to rearrange the night table to make room for the collection of pink and white lilies and blue irises. Dugan leaves without saying a word.

"I hope she's not left with a scarred face," says Verda Carberry. She's talking to Miriam, Mr. Carberry's younger sister. Verda visits once a week when she has a driver to take her from Wakeham to the regional hospital in Salaberry-de-Valleyfield.

"Golly, Verda. How can you think of such a thing? Her life's in danger."

Miriam is driving her sister-in-law home. Verda's husband, Jake, died suddenly five years ago from a brain aneurysm while working in his workshop and Mrs. Carberry, badly crippled with arthritis, now lives in a nursing home. It is Aunt Miriam who visits Isabelle regularly and who, along with the doctors, thinks her chance for recovery to be slight at best during the first two weeks, then anxiously watches her progress.

Geffun

At the end of April, wheeled onto the elevator, through the hospital corridors, and out into the fresh air by Aunt Miriam, Isabelle leaves the hospital. It has been six weeks. Isabelle is able to walk, with the help of a cane, to Miriam's car in the parking lot. The left vocal chord is paralysed, inexplicably, hence the whiskey voice, making it difficult to pronounce any word with a long 'e.' The vowel slides up and down her windpipe trying to find a place to land, garbling the already dusty sounds that come from her larynx. Aunt Miriam looks after her at her home in Salaberry-de-Valleyfield for a week before Isabelle returns to her own house in Wakeham. The last Saturday afternoon that she spends at her aunt's, Isabelle calls Dugan. "I'll be home in a few days, Dugan. I just called to let you know. Is Toulouse okay?"

"Sure." The one word reply puts a damper on her attempt to begin a friendly conversation and she suspects that Dugan's reticence to cooperate is related to Vincent. "Has the garage sold the car to the scrap yard?"

Dugan hadn't come around for a while with an update on the local happenings. Isabelle listens, quite unable to believe that she is hearing correctly since what he is saying has nothing to do with her question: "I have sexual needs and money needs. My sexual needs are more important to me than my money needs. And since you don't seem to have any intention of fulfilling my sexual needs, I want my money needs looked after."

"Have you taken leave of your senses, Dugan?"

"What?"

"I mean, can I quote you?"

"Ummm. Yes. I guess so."

"What do you want?"

"A lean on your house, or something. I have nothing."

"You have a paper. Anyway, some people–a policeman and a man from the school commission–are interested in putting a Youth Center in that building. They came to see me the week before the accident and they want me to help organize it."

"Yeah, sure. I've heard that before. You shouldn't be in business. You can't organize anything. I'm fed up waiting. I want some action."

"I'm not even home yet, Dugan. What can I do?" her voice starting to give out.

"Well, I'm going to see my lawyer. Like I said, I'm not waiting around for the sky to fall. You'll be getting a legal letter in the mail one of these days."

"I don't have any voice left," she rasps.

"You never said anything anyway."

"Fine. Goodbye," the salutation like a hoarse whisper.

By the second week in May, Isabelle is on her own again. Friends drop in a few times a day to help with the cooking, cleaning, and laundry. Agnes brings the occasional meal from the Old Folks' Home in LaViolette and news of the business. "Mme Dupuis wouldn't come downstairs for her meals again last week. Her daughter stopped in the Sunday before, I don't know if that has anything to do with it, but after she visits Mme Dupuis always complains of arthritis in all her bones and pains in her stomach and won't come to the dining room to eat with the others. … And Fred helped me to get Chloé into the bathtub last Friday, it was her turn for a bath, and I gave her a shower instead. I got in with her so she wouldn't fall and you should've seen her face when she felt the water running on her bare skin! I've never seen such a happy look. … And Mrs. White's blood sugar was sky high on Monday. She almost passed out on us. Every time her boyfriend takes her home for the weekend she eats what she pleases and then she doesn't feel well for the rest of the week. … I sent Marnie to the hospital by ambulance again yesterday morning but she was back in the afternoon. Poor Marnie. She couldn't get her breath. It was pretty scary for a while. If you ask me it has something to do with that lump on the side of her throat. I swear it's getting bigger. … And we're nearly out of steaks and laundry soap and chickens are on special this week at ninety-eight cents a pound. Can you give me four hundred dollars? I'll have to do a big shopping on Thursday."

After several days, Dugan telephones. "Aloha! Back home, I see."

"Hello, Dugan."

"Do you want me to come over sometime for a coffee?"

"No, Dugan. I'm not up to a visit from you."

"Aw, come on. I just want to see what you look like."

Afraid of what he might do if she refuses to see him, Isabelle agrees. "Okay, Dugan. You can come. But only for a few minutes. And I don't want to discuss anything upsetting."

A few minutes later, the bell on the front door, which is as old as the house, rings with a noise loud enough to cause a flock of birds to whoosh into the air from the tall maple tree at the side of the driveway, their plumage flapping in angry unison.

"Well, hello. You're looking not too bad. I haven't seen you for a week. Talked to you a few times on the phone though."

"It's been more like four weeks, Dugan."

"Here's your license plate. The garage gave it to me. … Hmmm. Nice flowers. ... Eddie Lucas is sick and dying. Did you know?"

"No, I didn't. That's too bad."

"So you don't want to talk about anything."

"Dugan, I'm tired."

"Tired! Did I hear right? Did you say you're tired? You never did an honest day's work in your life! You never held a regular job, never contributed anything to the community! You earned all kinds of degrees, but just for yourself, not to use them for society! Your life has been in a tailspin for years, ever since you were in that insane asylum. You gave your son away, for God's sake! Don't you have a soul?"

Isabelle says nothing, thinking she has just swallowed a cup of crushed glass that is still slashing her insides.

"Well, I must go back and look after my house. Call me if you need anything. I still have an affection for you, although you may not believe it. I was just trying to settle things."

Again, silence.

"Well, good evening, then."

"Good evening."

Head reeling, heart palpitating, Isabelle closes the door, the tightness attacking her stomach. In an automatic gesture, she goes to her desk, sits, reaches for her journal, opens it where she left off in the morning, then records Dugan's angry tirade to get rid of the words that still circulate in her thoughts. She continues writing:

I give up. Why did I let him come over? I don't wish him any harm. I just want him to stay out of my life. I'll never be able to talk to him. He's like my mother. I can't talk to her about anything either. Well, I've got Winona. I'll talk to her.

The next day is Sunday and Isabelle calls a taxi to take her to the nursing home in the village to visit Mrs. Carberry and her friends, Stella and Pearl. Pearl is a kind soul with thinning beige hair and a weak faltering voice that makes it hard for the others to understand what she is saying, causing her to be ignored in the usual run of talk amongst the residents. Stella, somewhat younger than Pearl, has had one leg and several fingers amputated and is wheelchair bound, but in spite of all her problems, she has a jovial nature. A favourite ploy of Stella's is to ask a handsome bearded man, tee hee, who happens to be visiting relatives or attending one of the Family Day celebrations at the home, if, tee hee, it tickles to get a kiss with a growth like that on his face. This brings giggles not only from Stella herself but from those close enough to have heard the question, and Stella always gets a kiss so she can decide for herself if the bush is kissable or too scratchy to touch a feminine face. "O-o-o-o-oh, it's soft!" she manages to coo before being overcome by gales of laughter.

This Sunday at lunch, sitting at their usual table in the dining room, are Pearl, Stella, Stella's husband, Isabelle, and her mother. Stella is bubbling over with news of her daughter's teenage daughter.

"My granddaughter's graduation from high school was last weekend," she begins. "What a show! You ought to have seen it! Her boyfriend picked her up in long white limousine to go to a fancy dinner in Montreal. I'm not kidding! It was about fifteen feet long and all white, straight out of Hollywood. And you should have seen the special hairdo. Long hair all piled up on top of her head. Little ringlets hanging around her face. First time I saw her wearing lipstick. My, but she was pretty. And what a dress! Velvet. Dark navy blue. Puffy little sleeves that lay just off the shoulder. Tiny gathers made with stitches so small they could have been my own in better days. Long skirt. Oh! You should have seen her!" Stella's face lights up and her eyes sparkle as she imagines the beautiful sight with her hands.

"Well, Stella, I hope they took some pictures."

"Of course, they did, Verda. Lots of pictures and portraits under the trees, you know, the way they do them now, natural poses, romantic like. And there were all-night parties," Stella continues. "The trend now is all-night field parties. In some farmer's field! What a hoot!"

"Oh, no! Getting dirt on a tuxedo! Imagine that!" adds Verda.

"They had a wonderful time, all those young people together. I wish I was young again." Stella finishes her story with a big smile on her face.

"That's not like the graduations our girls used to have–a nice dinner in the cafeteria, an award ceremony, and dancing afterwards in the gymnasium."

"Mum, that was thirty years ago. Besides, we used to party all night too. Remember? Six of us ended up at our house for breakfast at five in the morning."

"I don't remember that at all."

Stella and Verda don't get into conversations with each other. It turns into an argument so they keep their interactions to who's related to whom and the weather. That's pretty safe territory. Isabelle doesn't see so much as a hint of a smile this day. When Anna goes to visit a few times a year, Mrs. Carberry beams with smiles, smiles that continue into the week after Anna has left as Mrs. Carberry tells all her friends of the visit. Isabelle guesses that she didn't turn out the way her mother wanted.

"Iris and I went shopping last Thursday," she says, trying to open a conversation. "She took me to a doctor's appointment in Valleyfield. We had lunch and chatted a while then went shopping. I bought a dress for Angela's

126

wedding in June. And a hat." Angela is Miriam's granddaughter.

"A hat!" Mrs. Carberry looks at Isabelle. She obviously doesn't approve of the purchase and Isabelle waits for the next comment, which is not long in arriving. "You need that like a hole in the head."

With a shrug, Isabelle turns to Stella and Pearl who are nodding their heads and talking about how, when they were young girls, they were instructed how to angle your hat on your head to cast a flattering shadow over your cheekbone. No one of the feminine genre would ever have thought of attending a wedding without a hat, they were saying. Whoever did so must not have been invited in the first place, most likely would have been a straggler who had wandered in from the street, had watched beforehand the crowd conglomerating, and, out of crude curiosity to see something unusual, had wandered into the church. A hatless woman at a wedding was one of questionable nature, one with whom one would certainly not want to be acquainted. Mrs. Carberry starts to speak again, "Did you ask Iris to take you?"

"I guess I did."

"Isabelle."

"What's wrong?"

"You can't keep asking friends for help. You won't have any left."

"Good grief! She offered to help me anytime and stopped in to chat one evening last week. I had an appointment the next day, so she picked me up at ten in the morning."

Mrs. Carberry doesn't reply but keeps a steady gaze on her daughter. "I know Iris is your friend, Mum, but we get along well too." At a loss for anything else to say, Isabelle chats with Pearl.

Soon Verda has finished her lunch. She wheels back from the table, again fixing her eyes on Isabelle, and waits. Stop talking and take me to my room. The words aren't spoken, but they exist nonetheless, so cutting the conversation short with Pearl, Isabelle brings her mother back upstairs to her room.

Daydreams are bathed in sandy light, half-transparent and dimensionless. It's so easy to drift into this space without bounds or demands. *A silent spot, amid the hills, A small and silent dell!* ... *'Tis a quiet spirit-healing nook!* One day she is feeling up, full of energy, and is busy the day long with doctors' appointments, friends visiting, and life at the Residence; the next, she is tired and down, the simplest thing sending her into a quandary. Not dreaming at night bothers her. The doctor has prescribed a muscle relaxant to be taken at bedtime and it seems to interfere with the nocturnal fantasies in the rich domain of the unreal yet real. So, near the end of May, she stops taking the pills. She doesn't sleep that well, but she does dream, fresh delicate vernal dreams. The nighttime meanderings are disjointed, having very little to do with anything at all on which she can place a finger, however, being back in touch with that wealth of imagery is centering and grounding. Each day seems part of a slow and difficult transformation, not the swift magical change of a character in a harlequinade, but more like a butterfly wiggling out of a cocoon, the wings still sticky and unable to fly.

A dream catches her attention one night, waking her, and remains strong and persistent the next morning until she sits down to record it in her notebook. She is in a large arena riding on the back of a dark walnut brown horse. It's a magnificent creature, entirely graceful, superbly wise. A polo match is underway but there are no other horses and no ball is to be seen. Neither are there any reins to hold onto or with which to guide the powerful animal. Nevertheless, the horse seems to know what it has to do without anyone interfering or giving instructions and it carries Isabelle on its back through all the maneuvres of the game. Then she is riding through a green countryside and up a narrow lane towards a large three-storey house. The horse enters the house through the kitchen door, leaves Isabelle in the kitchen, and goes off on its own to explore the many rooms. Isabelle begins to search through the building, looking for this animal friend who seems to be leading her. She climbs a set of stairs into a spacious attic that is filled with priceless antiques, then finds the horse lying down, its head resting quietly on the floor of a room on the second floor. No one else is in the house that apparently is Alex's home by the lake on his grandmother's farm where, likewise, the attic is enormous, a storage for boxes of old books, broken furniture, and weary steamer trunks filled with dusty chandeliers.

"I'm going to see a psychotherapist, Vincent. His name is Léo Lévesque."

It's the first time that Vincent has been to see Isabelle since she is home from the hospital. He arrives, stays a few minutes, and leaves just as quickly. She has time to tell him about Léo and not much else since he's pressed for time and has stopped in only briefly to say hello.

"Why would you want to do that?"

"It's the depression I get."

"I hadn't noticed."

"There's something angry inside that scares me and I don't know where it's coming from."

Vincent telephones the next morning, apologizing for the short visit. "I had a client to see."

"The time you were here was like a fleeting moment–you were gone so quickly," she says.

"But you knew I wasn't gone."

"Yes," she murmurs, melting slightly.

Léo's office is on Laurier Street in Montreal, part of a second floor consortium of psychological services. A flower shop occupies the corner of the building at street level and, this being the last Friday afternoon in May and a pleasant one at that, the owner has moved his decorative wares and exotic flowers out onto the sidewalk to attract the passersby. Isabelle wishes this is why she has come to this end of the city–to check out rare blooms and signed pottery–since she's not at all convinced that anything will result from these encounters with Léo. At that moment, she would prefer to be out of reach of hope and fear.

"Do you understand the difference between a psychiatrist and a psychotherapist?" begins Léo, settling into his chair across from Isabelle.

"Not really."

"Both try to understand how the psyche works and why emotional disorders develop, but a psychotherapist tries to find the problem and control it without drugs or medicine. I'll act as a vehicle for the healing process."

"Is that what the therapist said to the German poet, Rilke? Rilke replied, 'If my devils are to leave me, I'm afraid my angels will take flight as well'."

"I don't know about that."

"Rilke never went back."

"But there's nothing to fear. If there are any devils around, my advice is that you'd better get to know them. Your devils hold not only your problems, but your strengths as well."

What does strike Isabelle from that first meeting with Léo, is a small framed photograph that is sitting upright beside a box of Kleenex on the low table between their two chairs. Her eye fastens on it as soon as she sits down. A muscular horse, its equine body sleek and brown with a long mane and flowing tail, is standing alone in a green and grassy meadow. The left side of the photo is filled with a luminous mist, a sort of celestial cloud, and the horse is looking into it with a gaze that attains stellar distances. It's her horse. The dream horse.

June. Beautiful leafy June. The front of the house is shaded from the hot afternoon sun in the west. Does a remedy exist to soothe and quiet the soul that is any better than planting flowers? Lowering herself on rather weak leg muscles by holding onto a rail on the veranda, she slides part way down, down a little more, then lets herself drop the last inch, her knees landing on a pillow she has set on the grass for just that purpose. Two or three impatiens aren't many to plant at a time, but by the end of the day there is a whole row of pretty pink and purple blooms. The next afternoon, she brings the lawnmower out of the tool shed on the back lawn and, after several attempts, starts it with the pull cord. At the same time, Dugan is outside working around his property and keeping himself within sight of whatever she is doing. She waves once, a small swoop with the flat of her palm, just to let him know that she sees him there. Dugan doesn't acknowledge the greeting, turns his head quickly, and begins pulling strenuously on a jungle of waist-high choking weeds that have massed and are growing recklessly on the line between the two properties.

Dr-dr-dr-dr-dring!

Vincent had stopped in for a visit. He and Isabelle are sitting in the kitchen talking about the Manoir–how to ease the ticklish situation, what could be done with the building, how to get rid of it–when the doorbell clangs. Isabelle excuses herself, leaves Vincent at the table with a magazine, and walks through the living room into the front hall to see who is visiting on an afternoon in mid-week. Through the voile curtain over the glass on the upper portion of the door, she can make out the figure of a well-dressed middle-aged man, unfamiliar, and her heart begins to beat with wild abandon. On opening the door, a bailiff hands her a sealed envelope. It's from Dugan's lawyer. *He's suing me! He's actually doing it! How could he!*

"I need your signature right here, Ma'am," the bailiff says in a detached practised voice, his gaze as unfathomable as a dog's or a cow's.

"There you go. Goodbye now," she says with a smile and closes the door. The document inside outlines the charges. Eighty-nine thousand dollars! She looks at the string of numbers. *This isn't happening. Is it? Tell me this is not for real.* Her head swims and she wishes she had the power of a goddess to make Dugan disappear or to transform him into something useful–she's thinking of Gefjun in the Norse legend who turned her four giant sons into a team of oxen so she could plow her beloved king's land–or if not into something useful then something benign like a cat or a canary. Placing the papers on top of the desk in the little office to the side of the entrance, she straightens her posture, lets her arms fall to her sides, closes her eyes a minute to regain her composure, tells herself she will deal with that matter later, and goes back to Vincent and the Manoir in the kitchen.

"Is everything all right?"

"Yes, yes. It was just a parcel being delivered."

"You look … I don't know … distracted. And pale."

"I'm okay, Vincent. I was just thinking about something else."

The moment the latch on the front door clicks into place as Vincent leaves the house to return to work, the legal threat looms large scrambling her senses, shattering the outer shell of control, and disintegrating the feigned calm. She goes to her journal.

I don't know what to do. Should have died in that accident. Everything is too difficult. I guess if I'd agree to marry Dugan, that would solve everything, all the material aspects anyway, but I'd be dead on the inside. So that's no solution. A dark hand weighs me down, makes a fist in my forehead, and bangs to get out. Why don't I scream and let it out? Why don't I let loose a blood-curdling call? It would make me more comfortable right now. Or would it? Maybe it wouldn't do a thing. Who said 'Sometimes a scream is better than a thesis'? What could a scream possibly do to change Dugan's mind? I can't handle all of this, this is too much, but I'll not find a solution in this state.

Okay. That's enough. That's enough of being too frozen to think. I'm going to handle it. I'm not going to let my nerves get the better of me. One little bit at a time, Vincent says. The strength to overcome adversity. I have an angel. I'll pray. That's what I'll do. I don't pray for tranquility or for all the trials and tribulations to cease, but I pray for the grace and strength to overcome them and for the patience to win my freedom. I've read that somewhere. An Indian poet, I think. Tagore. Rabindranath Tagore. Anyhow, if those aren't exactly the words, the idea seems right. I'll go into silence, into my mindspace. I'll remember those special moments with Vincent when he stands behind me and holds me and rocks me. I can stay in that space a few moments, fade into the feeling, feel his arms around me, my head leaning back into his shoulder, the rocking, the peace coming, the love, the safety. ...

... My mindspace is clear now. I see the partly open door on the other side of the room. Where's my little white light? Where are you? ... There you are. I see you now. Come closer. Come a little bit closer. Come closer and wink at me...Thank you. Thank you. Thank you. I'm calm now.

It takes three sessions with Léo before Isabelle loosens the iron-clad grip over her more tender sentiments and cries in front of him. Once the tears come she thinks there will be no end to them, each of Léo's questions bringing out feelings that she has kept tightly under seal. Suddenly, she is sad at just the whisper of a thought– *Go away. Don't bother me.*– and Léo asks, "Why, right now, Isabelle, did your face change?"

A new wave of emotion comes over her as the banished spot is addressed. Instead of being denied, disowned, and staked to the grave to prevent its ghost from walking, the orphan is accorded an existence, and a cold shadow, crusty around the edges, begins to take on a viable substance. The entity inside is being listened to and she can feel a morass of feelings start to distinguish themselves. Its spirit is sad, rather forlorn, burdened. There's an angry element as well, and a helpless one. This is a truthful moment. Like a shy child reluctant to step into a room filled with strangers staring at her, she faces the monster and, with a hesitant voice, tries to put words to it.

"It's when I was young."

"Yes?"

"I thought I was happy like everyone else, but I wasn't."

Touching this sensitive spot makes the hurt swell in her throat like a threatened bullfrog, blocking her windpipe, and making her gasp for air. Her lips feel numb, as do the fingers of her left hand as well as her jaw. She pauses a moment to collect herself, closes her eyes, places her arms on the chair rests, then enters a 'special moment' with Vincent before being able to relax and breathe normally. Her hand rises automatically to embrace her throat and Léo picks up the body language.

"I know there are real physical reasons why you're having difficulty to breathe, Isabelle, but I think that lump in your throat is a little girl trying to get out. Can you let her out?"

"I'm afraid of what she will do."

"Do you hurt yourself when you let her out?"

"Not physically."

"What is she like?"

"She's a wild spirit, like a Bohemian. She dances. And sometimes she stomps her feet."

"Is she like the horse?"

"No. She's wild. My horse wasn't wild."

"What does she do?"

"I never know. One time, Dan and I were on a holiday in the Caribbean and she felt like singing, so she sang on stage with a microphone."

"How did you feel?"

"Wonderful. Free. But Dan was mortified. I don't know how to sing. Afterwards, whenever I thought about it, I was humiliated."

"Why?"

"I'm not a singer. And straight people like me don't do things like that. I probably had too much to drink."

"Perhaps you needed some attention. I think you should try to get to know this wild spirit, even if it scares you."

"She gets an urge and there's not much I can do about it. I don't think I like her."

"All the more reason why you should get to know her."

A dreamgate opens during the summer. Somnus, reclining in a bed of poppies at the mouth of his cave, dispatches Morpheus with a display of imaginative power worthy of the happy king of gods and men. The day to day is reinvented in the otherworldly realms of sleep where will is suspended and the mind is free to fancy. Before the accident, the dreams had been difficult and struggling but now they explode with vital energy and gracious subtlety. Like luscious fruits falling ripe and sweet and moaning with delicious juice, dreamy allegories dance through the night telling stories filled with age-old wisdom and divine intrigue as they strive to illuminate a searching soul with truths from beyond.

In the middle of one night, Isabelle finds herself riding in a parade of mythical carts. They float above the ground in a wavy train, twelve wagons the colour of eggshell, each one connected to the next, like a magical mystical musical ride. The open vehicles are adorned with sculpted flourishes carved in relief, ornamental wings and flowers tossed with abandon. Affixed to the front of the first buggy, like the figurehead on a ship's prow, is a fiery looking ram. The animal form at the head of the second depicts a bull with horns shaped more like the horns of a goat. Leading the third carriage is a pair of happy twin children, neither boy nor girl. On the fourth is a crab carrying his home on his back, and, following the crustacean, is a proud lion, king of the beasts. It's a parade of astrological Zodiac signs and Isabelle is sitting near the end of the procession in the Sagittarius cart, a centaur-archer, half-man half-beast, perched in front of her and looking back over his shoulder.

She wakes wondering who is the person sitting in the parade cart just ahead of her, falls back to sleep, and awakens in the morning with another misty dream sequence filling her head. Observing this scene from afar, she looks at herself with a man who is not familiar to her as a daytime acquaintance, but whom she obviously knows very well. They're standing face to face, looking straight into each other's eyes, completely attentive one to the other, and talking in low murmurs that she can't hear well enough to understand. Each is wearing a long off-white filmy robe and the edges of the flowing dress are bound in shiny strips of ivory satin, clothing from another country and another age. In the next instant, they're in the same self-absorbed pose but stretched out on their sides and floating several feet above the ground in a surreal suspension.

Another night, she is living in Grandpa Davidson's home in Bruce

Crossing. A large white grand piano, a fine piece of work although not an elaborate model of the showmanship variety, is sitting in the kitchen occupying most of the room. A girlfriend arrives at the front door of the house carrying a suitcase in the same grey material as that of her winter coat. She hangs her coat in the closet at the back of the hall and places the suitcase at the bottom of the stairs leading up to the second floor, so it will be ready for her to pick up as she leaves. She goes to the piano straightaway, as if this was why she has come, sits down on the little bench in front of the keyboard, holds up her hands, and begins wiggling her fingers to loosen them. In the interval it takes her to remember the beginning notes to a melody, Isabelle says, "When the piano came, when it was born, I expected it to be white and blue."

Several nights later, before falling into a deep sleep, Isabelle asks, "What does the white piano mean, Winona? I'm having a hard time understanding. Could I have an explanation?" The dream that comes in response is in sharp contrast to the delicate tones of the previous nights and she observes a war on water between enclosed miniature warships, like covered seadoos, large enough for only one or two persons. There are no missiles or guns but the death toll is known to be large, hate being the biggest killer. The combatants are trying to maim each other by ramming into the side of the other's boat. It's impossible to tell the two fighting sides apart.

Along the shoreline of this watery drama is a string of boutiques selling trinkets and odd paraphernalia, the storefronts opening onto the sea. Isabelle is walking in the shallow water in front of one shop and is shocked when she looks down to see what is knocking at her bare ankles and churning around her feet. Silvery gleaming skulls with full heads of long black hair streaming out into the water like seaweed are jostling about in the slight current, vacant holes gazing up with horror, holes that used to contain eyes. Looking more closely, she can see that the bony spectres are not the full-sized cranial skeletons of adult remains, but are the heads of dead children. Gaunt white faces almost cover the sea floor at the shallow edge and the dreamer understands that the store owner is selling the skulls to make money out of the carnage from this dream war.

Farther inland, two fighters who were driving war boats arrive for a break. They're dressed in bright pink outfits that cover their bodies from neck to toe. One of them is struggling to take off the headpiece, which looks like a large black plastic box with slats on the front and sides, similar to an outmoded table radio with poor reception. He manages to remove it, revealing a nice-looking young boy with a dark curly head of hair, a heartthrob in other times, but then his comrade quickly replaces the polymer rectangle on top of his shoulders. Covered up with their flashy pink suits and black box helmets, both are automatons, incapable of operating at a frequency other than a single wave-length.

Then the setting switches to an old abandoned railway station. Dozens of ragged children, homeless and malnourished, are sitting on hard wooden benches, their eyes sunken and swollen, their short scuffed boots swinging in the air, legs too short to reach the floor. One is horribly sick and holds onto herself as she bends over retching greenish-grey bile, while others are crying from hunger and fear, and still others are silent, too weary for tears. The hapless youngsters are war orphans. General Roméo Dallaire of the UN Peacekeepers seems to have responsibility for these children. He's with another concerned person whom Isabelle doesn't recognize. Between them—General Dallaire and this third person—they're trying to find a solution to the sorry fate of these young innocents, victims of their parents' aggression. Engaged in conversation as they walk out of and away from the building, General Dallaire and his colleague leave Isabelle alone in the train station with the destitute children.

July arrives in all its summer glory. The blue sky is cloudless. Dappled shadows quiver on the front lawn as the rising sun in the east filters through the fluttering leaves on the tall maples, imitating the mesmerizing back and forth movement of waves lapping against the water's edge, ripples on a disturbed pond, floating and dissolving, or the rotating patterns of a uni-coloured kaleidoscope. Birds flit about in pairs from tree to tree filling the early morning air with sprightly trills and sweet songs.

Isabelle spends the morning on the telephone arranging for a lawyer to handle Dugan's lawsuit against her. She chooses a name from the yellow pages in the telephone book. He's a corporate lawyer in Montreal but has a small office in LaViolette as well. His name is Stéphane Debauve. A little later in the day, Léo telephones to move their next appointment into August.

"Good afternoon, Isabelle."

"Léo. I'm glad you called. I owe you an explanation for yesterday. Did your wife give you a message?"

"Yes, she did. She told me you arrived late."

"There was an accident on the bridge going onto the island."

"I waited forty minutes then thought you weren't coming, so I left. What happened?"

"My friend, Eva, was driving. We left Wakeham in good time but we were caught in the traffic jam-up. I must have arrived at your office just a few minutes after you had gone."

"That's too bad."

"I'm sorry for the mix-up."

"Were you resisting coming for that session? It doesn't appear to be your fault that you were late, but still, the energy you project does manifest itself somehow."

"Well, yes, I have been having a hard time continuing."

"I thought so."

"I think I'm going cross-eyed. I've been looking at myself when I was little for about ten hours a day for the past month. It's exhausting. I might have been giving the house a major spring clean-up. I'm worn out."

"I sensed something was about to happen. At the last session I could feel a swell of emotion rising to the surface and bubbling."

"It consumes me. I'd like some time off to absorb what has happened already."

"You have progressed quickly. I think you have been allowing other people to tell you what to do all your life and I could feel the anger build once you started to realize it. But, I really called, Isabelle, to tell you I'm taking holidays for a month now. My wife and I are going to a cottage in the Laurentians with the children. If you like, I can give you the telephone number of a colleague while I'm away."

"Thanks, Léo, but I'll be fine. Really, I appreciate the break."

"Good. I'll call you in August when I get back and we can schedule another appointment then."

"That's fine, Léo. I hope you enjoy your holiday."

That night, Isabelle dreams of a poem tree. A large brick building like a college residence stands behind a grassy playing field where a group of girls, brightly dressed in colourful shorts and tops, are in the midst of a ball game. Several sturdy oaks with far-reaching limbs are growing on the lawn to its right. On one of the trees, a finely formed specimen in all its leafy green voluptuousness of summer, there are many sheets of paper, each one tied to a branch with a little coloured bow. A message or a poem is hand-written on each. A wind blows. The air is pushed about in blasts and whirls and is soon filled with loose debris picked up and transported along by the swift currents, as if someone has shaken a glass water-filled bulb and the sphere is suddenly filled with swirling snow. But the papers remain attached to the tree, as if the birds were trying to make her laugh.

A poem tree–the messages and secrets of your being tied to the tree of life with unexpected knots, challenges, and twists. The wind, both cause and effect, doesn't allow the tree to stand still. Everything is blown about wreaking havoc in an instant. Leaves, twigs, refuse, bits of trash rush by in great gusts of air then settle anew, but the essence, the poetry of your life, remains firmly anchored to its roots, to the original myth that is nourishing your destiny.

It's the end of July. Just before waking, Isabelle is in her family backyard trying to clean it. She's digging a large hole in the ground, going about her business of shoveling, looking for something of which the dream observer is unaware. It snows. Soon the whole yard is covered with a foot-high blanket of white powder. Searching now for a path out to the road, she is clearing away the snow from in front of her, loses her footing, and tips into the cavity she has just finished digging, which is about three feet in depth. Undisturbed by the fall, she picks up the shovel once again and begins to heave the snow out of the small pit, aware that her father is standing by watching her dig deeper and deeper, although she doesn't see his person.

The next night, an English manor-style residence, once again of red brick construction, lawns manicured and trees trimmed neatly, sets the stage. Looking out the window towards what appears to be the east, if north-south-east-west designations have any meaning in dreams, she can see two long rows of tall elms lining each side of a shady green lane, like a romantic passageway in a fairytale where the long-lost lover makes his way to the fair damsel waiting for him at the end of the road. Isabelle goes outdoors to another side of the house. It's dark on this side. She comes to a subterranean cave, the entrance hidden in a grassy mound of earth where she follows a wagon load of young people that has just entered the cave mouth and is descending into the dark depths beneath the surface. Apparently, the youngsters are tourists having a good time, an underground adventure. They're laughing, shrieking, and waving their arms high in the air as if on the down slope of a roller-coaster ride. Isabelle stops inside the opening to the sunken hollow, just at the beginning of the rapid descent into the ground. At the bottom, the trolley full of children disappears around a curve into the cavernous darkness. Crouching on the steep incline, her eyes taking time to adjust to the shadows in the thin light, she can see many animals, large and small, wandering about and nuzzling in vain for food and water in the barren dirt and rocks of the cave. Their fur coats are mangy. Battle sores ooze openly. Protruding bones bespeak suffering. A sandy coloured lamb is climbing up the rocky path towards the entrance. When he approaches, Isabelle tries to hold the little body but he squirms out of her arms, not wanting to be touched, and scrambles back down with the others. A black cat isn't so afraid, although his mean and tattered appearance makes him out to be wild and a fighter. She feels sorry for the poor creature and tries to befriend him with a saucer of milk. Wary at first, he sniffs and stares at the whiteness, takes a tongue lap to taste the liquid, then drinks hungrily, allowing her to pet his wretched fur. Other curious animals approach cautiously to investigate the stranger but are easily startled and keep their distance. All are free to go, there are no restraining fences, yet none leave the dark confines of the underground.

Knowing that Dugan is watching from next door makes Isabelle uncomfortable. Her life wants to come apart and start over again, and her house is part of the upheaval. She wants to leave it. A home sitting in the midst of trees by a river where she can see sunset after sunset, sunrise after sunrise, with plenty of light and space for her loftiest thoughts is such a delightful notion that it often causes a momentary losing of herself in a daytime reverie. It would be a refuge for her soul, a dwelling where her spirit could renew itself. This is where she could create her own space, an abode where she could write her own tradition. It would have an artistic bent. It would be an islet of her own, alive with beautiful music, a place with the sensitivity of a fine painting. The very air would be filled with dreams. Here she could live unhampered by the weight of a house that is quaint, charming, cozy, and heavy with ghosts in the closets and talking walls.

August is a waiting time. Restless and impatient, she centers her thoughts on her vision of a Community Center, a place for youth to hang out. She meditates on the vision she would like to see. There are rooms for jam sessions and play activities, a grand hall for giving concerts, a sound stage with excellent acoustics suitable for recording, a facility for sports and exercise, meeting areas in which to sit and rap with friends–this is a place to identify with. Something special has to happen in that sad magnificent building.

One afternoon, while putting through a load of washing in the laundry room off the kitchen, Isabelle senses a movement outdoors. A feeling of uneasiness makes her look out the window onto her neighbour's property. At one time, when she and Gaspard first moved to the house, she could look out this window toward the west and see for miles down the country road to cornfields and cattle grazing on lush farmland. Soon after they arrived, however, Dugan planted hundreds of young Scotch pines and now, almost ten years later, the foot high seedlings have grown into a veritable forest that obstructs the view. Some branches swishing near the crown of one tree immediately catch her attention and she looks closer, expecting to see a couple of squirrels having a skirmish. But instead of some furry creatures romping about, there is Dugan sitting high in the treetop holding onto a handsaw. He's looking straight in the window at her. Quickly averting his eyes when her incredulous stare meets his, he begins vigorously sawing on a branch and the entire pine shakes and sways with vengeance, the black sheep of this green and placid wood. Enraged and affronted, Isabelle snaps shut the window blinds and decides now is the time to call Peter, the real estate agent, and ask him to sell the house.

By the end of August, a deal has been struck and the new owner wants to take possession at the end of September.

Peter guides Isabelle through five houses in and around Wakeham one afternoon. It happens to be a fine summer day, even houses positing their best look. The last one is the one she wants. Situated right across from the small hospital in the village, the property isn't so isolated as a country location and the back yard steals her heart. Tall hedges and trees line the land behind the house creating a private court and, just past a tiny forest glade at the back of the lawn, the river quietly makes its way downstream through the town. The two-storey home has oversized rooms and many windows so that a view of the outdoors can be seen on two or three sides from almost every room in the spacious home. It's much too large for her alone, but it's her dream house and the place where she wants to be.

Up early at six on the morning of the move, Isabelle goes over to the new house with a stepstool, a bucket, and a pillow slip filled with rags to wash walls and closets and wipe ceiling fans with soapy water. Eva joins her at noon with another mop pail and the two women scrub high and low until their necks pinch from tilting back to face the ceiling and their backs groan from bending down to the floor. They clean until the movers take over in mid-afternoon. The next day, Alex drives from Willow River in the green pick-up to help his mother move the last loads from the country house into the village. Ten days later, two young men still in their twenties, Jean-François and Louis, come to see Isabelle about the Manoir. A grand Music Hall fills their dreams and Isabelle hopes that everything will work out for them so she will finally be rid of the building.

Many October days are extensions of the summer without the crushing humidity, and this year is no different. Everyone longs for a complete season of these dry sunny afternoons, even the chill, which permeates the air after the light begins to fade from the sky in early evening, is acceptable. In fact, it's rather nice to snuggle into a warm sweater and remain outside in the cool twilight that is almost mystical with the play of indefinites. Isabelle works outside into the dusk cutting grass and trimming bushes until the low light is so dense she can no longer see what she is doing. As the weeks turn colder, ushering in November, wallpapering, painting, and decorating become the principal activities after sessions with Léo, the Ovila Street Residence, and the Rotary Club.

The first heavy snowfall of the season arrives one night near the end of the month. By morning, the soft graceful fall has changed the countryside from the dull bleak tones of late autumn into the pristine white of a Canadian winter landscape. The children who live along the street hurry outside to make snow angels and snowmen in the fluffy white down. Bundled up in their suits, boots, and woollen hats like little snowy elves and pixies, they mimic the charm of a Norman Rockwell painting or a set of Hummel figurines, enchantment spilling over onto sentiment. Rosy cheeks reddening in the cold air and bright eyes peering out beneath a forehead scarf dance and twinkle to their own music. Isabelle, watching through the window, her heart stirring and beating with simple sympathy, can't help but smile to herself at their youthful exuberance. How they enjoy themselves! How they wrinkle their faces! She can't exactly hear them shouting, but their waving arms and pointing mittens and excited motions are asking each other who can catch a snowflake on the tip of a nose. "I can! I can! Watch me! No, watch me! Here's one! I've got one too! Look! Can you see it? I can, but look at mine! It's even bigger than yours! Do you see it? Hurry! Look before it melts!" the squeals of wonder and laughter defining their world.

Isabelle goes to visit her mother at the nursing home one afternoon.

"You need a car now that the snow is here. You won't be able to walk everywhere and I'd like to get out for a drive and go shopping every once in a while. Here's four thousand dollars. I made a cheque out to you."

"You're giving me four thousand dollars to buy a car!?"

"Can you find one for that amount?"

"Sure, I can find one for that. ... I don't know what to say. Except, Thank you. And thank you again."

Within a few days, a little second hand car, with an engine about the size of a lawnmower's, is sitting in the driveway–just waiting to take Verda out for barbecued chicken at St. Hubert's on her birthday. Isabelle arrives at the residence fifteen minutes late. A longtime acquaintance, Claire, stopped in about eleven o'clock in the morning and the two talked away without regard for the hour. They hadn't visited for some time and there was a lot of catching up to do, so Verda is as pleased as a disgruntled Jemima Puddle-duck at being left to worry and wait in her room past the scheduled time.

"I don't want to go to Valleyfield now. It's too late."

Isabelle telephones the only restaurant in Wakeham that has a wheelchair ramp, but they're not open for lunch.

"Oh, lordy! Imagine that. How do they expect to stay in business if they're not open on a Saturday? I suppose you don't want to eat here."

"Come on, let's go out. It's your birthday."

Verda gives in, gets into the little car quite easily, and is able see out the windows without straining her neck as they drive ten miles through the countryside to St. Hubert's in Salaberry-de-Valleyfield. She has to admit she has a fine time. A bevy of waiters and waitresses group around the table and present her with a bowl of ice cream, a tall sparkler sizzling on top of the highest scoop. Then they break into a rousing rendition of *Happy Birthday* and one of them takes a Polaroid picture and hands her the photograph. Mrs.

Carberry is thrilled. A lady sitting at the table next to theirs happened to win three million dollars in the 6/49 lottery the week before and is lively and talkative to Isabelle who chats away with her in French. Verda is intrigued by the woman's excitement so Isabelle translates the conversation back to her.

"How do you say 'congratulations' in French, Isabelle?"

"*Félicitations*. Like felicitate. She'll understand."

Verda tried. "Felicistashions."

"Not bad, Mum."

Neither does Verda complain too much about the car, that it's too this or too that or not like the lovely cars that Anna rents when she comes to see her.

Once again in her room at the nursing home, Verda opens a gift that was left for her while she was out–a bottle of Harvey's Bristol Cream from some friends in Fall Creek. Isabelle has brought a prettily wrapped gift also–a soft blouse in her favourite shade of blue and a rosewater bath gel. Attached to the parcel with a curly ribbon is a romantic greeting card of pale pink roses sitting beside a nostalgic picture frame and a throw of cream coloured lace. Verda is pleased with everything and is full of thank you's and says that she feels better now than she did before they left.

Before Isabelle arrived she was mad at the girl who helped her put on her dress. She didn't button it up right and had done something wrong to the collar. Verda swore up and down that before today that dress had a collar. Now where in the world was the collar? "You don't remember this dress having a collar? Well, I do. Maybe it's turned inside... Well, if it's not there, what has she done with it? Isn't that the limit? This dress always had a nice little collar. You never know how something's going to come back when you send it to the laundry here. What a way to start the day." Oh, boy. This is going to be a difficult few hours, thought Isabelle, but the dress looked fine and Verda soon forgot about the missing collar.

Later on in the afternoon, Phoebe arrives for a visit before supper is served and hands her old friend a small gift. "Happy Birthday, dear."

"Oh, thank you, dear. You didn't have to go to all that trouble for little old me."

"Trouble? Now, Verda, you know that's no trouble. You're looking good today, dear."

"Thank you, Phoebe. You're looking pretty spiffy yourself. Did you have your hair done?"

"Just yesterday. You know, I've been a little under the weather lately and it helps to have Sharon fix my hair for me."

"It does give you a lift, doesn't it? Rachelle came and did my nails this morning."

"Boosts you right up."

"Sure does. The old aches and pains are forgotten for a spell."

"How many birthdays is it, dear? Not that we want to keep tabs on them."

"Eighty-three and I think that's enough."

"If you ask me, birthdays should be easier to take as you get older, not harder."

"Rare as hens' teeth would be more like it at our age."

"It's the principle of the thing."

"The very idea that we would want to be reminded of how old we are."

"Indeed, indeed."

"You know, Phoebe, I think we ought to open that bottle of the Harvey's Bristol Cream that's sitting right over there on the dresser. It's a special one."

"You just might have something there, Verda. We need a special drink on a special day, don't we now, two fine-looking spring chickens like us."

"Without a doubt."

"Too bad there aren't any old roosters around."

"Holy-moly! The old roosters around here aren't worth a hoot."

"Anyway, that's why I came over at three-thirty…"

"To look for a rooster?" Verda and Phoebe break into laughter at the same time.

"To give us plenty of time to enjoy a little liquid something or other before you go downstairs for your meal."

"That's what I thought you meant."

"Not that I have anything against the old devils, mind you."

"Nor I. But you know, they probably call us old crows."

"We can do without that."

"Can't we though."

"But even thirty years after he's gone, I've still a soft spot inside for my old Henry, delinquent that he was."

"You can't live with 'em and you can't live without 'em."

"What a fix."

"Somebody ought to do some rearranging, don't you think?"

"I'll say. Why in heaven's name do we have these big heavy old breasts when we're old and want small ones and cute shy things when we're young and want big ones?"

"They're a bother, all right, the way they droop about and hang in the way. Heavy darned things too. You know, they've got an operation for that now. Gerdie had hers cut back to size."

"I heard. But, you know how Gerdie's hung down so you couldn't see the belt on her dress. The poor dear had back pain because of the heavy load she was carrying around."

"It's not right. Let's put a note in the suggestion box upstairs."

"Why not, but I think it's a little late for us, Verda dear."

"I suppose you're right. Well then, let's forget about our ample fronts and have us that treat."

"Three cheers."

"Nobody knows how to look after us any better than we do ourselves, Phoebe."

"By golly, if that ain't the truth, I don't know what is."

"The glasses are in the cupboard."

"All washed and shined up, I see."

"I was just waiting for you to arrive."

"Tch, tch."

"Will you do the honours, dear?"

"With pleasure."

"Feel like a few cheesies to go with your sherry?"

"Humpty Dumpty?"

"Yes, dear. They're the best."

Phoebe arranges the glasses on top of the portable writing desk, opens the bottle of Harvey's, makes herself comfortable in a chair facing Verda, the small table with the sherry and cheesies standing between them, and fills the glasses. They raise them, smile at each other, eyes twinkling, and repeat in unison their favourite toast:

"Here's to you,
And here's to me,
And here's to those who wish us well,
And all the rest can go to hell."

They clink their glasses, have a sip to their health, and barely have time to set down the tumblers before their heads tilt back, their mouths fall open, and Phoebe and Verda laugh, hoot, howl, bray, slap their thighs, and wave their arms until tears run down their faces and they have to stop to blow their noses. So finally, Verda has a wonderful birthday and Isabelle is happy for her.

Back at home, Isabelle makes herself comfortable on the sofa, bringing her legs up onto the seat. It's a favourite position to read in or do some writing, wedged into the corner, the upholstered arm supporting her weight. Toulouse jumps up as well. He can't get close because of all the papers and magazines scattered on the seat, so he lies gingerly on top of them, placing his body just so, stretches his furry white paw far enough to reach Isabelle's leg, and leaves the little cream-puff end resting on her, contracting and releasing, contracting and releasing. Content at having made contact with his mistress, he stares at Isabelle with a steady gaze until she looks at him, then benignly blinks his eyes.

Claire arrives early one morning to help wallpaper the dining room. After lunch, they look at dozens of paint samples for the walls in the downstairs central hallway, the high stairwell, and the upstairs hall. They decide on a soft shade of rose that looks more grey than pink at night and more pink than grey in the daylight. A wide wallpaper border of tumbling Florentine flowers in shades of antique blue and rose on a background of rich taupe looks magnificent with the muted tones for the walls.

It has been snowing all day. The roads are icy and there's no sign of the storm letting up, so in late afternoon Isabelle calls Léo and cancels the appointment that is scheduled with him in Montreal for seven that evening. After dusk has settled, the skies clear unexpectedly, the temperature drops, and the air is still, letting a bright full moon turn the evening into a numinous landscape redolent with slanted sheen, a patina of moonlight. Snow like cotton batting has mounded high on the bare branches creating a forest of small clouds. The dark bark on the massive tree trunks stands out like forged iron from a blacksmith's hearth against the soft white blanket. A path of gleaming moonshine makes its way from the back of the yard across the surface of the sparkling snow directly to the back door of the house where Isabelle is standing and looking at the scene through the window. And beyond the wooded glen on the riverbank, the river flows quietly by.

Times like that of peace and wonder lift her into her mindspace for a few moments, into the big empty room with the partially open door at the back. Tonight, the door is open wide. There's no barrier at all, only brilliant light beyond the opening. A filmy white shroud leaves her body and floats up and away as she watches. It wafts through the clear passage, drifts higher and higher into the light, then, after a few minutes, the spirit returns to its rightful place within her self.

Vincent leaves for a month's holidays. The night before leaving, he picks up Isabelle and they drive to a quaint restaurant with an old-world cachet in a nearby village where they spend several hours over a gourmet dinner with candlelight and a bottle of fine wine. Back at Isabelle's, Vincent makes a roaring fire in the fireplace and they sit on the rug in front of the flames relishing the warmth and their friendship. Their love is treated delicately, they speak not of it. Perhaps they are afraid that words will further tarnish its fragility. Nor do they acknowledge the pulsing interior, that ardent throb so acutely aware of the dust and ashes of mortal endeavours in search of bliss.

"I'll miss you, Vincent."

"I'll miss you too."

"If you feel a little twinge in your thoughts and a smile comes on your face, that will be me thinking about you."

"You're my best friend, Isabelle."

It's a cold and silent winter evening at the end of December and Isabelle is sitting in her favourite corner of the couch with her legs curled up beside her. An inviting fire of maple logs burns quietly in the fireplace, the brilliant orange-red of the steady flames reflecting on her face and flushing the area about the mantelpiece and the hearth with a reddish glow. A blank writing pad rests on her knee. Mozart's twenty-first piano concerto, the second movement, *Andante*, is playing over and over. The muted strings and the serene wind instruments lead into the dreamlike and untroubled notes of the solo piano. From time to time, urgent complexes of harmonic triplets disturb the outward radiance and suggest a great depth to the stillness. As she closes her eyes, she is carried away with the beauty of the music into the lightness of peace and harmony that fills her mindspace. She looks into that space and, as she does so, she looks at Jake, her dead father.

He's wearing a wrinkled plaid shirt and his old frumpish cap with the worn spot on the brim where his fingers had always lifted it off his head and given it a shake or two before readjusting it in place. Wine-coloured suspenders hold up his baggy brown trousers, sprinkles of old sawdust making light patches on the dark material. The legs of his britches are tucked sloppily inside the top of black rubber boots that reach to mid-calf. Tears begin to moisten Isabelle's face. Jake stands up, his glance downcast as he lifts himself off the small child's chair on which he has been sitting. He turns slowly to his left, raises his eyes, removes his cap to place it on the chair, stretches out his arms as if to welcome someone, and begins to dance gracefully with Isabelle's angel, Winona, a most peaceful and happy expression on his face.

Pure emotion washes through Isabelle and resonates in every cell in her body. She is stunned by the scene that plays in front of her eyes. He knows. He knows I was hurt. He feels for me. He does. He really does. The words run over and over in her thoughts and the tears that fall spill a lifetime of sadness onto the empty page that rests on Isabelle's knee. She weeps out of the sorrow of misguided yearning and the joy of releasing an ancient pain that suddenly doesn't matter any more.

The drama continues to unfold as she watches. With flowing steps and refined style, Jake waltzes to divine melody with angelic Winona who is dressed for the occasion in a long white gown that falls softly about her in gossamer folds. After a moment or two, Jake turns his head. He looks directly at Isabelle and says in a voice that rings as clear and unexpected as a stretch of still water in a mountain stream, "I'm dancing for you."

Part Three

The Notebook

"Risk is whatever scares you. It is the threshold
we are required to cross before we can lean down
to our passions lying dormant and kiss them awake.
… It takes … courage [to] look straight into the
dark gate of whatever is unknown to us and know
that our fate lies in there, that our lives won't
be complete and won't make sense until we go
through. A calling is not so much something in
our path as we are in *its* path. … We need the gods
to bring us our callings."

Gregg Levoy,
Callings

January

Magritte's Pipe
"Ceci n'est pas une pipe"

Friday, January 3, 1997.

Seems to me the first diary entry of the new year ought to be something special, filled with grand plans and vows. Not this year. This beginning will be very ordinary, the way it is. Bear with me, dear Diary, because I'm going to do a lot of talking to Winona this year. Don't ask why. It just feels right. She has always been there, haven't you, Winona? Listening. Hovering about. I have a question for you, Winona: Do you think Vincent is like me? Don't you think he's trying to impress? Oops. That was two questions. You don't have to answer if you don't want to. They're silly. But please tell me if I'm on the wrong track. 'Cause I think he is like me. A lot. Not exactly, of course, not like two peas in a pod. But the similar part is eerie. I mean, it's spooky to be alike this way, not anything edifying, not *WOW! Can you imagine that? We like all of the same things! We even sneeze at the same time!* It's more like a screwed, blued, and tattooed kind of similar. He works hard to maintain an image of being strong and in control, having everything at his fingertips, and not needing to be loved. But he's crying out for love, trying to fill an emptiness. This relationship disturbs me. It does. It's getting under my skin. I want it terribly, but I'm not allowed to say what's inside. Vincent doesn't want to hear the word 'love' so I push a part of myself underground. I have to bury my emotions again. I'm tired of relationships where I don't count, where I have to hide half of myself when I'm with him and wear a camouflage when I'm not. I change colours according to the surroundings like a chameleon, light up this or that scene like a stage director working on a set.

I had an appointment with Léo this afternoon. I wanted to tell him everything, just let it tumble out in a garble of pointless episodes, vivid and hurtful, random eruptions hardening like lava. I wanted to stand still for just a moment, detach from everything I knew, separate from my life, put it all out there, give the odds and ends to Léo, cleanse them of emotion and make them impersonal so I could have a look from a distance. So he could help me.

There's a reason for everything, so why did I go through what I did? Why were there years of loneliness and confusion? I tried to do normal things–get an education, marry, raise children, work at a profession. Even the normal things didn't work out the way they're supposed to. Was I so different? What am I to do with first hand knowledge of meeting death face to face, willing, wanting to walk into oblivion because it would have been less painful, more peaceful than living? Do I have a reason to be on this Earth? My whole life looks like a training session to get me to stand on my own two feet instead of following the crowd. Don't get yourself too comfortable because something's about to go awry, sure as the mouse runs up and down the clock or the rattle of a rattlesnake. And why were there always two extremes that played back and forth? Such sadness on one side, such rapture on the other. I tried to surround myself with beautiful things. Didn't find people beautiful. Disappointing, was more like it. Or rather, what I saw on the outside impressed me, but inside was a tangle. I guess I didn't attract the right ones. Here I am, forty-nine years old, realizing that I've been dragging around a sack of untouchables all my life and thinking that it all happened for a purpose. I guess there are worse conundrums to be in than that.

Tuesday, January 14, 1997.

Last night, I dreamt of a baby. Pregnant? No way. But it was my baby and I loved it and hugged it and smiled at it. It reacted back to me with babyish delight, with a lot of gooing and gawing and the unwavering eye contact of the child who feels a connection. I was talking to someone, my sister I think it was. We agreed that the child looked like Alex when he was little, but it wasn't Alex. This baby was so heavy and oversized that I had difficulty lifting him. Or her. I think it was her. I spoke to the baby that the back of her head was flat from lying too much and not receiving enough love and attention–an old wives' tale. I heard that at a neighbour's when I was eight or nine. As soon as I was home I headed to my room and the mirror above my dresser, to check out the back of my own head. "But that's going to change because I'm here to love you now," I said to the little one. And, miracle of miracles, her head did change during the dream. The flat part filled out.

Wednesday, January 15, 1997.

I fired Agnes today. Over the telephone. I didn't want to see her face. She almost destroyed the entire Home. The staff as well as the residents were upset and nervous, wondering what was going on, where all the commotion would lead. 'Black Agnes' flashed through my mind whenever she appeared at the door to my house in Wakeham with her long jet-black hair and eyes as black as two coals peering at me from some uncanny place. Lately, she had been wearing a new long winter coat that reached to the floor. Pure black. I put the undercurrent out of my mind because I thought I could trust her. Head before heart. I see now that she had other plans, and that I should have put my heart before my head.

150

Thursday, January 16,1997.

Earlier today, Vincent arrived to say hello after his long holiday. The mid-January morning was sub-zero, the air taut and crackling with static. I made a pot of coffee to take the chill off the cold. We stood in the kitchen, our backs resting against the edge of the countertop, talking over several cups of the hot brew. I wonder that I didn't offer him a chair on which to sit. Maybe it's myself I was thinking of. Maybe if I got too comfortable it would have taken the edge of what I wanted to say or diminished the words somehow so they could slither by unnoticed like a garden snake in the grass. Mother would be disgusted at the breach of etiquette. *Merciful heavens, child! Where are your manners?* She'd be a lot more disgusted to know I'm having a fling with a married man. Anyway, standing seemed to suit the exchange.

"Our relationship has to come to an end, Vincent."

"What relationship are you talking about?"

"Ours!"

"Relationship?"

"Well, what do you think it is?"

"I didn't think we had a relationship. I thought we were just good friends."

Holy Mother of Pearl. Who's the loon here?

When he left, I drove to the Residence. What a day again, although it was calmer than yesterday, like a bit of quiet descending after the turbulence. Everyone is much happier today. I didn't have time to think of Vincent. When I do picture him, he's still the same sweet soul that I love. I think I'm the loon. A drenched and dippy loon.

Friday, January 17,1997.

Falling! Falling! I'm glad it was a dream. I was a passenger in a small airplane of perhaps fifty seats. The driver was invisible. I was sitting alone in a row near the front of the craft and looking out the little round window beside me. Suddenly, the plane took a plunge and dove wildly down through the air like a hawk aiming at a mouse. I didn't wake, didn't feel the need for it. I felt the impossibility of an ugly crash and just waited. Soon the engines roared, the craft picked up speed, straightened out, and soared high, seemingly effortlessly, as if the freefall was a routine event.

I know why that plane made a nosedive–more residents say they are leaving to go to Agnes's place. She offered them a cheaper rent. The staff tells me more rumours of Agnes and one of the old men. *Shshsh!* The fiasco seems to be never-ending, a contagious plight. I'm trying to be the rock in the middle of this storm. Everyone thinks the Residence is dying and the girls on the staff are afraid for their jobs.

Saturday, January 18, 1997.

Awake the entire night. So draining to listen to yourself babble on and on. So monotonous. Early in the morning, around five o'clock, let's be honest now, I cried, giant wet tears. I had to feel the pain. When the tears wore themselves out, I began to feel mad, and madder, and then fighting mad. No person like Agnes, using deceit and dishonesty, planning for months behind my back, was going to be allowed to get her way. I was so angry that I wasn't going to allow it to happen. This isn't going to happen to me! It felt like a mission. I was going to fight. *Hoist the flag! Polish the rifles! This is war!* I loved the hate. Fury was glowing like a brushfire. Mad was burning wild.

Monday, January 20, 1997.

"Let me know if it goes to court," the editor of the local newspaper, *The Reaper*, tells me. No interest there. More stories are circulating about Agnes reporting me everywhere. Where? Why? This is what Agnes told Alice. And Alice told me because Agnes doesn't want Alice to work for me; she wants Alice to work for her, in her new Home, because everybody knows that old people like Alice, and Agnes thinks she will have more residents that way. It turns my stomach. Maybe it was an empty threat, like a conch shell on the beach, empty of life but filled with sound vibrations. Agnes does say whatever she pleases. Maybe it was another of her stories.

Tastes like eyeball soup. Little bits of gooey nonsense, formerly distinctive, floating in a gelatinous semi-liquid, equally nondescript. Disgusting. Can it possibly lead to something? Perhaps it's to challenge, to see how much I can handle. Old Mrs. Lavoie said to me the other day, "Oh, dear. I wish I knew what was going to happen. I'm too old for this. You've got pretty big shoulders, handling all this stuff." Maybe it's to see how big they are. I was feeling such a thrill at discovering a little child within me and beginning to know this small person. A new world was revealing itself. It was an intriguing place, measureless, faceted like the inside of rock crystal. Then pandemonium broke loose. Chaos is in charge here. Bitterness, lies, gossip, and betrayal have become part of the daily routine.

Wednesday, January 22, 1997.

I seem so detached I wonder if my reaction is real. Agnes has arranged to take away my business. She's convinced the residents to follow her into her own home for the elderly. I'll have to close the Residence after they leave on the sixteenth of February and I'm not devastated or having anxiety attacks. Last week, I readied the troops for battle. I felt a strength and calmness that helped me to reorganize the staff, give them hope that they wouldn't lose their jobs. I was convinced that the Residence would not close. I had faith on my side. I could believe it into taking place. I thought Agnes would give up, couldn't understand that it was actually happening, but with a little bit of time rearranging the perspective and settling the dust, I'm not so sure that the place will stay open.

I allowed myself to be manipulated again, didn't I? Same old story–let others have their way to avoid the unbearable discomfort of being challenged and put down. I avoided confrontations with Agnes, knowing she would be angry and would needle away at me until she got whatever it was she wanted. I listened patiently to her tell me one sob story after another about who did everything the wrong way. She said. You said. He said. I said. She did this. She did that. And they were probably all lies, all fabrications to get me to give her complete control, to get her own way unhampered by a boss, one that was gullible and too willing to trust. A fine combination, like sending disaster a personalised invitation with a time and place. So I gave, wanting to please and expecting thanks in return. I thought I had to be tough as nails to get my way and I wasn't tough.

Thursday, January 23, 1997.

Dugan telephoned.

"Hi,Isabelle. I hear you're having some trouble at the Residence."

"Where did you hear that?"

"I heard rumours before Christmas that Agnes was going to take the residents away."

"You did? From who?"

"Everyone knows."

"So why didn't anyone tell me?"

"Nobody likes to interfere."

"That's a good one."

"Maybe they figured that you already knew."

"I probably wouldn't have believed a bit of gossip anyway. I trusted Agnes. She was my right hand at the Home."

"Is there something I can do?"

"Can't think of anything. I've spent most of the last two weeks there, talking to the residents and their families and the girls on the staff."

"I'd like to help."

"Thanks anyway, Dugan."

"I can go with you to the Residence, if you like. Maybe there's something I can do around the house."

"Not really. Everyone is upset, but carrying on."

"I see."

"We're short-staffed now too, because Agnes had most of her family working there."

"So I heard."

"You don't miss much, do you?"

"Not much."

"After I fired Agnes, I called her sister to see if she was still coming in for her shift the next day. She told me to f.. o.. and hung up."

"Nice, eh?"

"So nice I forgot to thank her. The mother used to do the cleaning, and Agnes's daughter also worked several shifts a week. None of them are there now. The other girls are working long hours and I'm helping out as well, so we'll manage."

"Okay, Isabelle, if you ever feel like discussing anything, you can call me anytime. I have an open mind, you know."

"Sure you do, Dugan."

"Can I call you again to see how things are going?"

"Well … okay, you can call me sometime during the week."

Monday, January 27, 1997.

So Agnes has a lawyer. She wants her last pay. Maître Debauve will call me later this afternoon.

I sent a letter to each of the residents and their family today, accepting their notice to leave. "I am truly sorry for whatever has happened to make you move away… I will be here at my house in Wakeham next Sunday afternoon to meet anyone who might wish to discuss recent events." I concluded the letter by wishing everyone the best. Now I want to put all this behind me. I wish Agnes the best and hope she can transcend her own difficulties. I'll close and take the loss, but that's enough of putting my time into something that isn't rewarding or fulfilling. Half of my life is in front of me. *It will be the better half!* It's an opportunity to move on. At least I'll be a step closer toward a new way of living, although it sure is a strange way for it to happen.

Maître Debauve just left. He tells me that Agnes can get away with coercing the residents to leave while she was my manager. The girls on the staff knew what was going on but no one said a word, not even when food from the Residence mysteriously disappeared. They were afraid Agnes would fire them. She had free reins to do as she pleased, even more so since the accident, a headstrong horse without a bridle. I trusted. Blindly. I'll lose fifty-five thousand dollars but there's no point in suing through the legal system. She has no money.

Tuesday, January 28,1997.

I wonder if my past was so woolly as to warrant this attack. I don't know how much more I can take. Now Eva is sending me a lawyer's letter telling me that I still owe her money. It arrived in this morning's mail but her lawyer doesn't seem to understand much about preferred shares. I filed the letter away in a drawer. She telephoned this morning:

"Um, Isabelle, I've been meaning to ask you something."

"What is it?"

"I've been talking to a lawyer and... do you think the Manoir will be sold soon?"

"Don't I wish."

"Well, whenever it happens, what do you say to my lawyer sitting in on the proceedings? You know, just to be sure it's done properly."

I feel like a criminal who is trying to take everyone to the cleaners and can't be trusted out of sight. Maybe Eva and Agnes are jealous. Is that possible? I do appear successful. But who would want my debts? Are they jealous of my new house with the huge mortgage? I don't understand this at all.

Wednesday, January 29,1997.

Agnes, Eva, Dugan, Vincent, Mother–the people around me right now–what accident of grouping brought them all together in this particular time and place? They seem like players in a huge drama who have gathered together to play out a scene on the brink of a ragged cliff and are roaming too close to the edges, each one acting out a specific role that forces me to look further, to ask why. Does the scene have a sequel? A beginning? An ending? Any earlier than this, I wouldn't have looked for interior meanings. I wouldn't have seen the darkness as an invitation but rather as an annoying hindrance, an obstacle to be swished away from in front of my path, wiped out of memory. In my academic way, I would have rationalized the outcomes based on the surrounding circumstances, fought back with a winning argument to appease my wounded ego, accepted the cruelty and irrationality of the fates, and then grudgingly moved on, silently registering another defeat.

Life is presenting something. Why don't I listen to what it is saying? Other currents are traveling beneath the day to day dramas. I can feel them. We lock ourselves into a stranglehold of activity, we write our own operas of misconstrued importance, we build an entire frantic theatre. Activity suggests purpose, but activity is a whirring maze that blinds and numbs. Beyond the pressing obvious is a hidden terrain that is beckoning from the unseen. Normally our vision stops in front of the façade in a fumble of unruly

155

characters with apparently divergent aims. I want to know what is behind that screen.

February

"The great malady of the twentieth century,
implicated in all of our troubles and affecting us
individually and socially, is 'loss of soul'. When
soul is neglected, it doesn't just go away; it
appears symptomatically in obsessions, addictions,
violence, and loss of meaning. ... The root problem
is that we have lost our wisdom about the soul,
even our interest in it."

Thomas Moore,
Care of the Soul

Saturday, February 1, 1997.
Strange and unsettling voices are trotting through my head this morning. Once, a long time ago, I found an odd piece of paper in the high walnut secretary desk that stood in the front hallway of the red brick house in Wakeham where Anna and I spent most of our school years. A wide glass door decorated with wooden scroll work closed over the bookcase section on the top of the cabinet. I used to remove the books one by one, look at the title and the name of the author, flip through a few pages, and replace it on the shelf in exactly the same position. On the bottom, three drawers were stuffed full of papers and old photographs. A slanted lid covered a workspace in the center of the desk. Inside the work area, there were four cubbyholes on either side of a cute little pen drawer that lay underneath a small shelf for the ink well. It was fun to snoop through the desk and pretend when no one was around, although it was forbidden to disturb anything. The lid opened flat into a writing table and one day, when I was giving the contents a good going-over, this little piece of paper made me stop in my tracks. It read, "Mother, I wish you were dead." I thought Anna wrote it and had left it there for Mother to find. About a year ago, I asked Anna if she remembered that note but she doesn't remember it at all, and she has a good memory of the past. It's better than mine, perhaps because we remember different things. Maybe I wrote that message myself and forgot. Why did I say that? You're not supposed to say things like that about your mother. Whoever wrote it, that angry expression revealed a little spirit who was sad, split apart, and shattered into several pieces that didn't know what the other was doing. One part was bad. A good part wanted love. A sad part was angry. The good part forgot

157

and wondered where the anger came from.

Monday, February 3, 1997. 4:00 A.M.

A parade of 'what if's' chug relentlessly along with their own judgmental dialogue that tears me apart. The self-critic inside tells me that if I were a better person and had looked after my business better, this attack wouldn't have happened. The edges are brimming with rebellion and betrayal like a mutinous pirate ship. But who's to say that if the assault hadn't happened one way it wouldn't have happened another?

In November of last year, I was helping Agnes buy the Residence and was ready to make a time arrangement with her since she wasn't able to finance it. "It's been my dream for I don't know how long to own my own home for the elderly," she told me, her face breaking into a smile and her gaze wandering up to the ceiling, not seeing the ceiling but a vision in the middle distance. We often sat at the kitchen table to have a discussion. I gave her a professional evaluation of the house and business and a cost and revenue projection of how lucrative it could be for her, especially when she was working there herself and not an absent owner, as I was. But wasn't it her own prerogative to twist and turn and do it her way? Not for me to choose. Still, she didn't have to do it behind my back.

The residents' families confound me even more. Only one family member, Lydia, came to see me yesterday afternoon. She wanted a receipt for income tax purposes more than anything else and to see where I lived, I suppose. "Agnes told me there was a better place, better arranged, and with a room to wash hair. I just went along," Lydia said. Now each of the residents is splitting their rent according to the number of days before the sixteenth of the month. There won't be enough money to pay the staff more than one week.

12:00 noon.

Maître Debauve was passing through Wakeham and drove by in front of the house. I like his style. He's like an old-time country doctor making the rounds to see his patients directly at their homes.

"Hello there."

"Stéphane! Hi. How are you this morning?"

"Just fine, Isabelle. I saw your car in the driveway, so thought you must be home. Am I disturbing you?"

"Not at all."

"Good."

"Would you like a cup of coffee?"

"Thanks, but no thanks. I'm on my way back to Montreal. I'll stay only a minute."

"Will you have a chair then?"

"Thanks again, but I'll not sit today. I just wanted to tell you that I had a conversation with Dugan's lawyer, Maître Chardonnay, at the courthouse this morning and she is really going to push now."

"What does that mean?"

"She'll probably want a cross-examination."

"When?"

"I'll let you know as soon as I know the date, if she does in fact want one."

"This is new to me. Can you give me some lessons?"

"Sure thing. I'll go through the procedure with you ahead of time. Me Chardonnay will want to go through all the points in our appeal."

"That's all right. It's kind of complicated, but it's the way it happened."

"I think you'll be a good witness."

"How's that?"

"You're calm. What's going on with the Manoir right now?"

"It seems like everything's up in the air."

"Not again."

"Jean-François told me he had a rich brother-in-law who was interested in helping with his Music Hall project, but he doesn't come forward with any money."

"I think those two boys are just dreaming, Isabelle."

"I'm beginning to wonder myself if that's not the case."

"If the Manoir isn't sold soon, Mr. Dutil, with his notarized second mortgage, will start demanding to be paid. How long has it been since he received a payment?"

"The last cheque I sent was when I was in the hospital. So that was last April."

"When he decides to take action, there's nothing you can do to save your house. He's got a legal title to it. Sorry to be so blunt, but I want you to know where you stand."

"That's okay. I want to know."

"Well, I have to get on the road. I have an appointment at one o'clock. I'll be in touch with you, Isabelle."

"Thanks for stopping in, Stéphane. Bye."

What am I to do? I don't understand, Winona. Everyone is demanding money I don't have. My stomach's in a knot. My head is swirling. Somehow I must find myself in all of this.

8:30 P.M.

Just returned from a Rotary meeting. It was good to be among friendly

159

faces instead of feeling helplessly caught inside a den of hungry lions. I feel good conducting the meetings, at ease. My mood has made a complete reversal from the muddiness of this afternoon, the dull sinking and heaviness. The threatening miasma has turned about to an air of pleasant confidence. After Stéphane left this morning, I went straight to my writing desk, made myself comfortable in the chair, closed my eyes, went to the still place in my mindspace, and found the strength I needed.

Tuesday, February 4, 1997.

Visited with the boarders at the Home today. Old Wilfrid hugged me and told me if I ever needed someone to talk to, he'd listen, even at three o'clock in the morning. Such a pleasant bright house, it's too bad to see everyone leave. If there's a victim here, it's the older folks. They don't like upsets and having to get used to new surroundings. Wilfrid says they'll all be sorry they left. I've told every one of the residents now that I'm closing on the sixteenth. So that's it. It's over.

9:00 P.M.

Phonecall from Stéphane. He called to say that Dugan's lawyer had presented him with two motions to reject our plea, which means that Dugan wants a judgment allowing him to take my house. My head spins.

I called Dugan. I think I made a mistake. He tells me I should have gone bankrupt a year ago.

"I'm fed up waiting. I want a return on my investment."

"But I'm doing what I can."

"Well, nothing's happening, so now I'm forcing you to settle."

"You mean you want to ruin me."

"Why not? You ruined me. I was investing in our future. I wanted to marry you. Instead of spending time on a relationship with me you cavort with a married man!"

Scary. Scary. How did this happen, Winona? I know I made a mistake accepting money from him. I was naïve in believing my project couldn't fail. The business plan took months to prepare and I included four years of pro forma financial statements. It was a good investment if it had worked. Big mistake. But Dugan's not innocent. He's made plenty of investments before this. He was trying to buy a relationship, purchase a marriage for himself not a piece of real estate.

"You never loved anybody! You're not able to love! You have passion, but only for money. And who co-signed the mortgage on your new house? Vincent with the deep pockets? He should pay."

"No one co-signed, Dugan."

"If there wasn't a co-signer, how were you able to get such a big loan?"

"That's none of your business."

"It is my business, now that you mention it."

"How do you know how big the loan is anyway?"

"I have my ways."

"Well, don't ask me, ask the Caisse. They're the ones who gave it to me."

"And why don't you ever ask me for advice?"

"Why should I?"

"I've got lots of ideas. I've been in business a long time, you know. Monsieur Jeanneau and Vincent and Eva run your life! You have no ideas of your own."

"You've gone overboard, Dugan."

"Me? You'll do anything they say ... and the auctioneer who rents space at the Manoir ... and Eva's boyfriend."

"I did ask him for advice on construction a few times. What's the matter with that? And the auctioneer has some interesting ideas on an antique market."

"You're nuts, you know. You should listen to people who have some common sense. Like your mother and me!"

Sweet Jesus.

Why do I listen to him? Why do I think he has something to say? My head reels. Why do I call him, try to talk to him, reason with him, thinking he'll understand? Is something else happening here, Winona? Jekyll and Hyde personalities are what I would call the people around me—each one a blessing and a curse at the same time. One version of the character has a quiet, welcoming intelligence that cradles my desire; sooner or later, the twisted version raises a grizzly head, chomping and tearing, hungry and shattering.

Thursday, February 6, 1997.

To: Me Stéphane Debauve

Fax: 210-414-3089

From: Isabelle Carberry

Message:

Hello, Stéphane. A brawl with Dugan last evening. He's a scary person— timid and withdrawn one minute, angry and accusing the next, spitting out an array of loverly threats that go from one subject to the next with scarcely time to take a breath in between. Over the past months, he has invited me out for dinner several times and I always refused, but last night I told him that it wasn't such a bad idea to have a meal together so we could talk about things. Then, he wasn't at all certain, afraid to go, he said, afraid to sit across the table from me, afraid he'd be taken again. "It's not the first time it's happened you know," he said to me. "You're the third woman I've tried to help with real estate, and I lost money each time. If there's no hope of a relationship there's no point in meeting, is there? Because there's nothing to talk about. Not a thing in the world. I wanted to marry you, for Christ's sake, and live happily ever after!"

Stéphane, Dugan makes me uneasy. You know all those trees that he planted in front of his house? As dense as a forest? He planted them so people wouldn't watch him, he told me, so he could be alone. He wants to ruin me. "Yes," he says, "I want revenge because you won't marry me! I don't care about the money. What else can I say? I'm still suffering from jealousy. How can you do that to a person?"

Is there nothing in the law to expose what Dugan is doing?

I'm exhausted. Thanks for listening.

I. C.

Saturday, February 8, 1997.

"That little girl who was hurt is getting better," Léo told me yesterday afternoon. "She is very important. Do you realize how important she is?"

"I don't think so."

"You still talk about her as a third person but she's a real part of you, a younger you."

"I do feel her with me much of the time now."

"Good, Isabelle. Is there a time when you feel her more than at others?"

"For sure there is. When an anxiety attack hits. I'll sit down and write what's happening–the spinning, the swirling, the tightening–then I look for her. I tell her, 'I need your courage and passion, your strength and grace now.' It's as if the fire for life came from this little person."

Sunday, February 9, 1997.

Imagine! I finally met my nemesis face to face last night over dinner. And he still has two faces. The first desperately wants to be liked. The second is cold and closed, pushes me away. At least I confronted him. *Hurray!*

Tuesday, February 11, 1997.

Went to court this afternoon. Me Debauve and Me Chardonnay had to argue their cases in front of the judge. I wasn't allowed in the hearing room, so I waited outside. It will be a while before a decision is handed down, but Stéphane tells me that our case was weak. He feared the judge would cut off his arguments saying, in a slow and reprimanding voice, "Maître, Maître," gently rapping his fingers for treating the facts of the case so lightly. Dugan had indeed loaned the money. I had written and signed a document myself,

162

albeit preparatory and full of mistakes, and I had, without a doubt, made myself liable in case of default. This wasn't a criminal case, it was a civil matter and you can't ask for a psychiatric evaluation in civil law, only in criminal law.

"If the judgment is not in our favour, a bailiff could be at your door the next day to seize your house and furniture. If I were you, I would prepare to leave," Stéphane told me after the hearing had concluded and he had joined me in the lobby.

"It feels like an end is approaching."

"Courts do that to a person. That's what they're there for, to put an end to the skirmishing."

"I'm happy. I'm even glad."

"Did I hear right? You're glad?"

"I am. These have been just more difficult times in a long string of struggling years. As long as I stay in Wakeham, I'll be fighting. It's a relief to think of leaving, to get away."

"Well, I have to say that you're the first person I've met, Isabelle, who is happy to be told that they may be forced into bankruptcy in the near future."

"If that's the way it is. I'm ready."

Wednesday, February 12, 1997.

My hands are shaking. I just got off the telephone with Dugan. "Leave me alone, you deranged freak!" I yelled at him. Then I hung up. Instantaneously, the self-critic kicked in and began yammering, *What's he going to do to me now? I called him names and I got angry, so much so I'm still trembling.* The next thought nailed me in a space where nonsense was not tolerated. I recognized old fear, old behaviour. That reaction is as old as I am.

I called Hydro to ask them to disconnect the electricity at the Manoir. Forty thousand square feet–how can I pay the electric bill for such a building? The telephone rang as soon as I replaced the receiver. It was Dugan calling back. "What did you say to me? I didn't understand."

"Don't tell me that, Dugan. You understood perfectly well what I said. I hope you can be happy sometime, but please don't call me anymore."

Before the hand piece was out of range of my ear, I could hear Dugan yelling into the telephone, "But I still love you!"

Thursday, February 13, 1997.

Driving along in the car, no telephone ringing, no knock at the door, gives one a special time in which to let your thoughts roam. I could see myself in a little white cottage by a lake, writing desk set up facing the water, a private space to write. (There's a little white cottage by the lake at Alex's farm.)

Perhaps I could put a story together, get away from the world of business. How inviting, this image in my head! How downright peaceful!

Friday, February 14, 1997.

A splendid mahogany Chippendale seven-foot dinner table, eight chairs, and matching china cabinet left my house this afternoon. I needed the money to pay my lawyer. One would think I'd be more upset. I loved their magnificent bearing and strength. "Be careful how you cover these chairs. Tie the quilted rugs around them. Hadn't you better put two blankets over the carving on top of the cabinet?" But I was willing to let the movers take away each piece one by one. But, surprise, surprise, it wasn't like a painful loss. Nor was it like a dire end. It was more like a new beginning. They had given to me, now it was time for them to give to someone else.

Hardly possible, but I swear I have more energy now. Toulouse had run out of his feline dinners so I walked through a gentle snowfall to the corner store to buy some cat food. The day was windless and the large soft flakes landed on my nose and eyelashes like little wet kisses. Coming back into the house by the entrance at the rear, I looked past the kitchen towards the front rooms and saw an empty space where that grandiose table used to be. The dining room is completely unfurnished now, but it's beautiful. I painted the ceiling a soft grey-blue that changes colour with the light. The wallpaper is moiré silk with navy and antique gold stripes on a creamy white background of raised etchings of vines, leaves, and urns. They're like Greek vases from a poem. The tone on tone is almost unnoticeable, but I examined the figures close-up. The polished oak floor reflects the evening sky ceiling. Outside, the setting February sun had peeked through a break in the cloud cover, casting a bronze glow on the falling snow and turning each window into a picture postcard of a winter wonderland. The space is even more beautiful without the heavy furniture.

Saturday, February 15, 1997.

This storm was supposed to drop ten inches of snow during the night but it didn't happen. The morning sun is warm on my face. I close my eyes and let the heat stream through me, from my face down my back, to my heart, into each of my arms, then through my body to my legs and feet. Warmth that loves and heals. I feel good, together, peaceful.

I'm fed up fighting. It's too hard to get a project going in that old hotel. I've done what I can. Need I continue? I'm going to let go. Mr. Dutil can buy Monsieur Jeanneau's first mortgage and get the building back. If he doesn't, he'll lose his investment because Monsieur Jeanneau will have it sold for default. Then both Dugan and Mr. Dutil could come back to me demanding compensation, take my house, but there won't be enough for both because the Ovila Street business is closed. All that's left is a big house with a big mortgage. Oh, well. The boys, Louis and Jean-François, with their concert hall project, can always buy the Manoir from me before Mr. Dutil or Monsieur Jeanneau takes it, but there's still the possibility that if Dugan gets a court judgment against me personally, that he could take my house and everything in it before anyone else moves. So be it then. But, if Monsieur Jeanneau has it sold by a sheriff's auction, it would be cheaper for the boys, but I'm still exposed, even more so if it's sold for less than Monsieur Jeanneau's mortgage. Not exactly a summer picnic.

Whatever happens to the Manoir happens. I'll not lift another finger to try to arrange it this way or that.

Mother just called. Anna has been in Toronto all week on business and is flying to Montreal tonight. She told Mother she would come for a visit on Sunday.

"Can you and Anna come here for dinner at noon?"

"I can't, but Anna can probably be with you. It's the last day at the Residence tomorrow."

"But Anna's never been here for dinner before."

"That's all right."

"But she doesn't know what to do, she doesn't know where things are."

"It won't take Anna long to find out."

"We'll be sitting at a different table and she doesn't know when to go for her meal. Here, they like you to go at certain times, you know."

"It's okay, Mum, Anna can manage for herself. Don't worry."

I'm losing something. I don't like this lonely and scared feeling. What's happened? Where did my strength go? Everyone will tell me I deserve to lose everything because I didn't do things the way they're supposed to be done, because I live alone in a big house, because I do things others don't. They didn't know my boyfriends. They don't like that, not knowing who is sleeping with whom.

Who will say this? Who are they? Am I hearing voices? Am I listening to the gossips? The ones who like to talk about other people because their own lives are stuck? The ones who are afraid to look beyond their own walls, who live in fear of the discoveries that might be made in the realm of the unknown? The ones who are frightened by uncertainties and comforted by the thought that if none of their fantasies come true then neither will their fears? Fear depresses your self and slows understanding. I'm so tired of this, I'm devoid of all feeling. I don't care what happens to me. How am I going to live? Where am I going to live? What am I going to do? What if I'm the one who is crazy and this is all my imagination?

Sunday, February 16, 1997.

My confession to Anna went over like a lead balloon. She arrived last night. We sat in the living room, each in a two-seater in front of the fire, and settled ourselves for a good conversation. I began by telling her I was going to move away from Wakeham and tried to explain the hole inside. I went on passionately and clearly, so I thought. Anna didn't make a sound as I was talking, not a muscle flinched, and her eyes didn't look at me, she stared off to her right above my head. I could tell she was preparing her defence, rejecting everything she was hearing. There was a shield in front of her I couldn't penetrate, as if the drawbridge to a castle had been raised and I was left standing and gaping, a dwarf figure on the wrong side of the fortress. She waited a few minutes after I had finished my monologue, then, "Don't get angry at me, Isabelle. I know you're in trouble. You tell me I don't examine my life. You've always had an answer for everything. I went far away from home after school to be on my own because I couldn't do anything as well as you could. I was always following in your footsteps. I think we've just got completely different ways of processing life. I think once we're adults we have choices we can make. You should have found a job and stuck with it, Isabelle. You learn to be tough and strong. It all pays off in the end."

I thought Anna had come a little bit closer in recent years. She always arrived in a flurry of activity–kids, bags, and a laptop in a rented car from the airport–but sometimes we would try to remember things from the past, like who sat where around the kitchen table in the little house in Bruce Crossing. Anna remembers. I don't. She doesn't remember the nightmares I had when we were in school in Wakeham. She doesn't believe Mother pushed me away, thinks it's my imagination.

I continued anyway. "There's an insidious cancer that strikes families and turns them into arid and dry places where children shouldn't be."

"You're crazy, Isabelle. I think you exaggerate. We must have grown up in different families."

That's not what I wanted Anna to say! I shouldn't have said a thing. Not a bloody thing. I guess she didn't like me. That must have been the barrier I always felt. It's still there. I had been talking about myself, saying, "Life's not about accumulating or about jobs," but she reacted to the comment as a personal criticism of herself. She thought I was criticizing her. I give up. Open mouth insert foot.

Anna left earlier this morning. That gate that keeps us positioned one on either side is still heavy and dark. Neither did it creak with any movement to open before she packed up her things and left for the flight home.

"Just because I don't believe what you believe, Isabelle, it doesn't mean I don't love you."

I can't answer.

"I'd like you to keep in touch. I don't want to lose you."

"I'll see you sometime."

"Oh, Isabelle, now what does that mean?"

"It means I don't know when I'll see you again."

So my business is closed. I drove to LaViolette after Anna left. The ending was more like a non-event than anything melodramatic and surcharged with raw emotion, like a penny floating lazily down to the bottom of a creek. The residents had already moved out the day before, Saturday. Just a few family members were picking up the last remaining items belonging to their parents and only one of the staff was there holding down the last shift. One emotion wipes out another leaving a big nothing, a benumbed smirch, like windshield wipers spreading dried bird doo, hurling and flinging the crusty parts but leaving a beaten smear. I'm sad at the way it happened though, the way I let it go, the way I let it be taken from me as if I didn't want it. Secretly, I knew that I didn't want it; it belonged to Agnes and Eva, not to me. They're the ones who ran the Home. But I didn't do anything to change the way it was.

Monday, February 17, 1997.

No nervous excitement, this morning. No anxiety in my stomach. There's just a peacefulness in seeing the end of a difficult time approach. I'm going to move, sell my house. Maybe I'll go to Alex's, live by the lake, try to write a book, just be with my angel, and let her lead me. Where are you leading me, Winona? Do you remember that dream? You were going to guide me on a journey that looked like a murky path up an ancient river flowing through a primeval jungle.

Yesterday was a day for dropping illusions. Not only did my business fade away without a cry of protest or a simple whimper (how important was it to me in the first place?) but Anna's perfect life–the perfect family, plenty of money, perfect children, one of each, both blonde, one blue-eyed, the other brown–doesn't look quite so perfect any longer. She lived in a perfect city, worked at an exciting job, and was surrounded by dazzling friends with equally glamorous jobs in the media. At least that was my rendition. Compared with my life, hers was exemplary. She'd fly in from Vancouver, overwhelming me with her togetherness and obvious success, to hear more of my struggling and give me a few dollars to help out. I always wondered why. What was the difference? Why couldn't I have that perfect life?

But the shiny exterior harbours a touchy interior. Barriers have been erected closing off forbidden areas where choices are made by balancing the pros and cons. Anna doesn't believe in a drama more powerful than oneself, doesn't believe that our life journey is to evolve as human beings. There's no place in her scheme of things for a world of interacting souls on individual journeys of self-discovery. It's just a little bit too crazy, too far gone into the fringe to think that all of my struggling was an attempt by my soul to find itself. "That's new age shit," says Anna.

But, Anna, hear me out! There are things I want to say. I too believe that we can all make choices. But before you can make the choices that will lead you forward, that will reward you with the lasting satisfaction and the happiness we all seek, you have to believe in a treasure within yourself, not in the stuff about you, in a little nugget of gold in the center of your being. And you have to hold it close to you, hug it, rock it, and listen carefully to what it is saying.

Tuesday, February 18, 1997.

And here's Claire telling me about another side of my successful sister, how she lives a hell on the inside trying to handle everything–raise her children, spend time with her husband, look after the house, and work full time at a demanding job so she can earn a good salary to keep her independence. Anna never spoke to me about her personal life. I assumed it was as distinguished as the rest.

These are days of mixing and stirring and turning the inside out. Before Claire arrived, Monsieur Jeanneau, polite and gentlemanly as always, telephoned to say he can't reach Mr. Dutil. "I've left a message with his secretary several times, but he won't return my phonecalls. Ça ne tourne pas rond. Something don't smell none too good about that fellow. Wouldn't be at all surprised if he disappeared altogether some fine day. Can you get in touch with him? Ask him if he's interested in buying my first mortgage and taking the building back. Maybe you'll have more luck talking to him than I have." Then, this afternoon, (why not another stir for good measure?) Eva and I end up signing a document together in a small room at Me Debauve's office with no antagonism whatsoever. Stéphane was surprised. Eva was chatty.

"How's Dugan these days?"

"He's a hard one to figure out."

"Tell me another one."

"He has his lawyer pushing to get a judgment against me in court and sends me a Valentines Day card saying how much he cares and signs it, 'Love, Dugan'."

"He's a strange one, all right. I don't think he liked you moving away from him."

"What do you mean?"

"I saw him the other day walking across the front yard of your new house.

He was striding right along, nose up in the air like he was sensing something, and looking for all the world like he was supposed to be there. Or, I should say, he was trying to make everyone think that he was supposed to be there."

"Why does he do that? It gives me the creeps."

"He's stalking you, you know."

"Stalking?"

"Oh, Isabelle. It beats me how you can be so smart and so dumb at the same time."

Aren't we all? Aren't we all mixtures of positive and negative? Aren't we all living in a state of duality? Don't we all wish for deviance to expose our nature? Don't we long for the opposite ingredient that will tell us who we are? That will close the gap that separates? That will transform and unite? No light without darkness.

A break away from this madness–that's what I'd like. A little distance ought to rearrange the angles in this picture. They've a cubist harshness to them like a Braque collage. On Wednesday of next week I'll leave for a few days, visit my Rotary friends in Ontario, and take the things I want to Alex's. Just my favourite things. I'll move out mid-March, even if my house isn't sold.

Wednesday, February 19, 1997.

"How do you think other people see you? What do other people think of you?" Léo asked me this afternoon. And I don't know. I can't say. My head fills with competing thoughts that blank each other out–happy and unhappy, strong and weak, successful and unsuccessful, subdued and wild, caring and callous–and I'm incapable of uttering a sentence that makes any sense. Nothing will come out.

"Isabelle, I see two people."

"You do?"

"One person tells me of dramatic happenings in controlled and logical speech, but I don't know whether or not to believe what she says."

"You don't believe me?"

"Just listen now. There's a wide current of emotion underneath the words that seems to be coming from an area in your chest. I don't know what those feelings are. One person arranges everything that makes perfect sense. Someone else vibrates in the undercurrent."

"It's funny that you say that today, because I've just noticed that I write with two I's–one is tall and straight and arrogant, the other is curved with artistic flourishes. I switch back and forth between the two when I'm writing."

"I see."

169

"How can that be? I don't think about what I'm doing."

"The one you use probably depends on what you're writing about and your frame of mind at the time."

"I've heard of split consciousness and mental dissociation, but I didn't think it applied to me."

"It happens in various degrees, some more serious than others, but, always, there is avoidance of something precious."

"Something precious?"

"Something that means a lot to you. Isabelle, there's a fire inside that has to have a stage. It has to come out. If it's kept inside much longer, ... what's that English expression? ... you'll spontaneously combust."

"Léo...!"

"Seriously, I think you've been denying your feelings for years."

Thursday, February 20, 1997.

Are images from twenty-five years ago floating in your thinking, Winona? Because they are in mine. This is a good one! I used to tell stories to try to get attention, to try to make others believe I was somebody special. I told my co-workers at the library that I had written a play and had shown it to a film producer at Crawley Films in Ottawa. What malarkey. Mr. Crawley had given me an advance of eight hundred dollars and was going to produce it. So the story went.

"What's it called?" someone asked.

"Black Chairs," I said.

"They'll probably change the name."

"Oh, do you think so?" I replied in mock oblivion as to why anyone wound want to change a name like that.

I had even bought myself a new long wool plaid skirt and matching blouse in powder blue, a gift to myself to celebrate, I said. But I suppose you already know that. Right, Winona?

And the story I told because I didn't go into work one Monday–I told everyone that I flew to Bermuda for the weekend with my friend, Ollie, in his little two seater Cessna plane and on the way back the engine caught fire.

I told stories, they were lies. I got right into them, lived them as if they were real.

This is even better! Sitting in school, one afternoon in grade eleven, I found my thumb in my mouth. Fifteen years old and there I was, in the middle of a lesson with the others, my elbows were on the desk and both hands were in front of my face trying to conceal the fact that my left thumb was in my mouth. *Embarrassing, or what?* The teacher interrupted her lecture, it was Hetta, to ask me where my thumb was and the whole class turned around in their seats to look. *Leave me alone you dried up old prune!* I wanted to scream at her. But I swallowed as inconspicuously as I could to get rid of enough spittle so I could answer, and I slowly took my hands away from my face that all of a sudden felt like a blazing inferno. I heard Moose chuckling beside me.

"What?" I said. The word slipped out of its own accord and I knew immediately that I shouldn't have said it. I shouldn't try to play innocent with Hetta, like she was the crazy one asking where my thumb was. No one ever addressed Hetta with a rude *What?* and she frowned. "It's right here," I said, slurping more warm spit that seemed to be gushing into my mouth from an open tap and I thrust out my left thumb, all pink and shiny and shriveled like knuckle skin. Hetta glared at me, then her glare swept around the class, then she stayed silent for a few more minutes until the students faced her instead of me before continuing to teach. It must have been during a literature or history class. I couldn't concentrate on those lessons. The mathematics and science periods were fun. I listened to them. But two o'clock every afternoon was my time to remember the dream I had the night before and, for a while, I don't know how long, I wouldn't hear what was going on around me. I was elsewhere.

Friday, February 21, 1997.

Why should I feel attached to this place? Why should I feel like I'm running away, being irresponsible, abandoning my mother? Why do I continue to struggle to try to bring something new to LaViolette when they don't want anything to be different? They don't want a seniors' complex in the Manoir. They nod their heads to me, "That would be wonderful." But amongst themselves, they talk about how it's too big for LaViolette, too wild an idea. They don't want a Youth Center, don't want to be bothered with other people's troubled kids. They would lock their doors and windows and fear leaving their property unattended. A home for handicapped boys was supposed to be built in LaViolette. The townspeople sent petitions around to their neighbours to sign in protest against the project. No one wanted it on his street as if it would blight the neighbourhood. Mayor Norman tries to see ahead, to attract new business into the town, but he's fought against by half of his councillors. They don't like change. Norman locks his door when I go to talk to him so the cleaning lady won't walk in to catch a bit of town tittle-tattle to pass around. She checks to see whose car is in his driveway and gears her impromptu visits accordingly.

Léo, I'd like to talk to you now. I know you'd help me sort through this jumbled muddle. I remember digging a hole in the backyard sandbox. How old was I? Six? Someone said Australia was directly underneath Canada, on

171

the other side of the world. My idea was to dig a hole in the sandbox until I'd get to Australia. That's silly to try to interpret anything from that.

What were you so concerned about, Léo, at the end of last session? You gave me a preoccupied smile, as if you were in such a rush to write you couldn't lose a minute. Or was it because there was someone else waiting to use the room? You changed somehow as soon as I told you about the vomiting–was that it?–it started when I was twenty, and the last time was once last summer, the only time since the accident. Dugan came to my house to see what I looked like after being in the hospital for a month and a half and stood in the front hall berating me for everything he could think of. After he left, I wasn't hungry, but I ate, then vomited, to get rid of the nervousness, the hate. What was it about eating? I was spooked. It felt as though there were demons and insects crawling and growing inside me like an invasion of alien earwigs. I had to get them out of my body.

And those times I can't remember? Why does the memory of wandering down the street on my own in Cornwall stop suddenly as soon as my mother arrives? I see her coming toward me, walking at a furious pace down the sidewalk, holding onto a shopping bag that's flapping in the wind, and clutching her handbag in the crook of her other arm. But after that is a blank. I don't hear what she says to me. I know it would have been something like, "What's the matter with you? I told you not to move. You're a naughty girl for leaving Mummy. You could have been hurt, a little girl like you alone in the city. Don't you ever do that again," the proverbial finger wagging. But I can't hear a word. Is that how I used to survive what I didn't like? Blank out? Ignore?

Mother must have hated to move back to Bruce Crossing when I was a year and a half old in nineteen forty-nine, leaving all her friends behind in Wakeham. She showed me some sad photographs of the last day. Florence and Phoebe were standing in the back yard, wearing forced smiles they had put on for the camera. The little one in white overalls (they were probably pale pink but the photo was black and white) with a bow in her hair and peering over the short picket fence is me. Mother told me how they cried together on each other's shoulder. How she must have hated that old brick house we moved into at first. It was at the end of a poor street, near the railroad tracks. Not Mother's idea of a nice home. I had two girlfriends–Rita and Marlene. They lived on the same street in a tiny box house that was covered with grey tin. It was built on one floor, had only a few small windows, and was dark inside. Mother tells me I never had such friends. She must have badgered Dad to move away from there. And how she must have hated even more to move back to Bruce Crossing just after Dan and I were married. That's when Dad started to drink. Mother didn't like that little village.

Saturday, February 22, 1997.
I've been in my new house only five months. There are still boxes I haven't unpacked, and, tailbender of tailbenders, this morning I signed the papers giving Peter a mandate to put it on the market once again. I wish whoever lives here loves the beauty and peace of the setting and feels the harmony and strength in its walls. It's a special place.

Lonely, lonely. Perhaps it's the nighttime. It's harder to face your fate at night. The silence is too loud, too shameless. One can't distract oneself with daytime antics, one is forced to be alone with the steely vulgar night, without a place to hide from its impudence. But, in spite of all, the darkness caresses like velvet. Underneath the brashness, it's soft and warm, but I long for the warmth to come from a person. Tonight, I'd like to be loved, feel loved, feel the touch, the closeness, the exquisite pleasure of floating in a dimension of such happiness. It makes me ache. An explosion shakes my whole body, a cry flees into the spaciousness of pure passion, but the joyousness turns into tears. The sobs travel throughout my body without restraint. I feel the sadness of being alone, of not sharing the depth of love and passion. It's the tragedy of a broken soul.

But here's a tiny change. I can put something in front of me now that just a year ago I wouldn't even consider–an abhorrence, a fear of gooey soft things, like worms and snakes. That's progress of some sort. Should one of these slimy or wiggly creatures touch me–panic! An attack inside my stomach! My heart pounded as if to break free from my chest, and my head was non-functional. It recognized only one word, *Flee!* The paintings and drawings of Melle and Bosch, the Dutch artists, brought on the same reaction. They depicted the landscape of the unconscious. It was ugly, deformed, frightening, hellish, sexual. I couldn't look. Why did I never know love? How I longed to be loved. How I wanted a kind, happy love. The men I met always wanted more, wanted to handle and control, wanted me to be the way they wanted me to be. I was more comfortable on my own.

Sunday, February 23, 1997.
Sunday dinner at the Nursing Home ought to be a harmless enough affair, but the faces around the table are angry, accusing, interrupting, and gossipy. I must get away. I'm imagining, conjuring up ghosts. A cold wariness or a mockery full of laughter and disgust poisons, attacks, and deflates me, as if I'm on trial accused of being a sinner and a monster with no feelings, horribly guilty of some crime that was out of my control. I feel judged by people whose concept of a good person is one who wishes to copy convention, who

doesn't step outside any limits, set the timbers to shivering, question the conformity authority, dare to stick his neck out and challenge the way things are, like a child too big for its britches, eyes bigger than its stomach, not content with the ordinary fare.

I'm performing. I'm a performer who has wandered onto the wrong stage, who's acting in the wrong play. How will I find the right one? Will I still have to perform? My aging face, even with a few telltale wrinkles, is still a nice face. And behind the face, in the eyes, I see desire, the longing to live a life that reflects me and no one else. All the self-examination is getting tiresome. I want to put analysis behind, in the past where it belongs. I see Mother today, oblivious to what is going on inside me, full of her own pain, going from day to day, leading her own struggle for survival. Is not the whole thing just my imagination? No, I've been down that road. Why do I choose to stay here when I feel only barriers? Why do I hold myself back from leaving?

Monday, February 24, 1997.

What is it that you really like to do? I asked myself. *What is it you could see yourself doing and loving so much that time disappears?* I think you liked those questions, Winona, because as I was sitting and watching the fire this evening, a waking dream played right in front of my eyes.

I watched myself enter a room filled with troubled boys around eighteen years of age and kneel down in the center of the group. One fellow in particular watched me intently the whole time, mesmerized, speechless. I spoke to them about how someone somewhere along the way told them they were worth nothing and stupid, incapable and incompetent. It created a hole inside and they were trying to fill this emptiness with dysfunctional destructive behaviour. I was so passionate in what I was saying, so clearly honest and loving that I reached through to them. The whole conversation ran through my head.

You're trying to fill an empty hole with alcohol or drugs. You will never fill it that way. The first thing you have to do is find a calm place in your mind, a space where you can go where it's still and quiet. I'll tell you how I found my space. I imagined a big empty room. It took on a shape of its own. It had walls, but no corners and no windows. There was a partially open door at the back of the room and beyond the door was light that was dazzling in its brilliance. I can go to this space anytime I wish just by closing my eyes. I had a little white light that changed sizes. I caught it one time at a baseball game in a dream. I was sitting in the bleachers behind the batter's box, stood up, and put out my left hand to catch a high foul ball. The ball got smaller

174

and smaller as it came towards me and when it landed in my outstretched hand, it had changed into a little ball of white light. It would come to me in my mind space, I would ask it to wink at me, it would, and it made me smile. It was pure energy, an invisible intelligence or consciousness that was everywhere and in everything–in trees, in snow, in rivers, in a stone, in animals, in us.

How do you think a tree knows when to shed its leaves, when to start the sap running through it again, how to grow branches? Because in its intelligence, it has a purpose, a destiny. As long as it is fulfilling its purpose, it grows into a magnificent work of art, perfectly balanced, beautiful, and in harmony with itself. When a piece of wood is cut off from its life source it begins to dry. It serves a purpose to us for a while in our houses and other wants, but as soon as it is cut off from its natural reason for being, it begins the process of decay.

And how do you think the simple dust in a tiny apple seed knows how to grow into a tree that blossoms with a flower so delicate and a scent so sweet it inspires poetry, and then produces a bright red apple, a fruit so delicious little boys will risk everything to steal it? Birds know when to change their habitat; nobody gives how-to lessons to a caterpillar on how to create a butterfly; a deer's antlers live and die every year according to the lengthening and shortening of the days; the young in the wild are born in the spring when there is enough food to nourish them; dogs have a destiny to be a dog–to stretch, to lie in the sun, to chase cats, to look out for their master, to procreate. When it comes to humans we each have a destiny too and when we're cut off from our true nature, from our inner guidance system, we begin a form of decay also. Everything on Earth is part of an enormous design and the key that locks us all together is in that little ball of white light.

As infants, as young children, we long to be loved, to be held close and smiled upon, and we love and trust the person who looks after our needs and we return their love. But things go wrong and the people who normally would love us, our parents, can't love, or don't like us. We don't receive their love; we don't see love around us. We're told we can't do anything right, that we're bad, good children don't behave that way, you're to respect your parents, you're not allowed to cry, big boys and girls don't cry, you're not supposed to question the family, that's not polite, things just are, don't ask or you'll get into trouble, you'll look stupid, don't think about yourself, if anything worries you shove it under the rug and work harder, you'll forget about it.

When we're not allowed to feel good about ourselves, we get into the habit of hiding our finer feelings and we don't let them out for fear they'll be hurt. Our true nature–to give love, receive love, and feel loveable–has been deceived, disappointed, and broken. Until we understand what happened to us, until we put the pieces back together, we suffer and struggle in an attempt to fill that emptiness. We search for love. If we were abused, it was fearful and traumatic. Often we don't remember; we blank out those memories. It's a survival instinct–when something is too painful to remember, too confusing to think about, we put it away somewhere, we forget until we're strong enough to handle the emotion. As we grow, we still want to be loved, because it's in our nature. Everyone in the world wants to love, so we do things to try to make up for the loss. We act out. We wear masks of behaviour to divert attention away from what hurts.

I just want to tell each one of you, from the bottom of my heart, that you're okay. I know you're okay. You're good, you're a wonderful person and a sensitive one, who got screwed up along the way by someone else who was screwed up. But you're okay. You're all there still. Your real self is just waiting to be recognized by you and to be welcomed back into your life, your real life.

Wednesday, February 26, 1997.

Nathaniel and Rosa are my Rotary friends. I arrived in time to have lunch with them at noon and they've fixed up their spare room for me to stay in tonight. They're so kind and easy-going that I seem to be in a different world. My other world of lawyers and creditors seems far away, makes me wonder what all the fuss is about. It seems like an exaggerated catastrophe that's not possible here, like a volcano in a sandbox. It's hard to put myself back into that space for Nat and Rosa, seems unnatural and uncalled for. I'd have to live through the trauma again and I don't feel like burdening them with a cast of strange characters.

Friday, February 28, 1997.

"Are you in a good mood tonight?" Dugan was at the other end of the telephone line.

"Look Dugan, as long as you have a lawyer to do your talking for you, I have nothing to say to you. Goodbye."

And I hung up. No sooner was the phone out of my hand but my head was spiraling, my stomach was coping with an old anxiety attack, and my arms were trembling. Can a dumb reaction like that be the result of sheer frustration? Frustration at an inability to penetrate that smooth deceptive mask? Whenever I try, he argues that I'm this or I'm that, my hands reach up to hold my head, and I ask myself why did I even try to get through that tough exterior. He sure stirs me up. The feelings are most unpleasant–anger at feeling manipulated, somehow being talked around and confused so that

176

I don't know what I think. I feel sick. I hate. I hate anyone who doesn't listen, who shoves me aside.

Maybe, like Léo says, the people in my life show me feelings that need attention, places that must have been wounded, touchy spots that were sectioned off and filed away in a special compartment with a label that reads, *DANGER - DON'T LOOK IN HERE*. Do you know that I can cry in front of someone now? It's a relief to know I can, even if it is only one person, Léo, my therapist. And I can speak now.

Is that why my voice was paralyzed after the accident, Winona? To bring attention to the voice that couldn't come out? Léo noticed the connection. The throat specialist tells me that it's ninety percent healed now. There's still a small piece that can't express itself, like the blind spot in a car side mirror, or a flute in an avalanche. I wonder if that's that blanked out part. Do I really have to know what happened there?

It reminds me of that dream I had last summer where I wouldn't go into the depth and darkness where children were frolicking with wild animals.

March

"We turn to God for help when our foundations
are shaking, only to learn that it is God who
is shaking them."
Charles West

Saturday, March 1, 1997.
Will you help me through this, Winona? Please?
I woke in the middle of the night with a tidy drama circulating in my head
and went over and over it, but I can't make my mind go where it doesn't want
to go. It's like trying to prod an elephant with a feather. There doesn't seem
to be even one coal left burning from that dream, just cool grey ashes, and I
can't find a thread of dream substance to pull on. Sometimes following the
thread from one impression to the next will bring the entire dream into focus.
All that remains this morning is a fleeting remnant where I was coming to the
end of some big event, was nearing the finish line, and I was told (I have no
idea who spoke, it was a voice I wasn't familiar with), "Put yourself into the
end part one hundred percent."

Monday, March 3, 1997.
"Hervé, I'm calling this morning about my Old Folks' Home on Ovila
Street."
"Troubles, Isabelle?" asked the manager of the LaViolette Caisse.
"Have you heard?"
"I did hear a few rumours, but you never know, eh?"
"Well, this time there's something to the gossip. I had to close the
business last month."
"I'm sorry to hear that."
"Hervé, can you take the building back? I can't pay the mortgage any
longer."
"That's a serious step. There'll be a black mark on your record."
"I'm not too concerned about a spot."
"Maybe you should ask a real estate agent to sell it. You might end up
with ten thousand dollars in your pocket. If I sell it, you won't get a penny
from the transaction."
"But it will be difficult to get a good price for it without a business
operating inside."
"Perhaps, but think it over again, Isabelle. Take a little more time before

179

you decide because, as I said, there are consequences that will affect obtaining another mortgage in the future."

"Okay, I'll live with it for a few more days."

"If you're still of the same mind after a bit of time, call me back and I'll start proceedings to repossess."

I'm ready to be left with nothing. It's okay. They're just things. What's important to me now is this magnificent strength that I feel inside. That locked box, the chest wrapped in chains and filled with hidden and abandoned parts of myself, seems to like all the touching and questioning. The cover has been thrown wide open, a grinning bear's den and the bear is emerging from a long hibernation hungry for nourishment. It's as if I'm just starting to live.

Me Debauve telephoned. "The judgment on the two motions was in our favour!" Stéphane could hardly believe the decision. "If you ask me, the judge didn't have time to read the case," he says.

Thank you God and my sweet Winona.

Tuesday, March 4, 1997.

This morning's air is compassionate but terse and abrupt, no suggestion of fumbling or teasing, the atmosphere is pregnant with meaning. This is definitely the junction at a crossroads. I've come to the end of an old pockmarked road, patched and bandaged in many places, the surface split and cracked into jagged lines serpentining like varicose veins. I have to continue. But what do I do? I've asked for directions several times, but I don't receive any indications of where to go.

And now you're telling me (am I right, Winona?) that I know why it is I don't receive any instructions. Because I already know the answer. You're telling me that I know what I'm to do but I don't start because I'm afraid of not being able to do it. Afraid of what the desire might demand of me. Afraid it will be too much. Afraid I might not be able to live up to the hope. How true! And how dismal! My sweetest dream is to write this book that's inside me. My eyes soften when I imagine it happening. It's a sweet longing of my new self. I have all the time I could possibly wish for to put my heart and soul into this story but the old me says, *You can't come up with a spellbinding tale. You won't be able to write it the way you'd like it to be. You're not good enough. You don't have a command of the language like an English master. You're not used to expressing yourself. You've never done it before. You'd never finish.* The list goes on with the breakneck enthusiasm of a can opener in overdrive, an excursus as dull as ditch water, an apology to justify my offence against myself, to mitigate the awful guilt of procrastination. I could research any topic, put together an A-plus report, but if the message had to come from me I waged a war and fought to pull the right words across a barricade that loomed in my head. Fresh original surprising thoughts lost out and were submerged in grey brain jelly before they could float across the barrier to grace my paper. The words I wanted wouldn't come, I couldn't form an opinion that was scholarly enough to impress a professor. I was very aware of the agony I put myself through trying to fight through that blockade and find the perfect expressions, modulated regurgitated thoughts heavy with doctrine, ones that would earn a note of praise scribbled in the margin of the text. I could envision tortured pages lying about helter-skelter, unfinished, yawning, gnawing, and groaning with my own internal inconsistencies. But I know better now. I know where that dynamic came from.

The evening was wearing on. Rather than heading upstairs to bed, I browsed through the bookshelves looking for something to read before falling asleep. I chose a book and held it in my left hand, about to leaf quickly through the pages, but before I had a chance to flip through, my eyes stopped at the frontispiece where the book had opened up neatly of its own accord. It was a comment from Goethe's *Faust*:

Until one is committed, there is hesitancy, the chance to draw back, always ineffectiveness. Concerning all acts of initiative (and creation), there is one elementary truth the ignorance of which kills countless ideas and splendid plans: that the moment one definitely commits oneself, then Providence moves too.

All sorts of things occur to help one that would never otherwise have occurred. A whole stream of events issues from the decision, raising in one's favour all manner of unforeseen incidents and meetings and material assistance, which no man could have dreamed would have come his way.

Whatever you can do, or dream you can, begin it. Boldness has genius, power and magic in it.

Begin it now.

Instead of turning out the lights and heading upstairs, I went to my writing desk to get a pen, walked over to the couch, settled myself in the corner, balanced a pad of paper on my knee, and began to write, "She added an 'e' to her name after she left home...."

Friday, March 7, 1997.
"How've you been?" I heard Vincent say when I picked up the telephone.
"Good. How about you?"
"Okay. It's been a while."
"It has. I thought you had left the country."

"Not at all. I've had a mess of legal problems with a building I sold a few years ago."

"You have problems with buildings too?"

"With this one anyway. I endorsed the mortgage in order to make the sale and now the guy can't pay."

"What are you going to do?"

"I have a choice to either pay the bank that sponsored the deal a hundred thousand dollars or to take the building back."

"Some choice."

"It's getting me down."

"Your voice sounds it. Perhaps it's a message to make some changes."

"What kind of changes?"

"To look inside your life."

"Inside my life? There's nothing to see there. I'm just sick and tired of long meetings with bankers and lawyers. I'm going to live in the present and not look anywhere."

"Vincent, that's not what living in the present means."

"What do you think it means?"

"Living now means dealing now with what's uncomfortable."

"How's that again?"

"It means looking back and trying to see what's out of synch in your life when events are sour now."

"That's not what the expression says."

"It's so misunderstood. Living in the present isn't an excuse to turn into a robot to avoid seeing something that you don't want to."

"Whoa. I didn't call to get a lecture."

"But once you've cleared away the nitty-gritty, living from that calm place in yourself, in the present moment, is *the* way to live."

"That's how I understood it, without the nitty-gritty."

"But that setback is trying to tell you something, Vincent, and it's not telling you that you didn't properly check out your buyer before you signed. It's telling you to take a look at your inner life, to stop ignoring your feelings."

"Well, if you say so."

"I do, Vincent. I mean it."

Sunday, March 9, 1997.

Chicken à la king today at the nursing home. I walked over just before noon to have lunch with Mother. The fresh March air was invigorating compared to the flat depleted house air, like a shot of good whiskey, or a blast of pure oxygen. The sun was noticeably higher in the sky these days, and stronger. The snow banks along the street were melting under the warm rays, turning what had been white cottony fleece into coarse dirty cheesecloth spattered with pebbles and road tar that the snowplow, in passing, had jettisoned from the street like gunshot. Mother usually has something in store for me after we're back in her room and I've settled in the chair across from her wheelchair wondering how to begin the conversation. Today was no different.

"You owe Dugan fifty thousand dollars that he put in the Manoir," she began. "I don't know how you got yourself into such a mess."

"Where did you get an idea like that?"

"Oh, Dugan's a good boy. He stops in to have a nice chat every once in a while and tell me all the news."

"Good ol' Dugan."

"Well, you never tell me anything."

"I can't."

"The poor dear. I'd cry my eyes out if I lost fifty thousand dollars. He worked so hard for it, going into work every day at that office place where he works in Montreal. What's it called anyway?"

"Dallaire Credit. He's been a clerk there for thirty years."

"There you go. Thirty years. You have to work hard for money. Hard-earned money. You think money grows on trees."

Wednesday, March 12, 1997.

I have no money for gas. Nothing is moving again. Cheques are bouncing. This afternoon I took out the glass gallon jar that's full of pocket change and started to count out pennies, nickels, dimes, and quarters. I'm still struggling. There's no buyer for my house. I can't move anywhere unless my house is sold. I do nothing but struggle as long as I stay around Wakeham and LaViolette, but I can't leave.

Why do you try to arrange everything yourself? Why do you always try to take control? It works perfectly well, better as a matter of fact, without you interfering. Allow life to happen to you. Look after what's important—your innermost places, your heart that wants expression. The little voice was in my head. Was that you Winona?

Friday, March 14, 1997.

Good Rotary meeting last night, although Thursday doesn't suit everyone—the meetings have been held on Mondays for fifty years. The directors met for their monthly caucus before the regular meeting at six o'clock. There was a lot of business to discuss and it went so smoothly I was astonished that I had covered everything on the agenda by ten minutes past seven instead of the usual seven-thirty.

There are still demands for payment but they're becoming few and far between. Yesterday afternoon I received a call from the Quebec Labour Standards office because they had a complaint from one of the staff that she didn't receive her last pay. True, I owe Adèle three hundred and thirty seven dollars but she knows the situation. Maybe she's in cahoots with Agnes. The other girls are waiting. So considerate of them, and patient. I don't have the money now, but I'll do what I can. Adèle doesn't have any money either. She probably needs it as much or more than I do.

Saturday, March 15, 1997.

The Ides of March. A fateful day. Julius Caesar's nemesis back in 44 B.C. He was stabbed to death in the senate in Rome. I hit a tree but I didn't die. Not a fitting comparison. Fun anyway. The accident was one year ago today. I drove by the tree this afternoon, slowing down as much as I could in passing by on the highway. I wanted to see if I would recognize it, wondered how much damage it had suffered, if it had any scars, and if so, if they were healing like I was. And I wanted to say to that chosen tree, "Bless you and thank you for changing my life."

Sunday, March 16, 1997.

Mother has had a hard time this week with more aches and pains than usual. I had lunch with her again. What a heart she must have! She must have inherited it from her pioneering ancestors. It's surprising how it can stand the strain on her body. There's hardly a part that isn't diseased. The blind eye bothers her with a constant pricking that gives her a tiresome blink; one ear is deaf; two ribs are broken; osteoporosis weakens her bones; rheumatoid arthritis runs rampant through her back, shoulders, arms, hips, and legs, deforming her hands and feet. Alex used to call her his 'bionic grandma' when she began to have her joints replaced with Teflon parts– first her knees, then both hips, and then a shoulder. It seems only her mind isn't affected. She's quick-witted, always has a good large print book on the go, loves to have company and hear all the news, and still plays bridge with her old cronies. It's amazing she can think at all with the medication she takes– twenty-six pills a day and eye drops four times a day. What a pharmaceutical onslaught! She and the pills seem to be codependents in vice, one supporting the misery of the other.

As I was leaving to go to the nursing home, my little car got stuck at the end of the driveway in a low ridge of dirty wet snow left by the snowplow. I shifted heavy shovelfuls of blackish slush spotted with stones away from the wheels but still couldn't get free. My next-door neighbour was walking home from church as I was spinning the wheels and a young fellow was watching the commotion from the hospital parking lot across the street. Both came running to help push and the metal sprite was on the road in five seconds.

At two minutes past eleven-thirty, I arrived in the entrance, removed my snowy boots, slipped into a pair of shoes, and could see through the sliding glass doors that the meal had already begun. Soup was being served to the residents; guests always help themselves in the kitchen, cafeteria style. I rushed to the empty chair beside Mother at the dining room table, out of breath from hurrying because I knew I was behind time.

"You're late!"

"I am." I explained the delay.

"So, you had an excuse for being late."

I let Mother be and joined in on the table conversation. When lunch was finished, I wheeled her upstairs, helped her with her room chores, watered the plants, filed her paid bills, straightened out her closet, and sewed on a button. I had done her shopping for her–a bottle of Australian sherry and a bag of Humpty Dumpty cheesies–so I arranged them in her mini-refrigerator the way she likes with the bottle cap unscrewed and sitting lightly, some cheesies, not too many, put into a separate little white plastic baggie that doesn't tear when she tries to take some out of the sac. The cellophane bag on cheesies rips.

What an ugly mess must be inside her. Whenever I'm around, I feel a mess inside me too while an obstinate and unruly goblin readies our defences like an old boxer resurrecting the moves that kept him from being pummeled in his last fight. At the same time, I see her as she is today, old and crippled, always my mother, and I question my cold heart.

Mother perched on the edge of the bed while I undid her shoes. She let herself fall backwards onto the bedspread as I lifted her legs. Inching herself into a comfortable position, she prepared to have a nap before the afternoon curling game began on the television. I adjusted the head of her bed and as I did so I looked at her face wondering if, when I looked at her, she would be looking at me and would consequently avert her eyes. It was almost an act of bravery to look my mother in the eyes. It was defiant and disrespectful and arrogant. Even after close to fifty years I was scarcely able to break this generational code. But her eyes were closed. The skin on her face was colourless, had a wax-like pallor without a line or a wrinkle to disrupt the moulded effect that was leaden as a corpse. It could have been her remains that were lying there motionless.

The sullen knot that had been tightening inside my stomach gave way, dissipated, released its claws like a lion turning into a pussycat. Something new was taking its place in a different spot in my body. It was a tug of sympathy. I felt sorry for this poor old soul who was valiantly fighting to live as her body was giving out on her.

Monday, March 17, 1997.
   There was a funeral service at the Anglican Church this afternoon. Not Mother's. Goodness no. Mother's battle to live is like a ten-year Trojan War where neither side will surrender until one of the opponents is reduced to dust. As in any war between gods and mortals, the vanquished is not the godly side. The funeral was for my old French teacher from the fourth grade, Mr. Graves. Claire picked me up and we went together. After the ceremony, we got into a conversation while sitting in her car in my driveway, about another world that was going on right here in Wakeham when we were both young and in school. I was so caught up in myself I wasn't aware of what was happening elsewhere, but Claire noticed everything–who was having an extramarital affair, who was violent and drank too much, who beat up his wife and children. The three kids, two girls and a boy, were in school at the same time as Claire and I. One of the girls, Belinda, later married a local boy, Paxton. Paxton had a screaming rage in him when he was little, a kicking fury that he unleashed against his mother. Belinda and Paxton were at the church this afternoon. Belinda denies any violence–her father never hurt her, only when she deserved it. Now Paxton beats her up and their two boys.
   What an absurd game we live! We know nothing about it until we face our black spots. The drama of living is overwhelming until you slow down to smell the roses, until you stop allowing the circumstances to control you and ask the circumstances what it is that they want you to know.
   I still love Vincent. Far beyond the possession and obsession, the one-sidedness, I'm still attached to something at the center. Maybe he doesn't know himself of his sweet sensitive soul. He's put that part away, buried his feelings deep inside. Even when the love isn't returned, I feel a strong connection, an unearthly bond. There's a sadness inside Vincent. I can feel it the way Léo could feel an unsettled emotion inside me. I know so well the pain of not living who you are.

Tuesday, March 18, 1997.
   The charm of the day was everywhere. It was in the beautiful clear blue of the afternoon sky, in the way the wide expanses of snow were whiter than white, in the way, as the day wore on, the lowering sun reached out in long copper shafts and bounced across the fields and the frozen river, in the way the light looked into the houses as it was waning, soft, bashful, milky. I went to LaViolette to do some errands, signed a rental agreement for a Rotary Brunch next month at the Academy, faxed some papers to Me Debauve, then went for a drive. I followed the rivers, circling back to Wakeham. Everyone

I looked at returned a smile, one that elevated, freed, connected.

Wednesday, March 19, 1997.

Hello God. It's me, Isabelle. Do you remember me? Usually I talk to Winona, but today my heart is full. I've got an earful and it's pretty important, so thought I'd go directly to You. I hope You don't mind. I'm sorry for those things I said to You when I was ten or twelve years old but it seems that was all I knew. I know You understand.

I would so like to be close to someone tonight but I don't see anyone here for me. There's nothing here for me, no relationship that really means anything, and no job is presenting itself. There's not even a hint of one, God. I always felt tied to this area, felt guilty if I thought about leaving. I see how I've struggled to fit in, always pushing to make things work out. It's been a fighting place. But God, it embarrasses me, but I have to ask you to provide for me as long as I stay in this town.

Thank you for this warm morning sunshine, for the calmness and peace I feel, and for the rest. I've slept nine to ten hours a day for the past month. Never have I slept like that. And thank you for all of the people in my life who help me to heal, who show me where the sad places are, so at last I can listen and hear them crying out to me. Thank you for the freedom, the lightness in my body, the openness in my heart. The heavy bag of do's and don'ts and can'ts and should's and mustn'ts and ought's that I carried strapped to my back all my life gets lighter and lighter. Living is no longer that threatening and exhausting place fraught with tension and anxiety. It welcomes me and I welcome living.

Thank you for listening, God. I knew You would. Amen.

2:30 A.M.

I haven't gone to bed yet! Vincent telephoned at eleven-thirty to say he was on his way from Montreal and would stop in to see me. The electricity was too strong to ignore. We hadn't spent a few hours alone together since early December. We talked, held onto each other, loved, talked more, hugged, looked at each other, told stories, kissed, loved, stoked the fire, held hands, examined our interlocked fingers, meditated, talked more. Heaven came down to earth.

Before he left, we stood in the hallway by the front door.

"I love being with you, Vincent."

"But?" He could feel the but.

"The time we spend together is special, but it makes me sad."

"Sad? Why would it do that?"

"Because your heart's not with me."

"Part of it is."

"Then the other part is with someone else." That was a purely jealous thought and I chided myself.

"No." He looked into the distance.

"I liked you too much, Vincent..." He held me close, closed his eyes, buried his head in the crook of my neck, and I felt, for the first time, a fleeting sense of caring, transitory as a tramp, but genuine. "Not the businessman, I mean the person who's inside here," I placed my hand on his heart, "this special person who's in here, who hides, who you don't show to anyone."

"I show him here."

"That you do."

So it was all right when he left. I was still in love with the person inside who was sensitive and loving but who had difficulty trying to come alive.

Thursday, March 20, 1997.

At our Rotary meeting tonight we presented the Breakfasts for Children organization in LaViolette with a cheque for three hundred dollars. It wasn't enough. The minor hockey league gets a thousand dollars à year. Hungry children should have at least that much or more. There was a small turnout tonight, only eleven members. We have to get back to Monday nights.

Friday, March 21, 1997.

"Isabelle. Hi, it's Vincent. I called earlier this afternoon around five o'clock to ask if you wanted to go out for dinner, but there was no answer."

"I was still in Montreal around five. The traffic on the bridge to get off the island was bad. Nothing but bumper to bumper cars and trucks for as far as you could see."

"Another appointment with the therapist?"

"That's it. Once a week, barring snowstorms."

"When did you get home?"

"Just this minute. I haven't taken off my coat yet. The phone was ringing just as I walked in the door."

"It's seven. Too late to go out for dinner?"

"Sorry, I don't feel up to going out now."

"That's okay. I'll call you again tomorrow evening. If you're at home I'll stop by. I'd like to be quiet, just relax and talk."

"Sounds nice. I'll be here."

Saturday, March 22, 1997.

A light dusting of snow, as yet undisturbed, is sitting quietly on the trees after last night's snowfall. It looks like a bright winter day, fresh and clean with the new whiteness, but it's spring. The warm sun is shining through the window on my paper and I can feel the strength of the sun's rays on my face as I write.

Sunday, March 23, 1997.

Vincent arrived about eight o'clock last evening. We sat at the kitchen table eating take-out chicken and talking about this and that. He made a casual comment that there were ten children in his family.

"Ten? I thought there were nine."

"Yes, but one died."

I looked at Vincent, not wanting to ask him to talk about something he didn't want to, but he continued.

"My brother, Roger, died when he was thirteen."

"How old were you?"

"Sixteen."

"What happened to him?"

"The day was a scorcher in the middle of a summer heat wave and we wanted to go swimming. I had my driver's license, so we took my father's car without telling him and drove to visit some friends who lived on the Ouananiche River near the U.S. border. Anxious for the cool water, Roger ran along the dock and jumped. The water was only six feet deep, but he couldn't swim. I was slower arriving. I stopped to put the car keys in a safe place. When I got to the dock where Roger had jumped, he was nowhere to be seen. I looked everywhere on the water, up and down the river, it wasn't a wide river, more like a stream at that point, and checked along the shorelines, wondering all the time if he was playing a trick on me and how he could disappear so doggoned quickly. Then a hand reached out of the water. Then a head with dark hair plastered to the skull bobbed above the surface. It was Roger. He called to me, "Vinnie! Vinnie! Help me!" I jumped in the river but couldn't swim either, and I couldn't find my brother under the water. Fifteen minutes later, a diver found the body lodged under the dock, but he was dead."

"Oh, Vincent."

"The body was exposed in our family home for three days. I lay in bed during the whole time. My body jumped involuntarily as if I was being given one electric shock after another. The incident was never mentioned around me and I never spoke about it to anyone. Ten years later, I asked my mother about the drowning and she told me the family thought it was best for me never to speak of it."

"I'm so sorry."

189

4:00 P.M.

What I thought would never happen, happened. I went to the nursing home to have lunch with Mother. Afterwards I brought her back upstairs to her room and sat waiting for her to go through her list of things for me to do. She started to tell me I needed a real job, that I do nothing.

"I'm writing a book."

"But you don't make any money. Everything you do is volunteer. You owe Dugan fifty thousand dollars that he worked so hard for."

"Don't you think I worked hard? I spent three years trying to get eight different projects going in the Manoir. When one didn't work, I tried another. I had the Residence to look after at the same time. There were government reports to send off every month, bi-weekly payrolls to do, corporate income taxes to prepare, staffing problems to deal with, empty rooms to fill. I had accounting clients too. I was on the Board of Directors of a music and theatre project, and I was the treasurer for the Rotary Club. Don't tell me I didn't work hard."

"Who's going to look after you, pay your bills if you don't work? People will sue you."

"God is going to look after me," I announced. "I've stopped fighting and I'm living wonderful days doing what I feel good at–writing, trying to understand myself, and thinking of how to help others find themselves. I know God will look after me."

Mother had been sitting in her upholstered armchair, her glance cast downward, shaking her head. She lifted her head with a jolt at my last remark and stared straight at me as if she hadn't heard right. "God? You haven't been to church in years. … Well, I hope you do pray to Him and I hope you pray hard! And every day!" She waited a moment then added, "I don't want you to lose your house, dear."

"It doesn't matter," I said. I added to myself, *I have a partnership with an angel.* She ignored my comment that it didn't matter if I lost my house– another ridiculous statement from a quarrelsome vixen of a girl she had never been able to fathom. She would have liked to knock some good ordinary common sense into that wilful head of hers.

"You need to make money so you can pay taxes."

"I'll sell my house and leave. It's a struggle each time I try to do something here. I'm always fighting. I'm tired. Things aren't the way they should be. I want to get away."

"You're a goosey gander if there ever was one."

"I've lived my life trying to be somebody I'm not, trying to be the person you wanted me to be."

"Don't talk nonsense. You always did whatever you wanted."

"But I tried to please you."

"What a brain you had."

"I could get good marks in school but I thought I couldn't do anything the right way because you always criticized me."

"We were so proud when you brought home those report cards."

"Don't you remember those nightmares?"

"We loved you. We used to get in bed with you."

"But you never said a word to me. You never acted like you cared about me, or asked what was wrong."

"All kids have nightmares. You probably wouldn't have known what was causing them."

"But it would have helped to know you cared about me."

"I loved you. I worked so you could go to college. I did my best for you."

"I know you did. You made me strong. You gave me your strength and determination never to give up. I admire your courage to carry on through thick and thin no matter what, but you never showed me that you cared. I don't remember you ever giving me a hug or putting your arm around me. I felt rejected, brushed aside. I couldn't do anything to please you. It hurt. It followed me around. I threw up or drank to fight back feelings I didn't know what to do with. I tried to kill myself because living hurt too much."

"Dan ruined your life for ten years."

"No, he didn't, I did. You can't blame anyone else for what happens in your own life."

"Well then, Gaspard didn't criticize you!"

"Oh yes he did. The first six months were fine then he started to show his temper. I could never do anything right for him. He was jealous, locked me out of the house if I worked late and ate supper with those I worked with. He didn't want me to visit my friends, he thought I was flirting."

"You're an accountant. You can get a good job."

"I don't want an accounting job."

"You went back to university for five years when you were forty. You worked hard for an accounting degree and now you're not going to use it? Lord love ya. What's the world coming to?"

"I want to do something I like. I want to write, to work with young people, help them find themselves because I know what it's like to be lost."

"I suppose you'll tell them you're mother didn't love you."

"No. I'll tell them I didn't feel any love."

"Oh, dear. I might as well die right now. I'll pray to God to take me right away. I can't take much, you know. It's not easy living in here."

I looked at her and waited, not knowing what to say. *Winona, please help me. What do I say?* I found myself speaking. "Just be the good person who's inside. That's all."

Mother levered herself up from her chair. I arranged her walker in front of her and it squeaked and thudded as she lifted and dropped it across the floor to the washroom. She came back and wanted to lie down. "Let me give you a kiss," she said, and she started to cry. She sat on the bed while I took off her shoes then lay back onto the pillow. "Well, I guess I'll just leave you alone, let you do what you want."

"Yes, please do."

"I don't know what to do. I don't know where I stand."

"Trust me. Just let me be. Allow me to create something and believe that everything will be all right. Believe me."

"I need you."

I was crying too. "I'll call you at four o'clock to see how you are."

Mother seemed small and childlike as she lay whimpering in her bed. I left, tears in my eyes, astounded at the dialogue that had just taken place. I couldn't have planned the event had I tried, it had a life all its own. I had unburdened myself and now I was as happy as a perfect summer day. She truly loved me. Deep down underneath a pile of dirty things, she did love me. She just couldn't show it.

The grandfather clock in the living room chimed at four in the afternoon and I called to see how she was. Aunt Miriam had come for a visit shortly after I left. She and Mother went to visit a lady they both knew who had just moved into the nursing home. Mother gave me all the details about Mrs. Carmichael's plight, about a sorry state of affairs that had forced her out of her home and into the nursing home. I listened, aware that Mother was back in her comfortable zone. She ended with, "I'm all right now, how are you?"

"I'm okay too. It's twenty past four so I guess you'll be going downstairs for supper now."

"Yes. Call me sometime during the week... I love you."

"I love you, too. Bye."

9:30 P.M.

My breathing has quieted to the slow and steady rhythm of existence. I'm sitting at my writing desk by the window, my head leans on my hand, my eyelids are heavy with their own weight. I just finished watching the video *Moll Flanders*. I cried. My breath came in short gasps of recognition of the wayward life, lost in confusion and searching for yourself, for freedom from the control of others. I felt I was Moll Flanders. She spoke to me of the indomitable human spirit, of the love it carries once you find it and once you have the possession of self-hood.

I'm spent from the trauma of reliving the past twice in one day. But I also feel a peace in a new sense of self, a quiet confidence that comes from a will to be who I truly feel I am.

Monday, March 24, 1997. 10:00 P.M.
"Hi. I'm in Toronto for a week." It was Anna. "I haven't called because I've been really busy with work. I was in Yellowknife, in the Northwest Territories, for two weeks giving management seminars. And, honestly, I didn't know what to say, since we had parted on touchy ground last month."
"That took courage for you to call."
"I've been thinking about you," Anna continued.
"I didn't think you had time to think about me."
"Sure I do. You're family and I love you."
That sounds so empty I can't respond. I told Anna about the unexpected reconciliation with Mother yesterday, how everything flew into the open and we both cried. I told her too how I called Mother back in the afternoon to see how she was getting along and she seemed to have forgotten all about it, or that it was over and done with and need never be mentioned again.

Tuesday, March 25, 1997.
Monsieur Jeanneau is back from a holiday in the south. He telephoned last evening and is ready to take action on the Manoir. To be rid of the building? I've scarcely allowed myself the luxury of that thought. As much as I would like one, I don't have a solution. Monsieur Jeanneau can force a sale, but there will still be enough time for the boys to buy it if they can get their act together. With all the legal work to be done, it will be late fall before a date is set. I wonder what has happened to Mr. Dutil. He's a strange fellow, changing offices and telephone numbers every so often. There's no fax. He did have one once. I guess he didn't like what he received. If he, Mr. Dutil, takes the building back, he can resell it, then he wouldn't lose at all. Actually, he won't have lost anyway, it would have been just extra profit from the deal. He bought the Manoir in a strange way, paid only fifteen thousand for it. At least, that's what's listed in the archives at the registry office. He would have had to pay forty-five thousand in back taxes that were owed to the municipality at the time, then he sold it to Eva and me in another contorted sequence of events, probably unethical, where he pitted a private buyer of his own against his real estate agent's buyer, namely us. We paid one hundred and ninety-five thousand. Mr. Dutil kept a balance of sale as a second mortgage of forty-five thousand, so he's made ninety thousand dollars already.
Why do I worry about him? It's shady money. I'm not going to interfere. It's all right whatever happens. I'm finished with running after everyone,

being the organizer, arranging and rearranging the details for everyone else. I don't care who gets the building. I don't care what happens. I wish everyone good health and happiness and thank you all for being in my life. *But I hope to never lay eyes on you again.*

Wednesday, March 26, 1997.

Me Debauve was waiting for me at the Salaberry-de-Valleyfield courthouse when I arrived at nine-thirty this morning. It's a stately old limestone building, traditionally arrogant and solid, the kind that makes you whisper inside. One hundred-foot tall elm trees stand on either side of the cement walkway that leads across the front lawn to the high entrance steps, bare winter branches reaching high into the sky far above the peaked-roof stone tower in the center of the structure. The austere aspect of the exterior professes less of an interest in itself than in those who people the interior. The building haunts with the strangeness on the souls of so many men and women who have passed between its walls, their concentrated burdens of lust and greed and bitterness stirring up thick vapours that disturb the courthouse air. A time had been set, eleven o'clock, for a cross-examination of Dugan. Stéphane wanted to meet earlier so we would have time for a short discussion before the proceeding.

"Good morning, Isabelle! Beautiful day, isn't it?" his voice echoed in the great hall.

"You're in fine spirits today."

"The questioning has been cancelled. I just received word."

Stéphane speculated that Dugan had called it off since it was very unlike Dugan's lawyer to cancel a cross-examination.

"That's just perfect," I said to Stéphane, and I silently thanked my angel. Just perfect, so it is.

7:30 P.M.

This morning's surprise made me feel so good that it was impossible to stay in the house. Outdoors amongst the sky and the trees was the only place to be, so I went for a drive. I followed my usual route, a circle around by two rivers that leads me back to Wakeham. It takes about an hour and a half. When I arrived home there were two messages waiting, both from Vincent. I called him on his cellular. He answered after a couple of rings.

"Hi, Vincent. Where are you?"

"At my sister's. We're having supper just now."

"I don't want to disturb you with your family. Would you rather call me back? I'm at home now."

"No, it's okay. Do you feel like coming to my place if you're not doing

194

anything else this evening? I'll be going there as soon as we finish eating."

"Your place?"

"Yes. Why not?"

"I thought it was obvious why not."

"No one is there."

"Still...."

"Still, what?"

"I don't even know where you live."

"I can give you directions."

"I'll have to think about it."

"How long will that take?"

"I'm not sure."

"Uh huh."

"Call me when you get home."

"Okay. I won't be very long. Bye-bye."

"Bye, Vincent."

I thought about whether to go or not, about the ethics and the non-ethics, and should and shouldn't got into such a scramble with agony and ecstasy that I didn't know what was right anymore. I'm tired of playing games with cunning deities that make right of wrong and wrong of right and chuckle at the confusion, and I would love to go to Vincent's place, so I'm waiting for him to phone back and tell me he's home.

Thursday, March 27, 1997.

Vincent does have a sad place. He surely does. Thank you for showing it to me last night, Winona. I guess you knew I would go, didn't you? Now I understand even more what he's swallowed up and buried deep inside. He hides it so well in his cool image of the wealthy and successful businessman that he himself doesn't think the thirty-year-old pain is still there. "That's life. What can you do? Sometimes you have to take a lot of hard knocks." He says it like a motto. Worse, he believes it.

Vincent showed me through his house. It was in the midst of renovations so the furniture was pushed away from the walls into the center of the rooms. A baby grand piano was covered with a dust cover because of the carpenters working about, but it hadn't been used for years anyway. Vincent used to play but had given it up. He also used to paint with oils–character portrayals–but he gave that up too. On one table, there were a lot of family photographs, nicely framed and stacked in a wobbly pile. He showed me a few portraits of his daughter, his grandson, his granddaughter, a picture of his whole family. Then he pulled out one frame that was sitting underneath several others, looked at it, and hesitated. After a moment, he held it out to me. It was a photograph of a beautiful looking little boy about five years old, obviously handicapped. "And this is my son. When he was born it was as if my brother had come back in him. He's thirty years old now and lives in an institution in Montreal. Ninety percent of his brain is damaged. He can't walk or feed himself. His blood should have been changed at birth–a mixture of negative and positive blood from the parents is dangerous–but the doctor forgot. My wife and I looked after him for three years before placing him in an institution. The doctor was sued and we won, but that didn't help my son."

Does anyone else know how he struggles? Not if he can help it. He lost a million dollars about fifteen years ago and not long after he almost died in a ski accident. Then he had a near death experience on the operating table! But he keeps on chasing money, scrupulously measuring and re-measuring it. He thought he wasn't careful enough about spending, so he holds on tighter, keeps track of it daily so it won't get away again. And he still struggles, toughening himself up against the knocks, an unnatural position to live in, like a tree trying to grow against the wind.

9:00 P.M.

I arrived home at four forty-five this afternoon after an appointment with Léo in Montreal, quickly prepared an agenda, changed into business clothes, drove to LaViolette, picked up some cheques from the treasurer, and went to the restaurant for the Rotary meeting. There were only eleven members in attendance again tonight.

Would that I could switch my thinking back to the hour spent with Léo, but I simply can't get into it. The time with him is always demanding–he throws another light on what I think is the real thing, as if I'm hearing with different ears, seeing with different eyes. Sometimes he takes me aback, makes me fortify my avoidance processes until I can spend some time alone with what he says. I have to keep him in his place until I stop yelling inside–*But you're not me and you never will be! You don't know how it is!*–until I'm comfortable enough to think, well maybe you do have a point there, maybe I don't have the whole story.

10:30 P.M.

Vincent phoned. We talked for twenty minutes about not much at all. I'm off to bed. Goodnight!

Friday, March 28, 1997.

I've been sitting here in the early morning trying to recap the time with Léo yesterday, but it seems far away. I know we talked a little about the long list of trials and disappointments–to me, the hardest time was the crisis that exploded in January and February. Perhaps because it was the most recent? Because the scars are still fresh? Had it happened any earlier, I didn't think I could have coped with the magnitude. It was like reaching a breaking point, an apex of strain where one of us had to give in–my ego or my soul. The threats sent shock waves through my entire system but being threatened was exactly what I needed to deal with. For the next session, Léo wants to spend more time on the struggles, not the recent ones, the old ones. "Something happened to bring you past each one," Léo said just before our time was up. "Try to think about what that something could be."

Saturday, March 29, 1997.

The betwixt and between, *entre chien et loup*–I like those expressions. Distorted light transforming. Silently, eerily. The indigo of the night sky turns gradually to violet, to the silhouette of early morning, then masquerades in shades of pink–purplish pink, rose pink, bluish pink–before changing to a blue haze. I woke at 5:00 A.M. and watched the ancient spectacle, but fell back to sleep before the sun rose high enough to clear the day.

The telephone woke me at nine-thirty. It was a voice message from the Bank of Commerce. "This is," pause, "C.I.B.C. calling," a longer pause. "All of our agents are presently busy," a pause again, then, "Hello, my name is Christine. Is this Isabelle Carberry?"

"Yes."

"I'm calling to know when you are going to make your payment. Five hundred and fifteen dollars is currently past due. I'd like to know when you can pay this amount."

"I understand, but I told the girl who telephoned two weeks ago that I'd send one hundred dollars at the beginning of April."

"Just a minute now 'til I find your file. Oh, that's right. I see the agreement. It's recorded here."

"You were supposed to send me a budget form in the mail, but it hasn't arrived yet."

I hadn't picked up my mail since last Wednesday. The letter was probably sitting in the Post Office box. After a sleepy conversation, she hung up.

I crawled in again under the bedcovers and was just dozing off to sleep when the telephone rang again. It was Mother. "I was wondering if you have everything you need for my income tax."

"Yes, I think all the slips are in now."

"Yes? But you haven't done it yet. Everyone around here is talking about income tax." A little laugh. The doorbell rang.

"Someone's at my door. Can you call me back?" I jumped out of bed, tousled my hair, grabbed a housecoat, and ran downstairs barefoot to the front door.

"Hello. My name is George. I have a landscaping company... Here's my card. I was wondering if you have anyone to cut the grass this season?"

"I'm not sure. A young fellow helped me out last fall and asked for the job, but I haven't heard from him since."

"Perhaps I can help you then."

"Maybe so. I'll try to get in touch with him to see if he's still interested. If he can't look after my lawn, I'll call you George. Thanks for stopping to ask."

Back upstairs, I was standing in front of the bathroom mirror, washing my face, when the phone rang again.

"Aunt Eileen and Sheila are coming for a visit this afternoon at two o'clock. They'll want to see you too. It would be easier if you could come here."

"Okay, Mum. I'll be there about two-thirty."

"Don't be late."

"I'll be there."

It was a little past ten-thirty before I arrived downstairs to make a cup of coffee and sit at my desk here in front of the window. I've been dying to tell you all about what happened last night, but it's taken me a while to get to the point. I'm afraid that the words I would like to write might not come now. You know how distractions are. All that stuff I wrote down first could draw me away from the real thing. Here goes anyway. Vincent arrived about seven-thirty last evening. Fancy a sea of waves. Don't forget now, this was real! The hard part is putting it into words. Well, those waves, huge and amorphous, are still cresting and bursting into millions of tiny spaces. They soar high and free then smooth into clear calm waters that run to the deepest parts.

Vincent and I sat listening to Michael Bolton's rendition of *Georgia On My Mind*, his amazing voice sounding the cry for love. It's an unearthly call that comes from the depths of his soul. I felt a possession that moved inside me to the waves of the sound, like a burning energy radiating outward, reaching, wanting, swelling, begging for that ephemeral touch of love. The dark sweetness transports me to that dimension where nothing else exists, where there is not a pain nor a sorrow that cannot be comforted by the unfolding of that lovely elixir. The tenderness, the melting, the desire touched deep within and deep without, healing, loving. But it wasn't like before. There was something else. It held a new passion, an overwhelming power that had an unshakeable truth about it, a lovely unshakeable truth. I could only be in awe of something so magnificent. My whole person was infused with a brilliance that could only be divine.

There's more. But I have to go out now so it will have to wait until tomorrow morning.

Sunday, March 30, 1997.

Now let me tell you about the rest of Friday evening. Vincent hasn't called since. I gave him a lot to think about–in fact, I probably overloaded him and that's why he's not calling. Maybe it was too much too soon. I had been saying things to him recently, dropping ideas in the course of conversation that there are no accidents, nothing is random, that he came into my life at exactly the right time, breathed life into me, and made me touch feelings I hadn't felt for a long time. Now it was my turn to give to him. I spoke to him about my angel, how she was always with me. He already knew about my mindspace and that I went there whenever I panicked, to calm down. Friday evening he wanted to meditate together, so we sat on the floor in the middle of the small studio room and Vincent tried to visualize a white light like the one that had become such a familiar friend to me.

"I don't see a white light, Isabelle, but I see two lights in the distance."

"Really? What are they like?"

"One is yellow and the other is orange. But they won't come any closer."

Later, we wandered into the living room and stood by my desk looking at the stack of journals that was piled on one side. I had bought a notebook for Vincent in which to begin writing his own journal.

"That's for me?"

"So you can have a private place of your own."

"But I can't write in a journal. I don't know what to say."

"Just start having a conversation with yourself and write down what you're thinking."

"You know, I do like to write, compose things. At work, I'm always the one who writes the letters."

"Then you'll love this because all you do is follow your train of thought without being a critic or editing your words."

"But what if the words don't come?"

"It probably means that you're trying too hard to find the perfect expression."

"But I want to write well."

"It doesn't matter here. You're the only one who reads it."

"That would make it easier."

"So relax and go to your mindspace, an idea will come."

"I'm having trouble to find my mindspace."

"Are you? Here's an image to go to."

"I'm listening."

199

"Remember yourself a short while ago–you were stretched out in the chair, relaxed, and listening to the music. My hands were touching you, massaging. Now remember how it felt–the comfort, the wonder, the peace, the happiness…" I hesitated but the next word had to be there, so I continued, decisive, confident, "the love. Hold onto that. Now let the visual part go and keep only the feeling. That's the atmosphere in your mindspace and you can go to it anytime."

I seemed to have his complete attention, so I ventured further.

"Vincent, your heart was broken twice and broken hard, first at your brother's death, then about ten years later when your son was born. It hurt so much you decided, probably unconsciously, to never let anyone get close to your heart again. You told yourself you were no good and unlovable and you never wanted to feel that hurt again. You were desperate. Love was in a state. So you put your feelings in a box and closed the lid. Then, to forget that part of yourself, you worked hard at business. Business is a safe place to go when you want to squash sensitivity, when you want your self to be anonymous. It focuses on the bottom line, hard facts, dollar signs. Your innermost feelings can remain untouched if that's what you want. You worked hard to make a lot of money and be successful so you could prove to yourself that you were okay. You met society's criteria of achievement and worth. The problem is, no matter how successful we become in accomplishing goals, we still yearn to love."

Silence.

"Most of us live a charade, we live within an illusion. We think a cruel spirited fate dumps bad luck on us willy-nilly, but nothing is further from the truth. It is we ourselves, who bring the situations and people into our lives. We struggle and twist to make difficult and complicated events work out in our favour. We pat ourselves on the back when we narrowly avoid a crash, saying, *Ha! You didn't get me this time,* but the obstacles are just an equal and opposite reaction to the discord within ourselves. What is happening on the outside is a reflection of what is happening on the inside. When the energy of your soul is being ignored, whatever you are trying to do will clash and clang and rip with thorny snags and dissonant notes, with a want of harmony."

"Isabelle, I would like to have an angel but I don't have one."

"But everyone has an angel."

"Everyone?"

"You just haven't looked in the right place yet."

"And where would that be?"

"In that box with the lid."

Monday, March 31, 1997.

I feel like a teenager again, having fits because my boyfriend is late. During the winter months, it was all right not to be with Vincent. The events around me took up all the space. But there's a new intensity. Instead of warring with feelings I'm checking them out to see where they want to go. Perhaps I'm going overboard again. I'm anxious because I don't know what he's thinking. He said he would call me on Saturday or Sunday, and there's still been no word from him.

8:00 P.M.

"I was supposed to call you on the weekend." It was Vincent, sounding quiet and distant. "Several times, I thought to myself, I have to call Isabelle, but I just can't. I need more time."

"That's okay. I threw a lot at you last Friday."

"I needed to be given a lot."

"I wondered if it was too much."

"No. I started to write and spend more time by myself. It's quiet here with my wife gone for a few months. I meditated and looked for the lights again."

"Did you see them?"

"Yes. They were there, off in the distance, but I can't make them come any closer."

"What else did you do in your space?"

"I asked whether or not I should telephone you."

"Did you get an answer?"

"Yes."

"And?"

"'No.' The answer was 'no'. I said, 'Okay, Boss'. I figured I wasn't supposed to call you then, so I spent more time being quiet and thinking. You were right. I do run all the time so I don't have time to think about how I feel. You showed me a part of myself I had ignored. I felt free, good. You're a giving person to want to help me."

"Thank you for saying so, but I wasn't alone."

"You weren't?"

"No."

"I understand."

April

"April is the cruellest month, breeding
Lilacs out of the dead land, mixing
Memory and desire, stirring
Dull roots with spring rain."

T.S. Eliot
The Waste Land

Tuesday, April 1, 1997.

The sky is ringing with anticipation this morning. I can hear the sound as high and soundless as gleaming tinsel. No dusty corners on the two lonely little clouds. No slight overhang skewing the blue that is as bright as lapis lazuli. No windy forces gathering to shape the snow that fell yesterday and, surely for the last time this season, left the ground pure white. The vastness is complete. But it's cold–minus three Celsius.

The telephone rang at about eleven o'clock last night.

"Is that you Vincent?"

"How did you know it was me?"

"I don't get many phone calls at this time of night."

"It is kind of late to be calling."

"That's okay. I wasn't asleep."

"How are you?"

"Fine. I was just doing some reading before turning out the lights."

"Did you have a good evening?"

"Sure. It was quiet. And yours? Have you started a painting?"

"Well, yes, now that you mention it, I have."

"Now that I mention it? You don't know? Did you set up your easel and paints?"

"Not yet. It's in my head."

"I see. The beginning."

"I was tired tonight, I needed a break, so I surfed the Internet to change my thinking."

"You've gone so far in a few days, I'm astonished."

"I think I am too.

"Does it feel good, though?"

"Very."

"I'm happy for you."

"Thanks. I'll let you go so you can get some sleep. I had nothing particular in mind when I called except to say, have a good night."

"I'm glad you called. Goodnight, Vincent."

The love magnet has been turned off! That frenzied obsession, that impregnable knot of frustrated desires, that avatar of a woman in love, those abject emotions that toyed with me are gone. The thought roving around my head after I hung up the phone was unexpected, to say the least. *He's on his way. I can let go now.* As if I couldn't let go of that intense attachment until I had touched his spirit inside, the piece that had been broken off and buried deep. I had to make him feel so much that he couldn't ignore his feelings any longer, he had to meet the energy of his soul. Only then did that winding hookah disengage itself and turn into a different sensation, one that was clean and calm and measured and asked for nothing, like those transient moments of the pre-dawn.

Thursday, April 3, 1997.

"It's been too long, Isabelle," Monsieur Jeanneau was saying over the telephone. "I'm going to go ahead and have the Manoir sold."

"Do what you have to do, Monsieur Jeanneau. Ask your lawyer to begin proceedings. I won't fight for that building anymore."

"If something was going to happen it would have happened by now. It's the only thing left to do."

That old panicky reaction? The one that used to invade my senses? Nothing today! I'm as calm as a piece of toast. Not long ago, it was unthinkable that the Manoir would be sold by a sheriff's auction for non-payment. I felt inexplicably tied to that building, felt I had a mission to bring a new life to the Manoir, to clean up the mess inside. Being unable to accomplish what I had set out to do would have been a crushing defeat and sent me wading through an avalanche of denial. But today, there were no nervous butterflies. I'm exposed again, but that's okay, I'm all for blow-ups. They dismantle your illusions.

Friday, April 4, 1997.

Mother had an appointment with her eye doctor this afternoon. I stayed in the examination room with her in case she needed help. She doesn't like that very much, says the doctor talks to me instead of to her. Dr. Lemaire asked her questions about the picking, examined her eyes, wheeled his chair to the desk, and began talking about changing the prescription for eye drops. A doctor she saw two weeks ago gave her two drugs that were contradictory. He corrected the problem, but I guess he wasn't talking loud enough and Mother thought he was talking to me.

"Talk louder so I can hear!"

"YOUR EYE NEEDS A TREATMENT, A LASER JOB, MRS. CARBERRY." Dr. Lemaire raised his voice to yelling pitch. "WE DON'T HAVE THE MACHINE HERE AT THIS HOSPITAL. IT WILL HAVE TO BE DONE IN MONTREAL. I'LL MAKE AN APPOINTMENT. I'LL CALL A COLLEAGUE THIS AFTERNOON BECAUSE I KNOW THE EYE IS PAINFUL."

"Oh, I don't like that! I wanted you to do something now."

Dr. Lemaire's head dropped forward and I could hear him muttering, She doesn't like it. She can't wait.

"Can you come back to see me in two weeks? I'll look at the eye again. The new prescription should have helped by then. If I can arrange the laser surgery before that time, I'll call you."

Mother still thinks the doctor is talking to me. "Hey, this is my eye, not hers! I can't live with this for another two weeks!"

Dr. Lemaire looked at me, "What more can I do? I've changed the prescription. She comes to me a month after the problem began and wants me to fix it immediately."

"I know, I'm sorry. She doesn't hear very well. I hope the rest of your day is better."

Mother is not pleased. There's no question about it. Her face is red and cross; her lips are pursed thin and trembling; her chin is frozen; darts are shooting from her eyes. As we left the doctor's office and I wheeled her along the corridor, Mother was still grumbling, "He talked to you instead of to me, as if I was some moron who couldn't understand."

"Mother, Dr. Lemaire has done what he can and the new drops should help the irritation. He'll call if the treatment can be arranged any earlier than two weeks."

"Phooey on that! I'd like to shake the livin' daylights out of him!"

There was no point in fighting that blockade of anger, still menacing and threatening at eighty-three years of age. Poor Dad. Living with Mother can't have been easy. He never would have told her to shut-up. Something gentle perhaps, like, "Aw, quit yer naggin'," or "Gol darn it, I heard ya the first time." But, nothing disrespectful. He went on binges instead, drank to escape. Then the expletives flew, stored-up invective released.

I don't want to hate. Hate has a sour taste that's ugly. It wants revenge. It swamps, consumes, takes over, annihilates the good and the peace that is so much a part of me now. Hate has the same ugliness as confusion. I don't want it inside me. It pollutes, poisons. There's such joy in allowing myself to spend my days on things I love to do—writing in my journal, working on my story, listening to music, going for drives to see the countryside turn into spring, reading, sleeping soundly, dreaming. Mother would say that's doing nothing.

It is nothing compared to how she worked in her lifetime and how her ancestors worked before her. Her only brother was crippled with arthritis at seventeen years of age and she had to take over his chores in the barn and around Grandpa Davidson's farm where they grew up. Grandpa Davidson's father lived with them until he died in 1938 at the age of ninety-six. He was born in Canada in 1842 after his parents had emigrated from Scotland in the 1830's. One day, when Mother was about ten years old, a local fellow was delivering a load of gravel to the farm. She was walking up the long lane to the farmhouse when the dump truck came along with its charge of crushed stone. The truck driver slowed down to speak, "Good afternoon, Miss, would you like a lift the rest of the way?"

"Yes, thank you, I would."

"You must be Johnny Shoemaker's granddaughter," he said to the young girl after she had climbed into the truck and sat tall on the front seat to see out the window. Mother wasn't at all sure that it was such a wonderful thing– being a shoemaker's granddaughter–but that's how she found out that her Grandfather Davidson's father had made shoes in Scotland before coming to Canada. "Anyway," she reasoned after asking her father what the truck driver had meant, "he made a mistake. I'm Johnny Shoemaker's great-granddaughter, not his granddaughter. Maybe he doesn't know what he's talking about. And Father tells me that shoemaking is a virtuous profession. So I guess it's all right."

Mother's grandfather Davidson had married a girl named Margaret who came from a large family of eleven or twelve children, mostly girls. The parents and close relatives had also emigrated from Scotland between 1830 to 1835 and settled about twenty miles north of Cornwall on the Saint-Lawrence River, about sixty miles west of Montreal. Margaret's father, John, his brother, Donald, and their two sisters, Ellen and Ann, undertook to transform the barren wastes and swamps, which were inhabited mainly by the dreaded wolves and brown nosed bears, into a civilized and productive state. They cleared the land, erected houses, planted and harvested crops, nurtured cattle, and built schools, roads, and Presbyterian churches. Margaret's Uncle Donald was the clerk of Stormont County for years. Her father, John, was a strong singer with a lusty voice and, in his day, led in all the church doings and Sunday School picnics in that part of the country. Margaret's mother's father was known in the old country as a great teacher and a man of learning. He arrived in Canada from Scotland well heeled with this world's goods and had built a grand stone home where the family lived in comfort.

Not too far away and a little farther inland was a part of the countryside that the local inhabitants called Sandringham, but you'll not find it on a map. Dad drove Mother and I back to see the old places a few years before he died. There was one dilapidated house–most of the white paint was worn off–and an old abandoned General Store with several windowpanes missing, a hand-painted tin sign hanging at an angle and slapping the clapboards with each draught of wind. These two buildings, standing on opposite corners, comprised the village center. Dad drove a little farther along a gravel country road, passing by Mother's old homestead without stopping. It was overgrown with trees and shrubs and barely visible from the road. They were both quiet as they looked gingerly at the grey-brown paintless weather-beaten house, as if they didn't want to see anything more than what a cursory glance would provide. We never did go to see Dad's place.

At the beginning of the 1930's, the country was in the midst of a full-blown depression and Mother lived with a family in the nearby village of Bruce Crossing to attend the school and obtain a high school leaving certificate. Then, boarding with relatives and friends, she attended Normal school in Ottawa and became a teacher. She was young and pretty and twenty-three years old in 1937 when she had her first teaching assignment. She taught all the grades, from one to eleven, to twenty-five or thirty youngsters in a one-room schoolhouse in rural eastern Ontario. "I earned an annual salary of six hundred and forty dollars and I thought I was rich," she said when she was eighty years old, memories sparkling in her eyes. "The older students were eighteen year-old strapping farm boys who didn't particularly like being in school, but I laid down the law and they listened to me." And her word stood.

A few of her former students still make a trip from Ontario to Quebec every summer to pay her a visit at the nursing home. She's so excited when they're coming that she gives me a call, "Do you know who's coming to see me today? Elmer and Delius and Walter. Elmer tells me they'll come once a year as long as one of them is still able to drive his van. He was a little rapscallion when he was young, that Elmer was. I used to have quite a time trying to keep him from misbehaving. Always had a trick or two up his sleeve. And imagine, they're bringing three or four others from the area too. He didn't tell me who they are, but I'll surely know them. Isn't that wonderful? My, my, what a nice surprise I had today."

Then she met Dad, who was apprenticing to run a cheese factory back at Sandringham, not far from the rural school where she taught. Mother used to hitch up her pet horse, Maggie, hold onto the reins, and ski down the road behind Maggie on her way to visit Dad on his farm. She once showed me a small black and white photograph with fluted edges. In it was a young girl wearing a long white dress. A full set of bangs stretched across her forehead and a large white bow perched saucily on top of her head.

"Hey! There's a big bow in your hair. It's just like the one I used to see on my head in all the old pictures!"

She was standing beside a tall muscular horse. "See? That's me and Maggie. And there's the hen house just behind and the pigsty's over there. There were four workhorses on the farm that the men used for plowing the fields and they'd kick if you were standing too close, so you had to be careful around them. But Maggie wouldn't kick me. All I had to do was pat her on the backside and she knew who it was."

In those days, during the winter, snow was plentiful and the young people skied across the fields gliding cleanly over the top of the rail fences. A small hill not far from the Davidson homestead was a favourite meeting place. "Everyone called it 'The Mountain'," Mother told me not too long ago. "In the evening, after supper was finished and the kitchen was cleaned up, I used to strap on my boots and skis and make my way over to the Mountain. I had three girlfriends–Mary, Gwelda, and Flora–who would meet me there and we'd ski at night under the stars and the light of the moon until we were so tired we couldn't make it up the hill any more."

Dad made a pair of skis for himself–boiled the wood, curved up one end, and polished the blades with homemade wax–because he couldn't afford a store-bought pair. "They were great skis," he said, "just as good as any pair of brand new ones you could find in a shop."

Dad's family was poor but they had enough to eat. And they came from hearty stock. His father, known throughout the district as Big Roly, was born in 1846 and died in 1936 at ninety years of age. Dad left home at a young age and his recollections of his father were mainly those of a large contrary old man who smoked 'Old Chum' in his pipe and was confined to bed through sickness and against his will for the last years of his life. Dad's mother, Chloe Maria, who was thirty years younger than her husband, looked after him. When Dad himself was eighty years old, a young cousin, knowing Father's prodigious memory and talent for regaling everyone with stories, came to visit one afternoon and jostled that great storehouse of things remembered and long forgotten. The words of a song that Big Roly used to sing around the house, on days when his health was better, began to quiver and shake, then rattle and chatter in the innermost recesses. Scrambled images and jaunty characters began to make a noisy racket, scenes emerged, the voices humming and rhyming, and gradually the lyrics tumbled out, verse after verse. It was a ballad from Roly's strong youthful days as a bushman and log driver.

You've seen a white tavern
Stands under the hill
At the head of the chute
Where's John Landon's mill.

It was often times there
That gay fellows did meet
To have a drop of good whiskey
And something to eat.

It happened one time
In the fall of '62
That gathered there once
Was a comical crew.

They cursed and they swore
And they laughed at tall tales
And thought a fine fricot
Would be good for what ails.

They went to the cupboard
But faith it looked blue,
There was nothing there
To make up a stew.

"But, hold on," said Grey Jimmy,
A jokish old man,
"If you listen to me
I'll give you a plan.

"I'll go up to John Landon's and steal a fat lamb,
I'll kill him, I'll dress him,
I'll bring him to you
And then we'll have something to make up a stew."

In the 1860's, during the spring, Big Roly drove logs down the Ottawa River. The long harsh Canadian winters were spent in the forest wilderness in Quebec, on the north side of the river, about one hundred miles west of the city of Ottawa. He and the others on the work crew cut trees and dragged the logs out of the bush to the shores of the river where, after the snow melted and the ice broke up, they would be rolled into the fast-moving current and sent downstream to Montreal. It was a man's world of dangerous hard work, of accidents and cruel deaths, of cursing and surviving. The tavern near Landon's Mill was their home away from home, their place to unburden and release the fatigue and tension of the day.

"That would be very nice,"
Said Miss Cousineau,
"For there is nothing like lamb
To make a fricot."

There was one, Hughie Bisson,
He was sparkly and lean.
Not to aid in the plan
He thought downright plain mean.

"I'll go up to Turcott's
Some onions I'll steal
And I'll bring them down here
To season the meal."

Chloe Maria, Dad's mother, had her roots in the early pioneering days of Canada also. Her father, Francis Sydney, began life in a manner unusual to most. When he was four years old, his father, still a young man, died after being kicked by a horse. It was 1842 and Francis' brother, John, was born not long after his father died. At his death, the boys' mother, Catherine Darlington, was left alone with her young family at George's Lake, a tiny colonial settlement fifty miles west of Ottawa on the south shore of the Ottawa River. In order for Catherine to lay claim to the property they were clearing in the New World and obtain a deed to the land where they had made their home, she rode by horseback to Cornwall through what was then Indian Lands to file the claim–a distance of more than fifty miles each way. A trail through the unspoiled bush was the only path she had to follow. Catherine was still nursing John when the hazardous journey imposed itself. She had no option but to leave her toddler and infant son with her sister, who had recently given birth to a child of her own and who breast-fed both babies until Catherine returned with the land deed.

So off to John Landon's
Jim quickly did run,
He told them all there
He was in for some fun.

"There is old Nero–
He's getting so old
That some day this winter
He'll die of the cold.

I'll kill him and dress him,
Bring to bonne femme
And she'll never know
But 'tis not a fat lamb."

Ten years later, in 1852, Catherine married Little Jimmy who claimed he stole his passage from Ireland since he was born a few days after his mother arrived in Quebec City. They had one son, James, who married Miss Lizzie and were the parents of four children. When Anna and I were young, I remember visiting two old bachelors who lived with their mother on a farm near George's Lake. Frank and Howard were men of few words. They rarely spoke and if they did utter a sound there was an instant replay followed by a great amount of head nodding. "Well, well. If it ain't young Jake. Glory be." "Glory be. Jake and his girls. Indeed, indeed."

Inside the house, it was hard to take several steps in the same direction without bumping into a piece of furniture or a cardboard box filled with old papers. There wasn't an empty space to be seen on a countertop or table surface. Uninterrupted clutter and a multitude of bric-a-brac right at eye-level, the accumulation of years, signaled a veritable treasure chest for three-year-old Anna. While the adults were engrossed in the happenings of bygone days, she wandered through an open door into a well-stocked pantry, found a gallon can of maple syrup sitting on the floor, unscrewed the cap without difficulty, and emptied the contents. It took some time for the sticky liquid to trickle out into the adjoining room where the others were sitting around the kitchen table. Meanwhile, Anna sat in the sweet nectar licking her fingers and staying as quiet as she could. "Well, I'll be. If that don't darn yer socks now." "Well, I'll be. Darn yer socks, don't it?" said Frank and Howard when the incident had been discovered. Mother spent the better part of the visit mopping up.

Lizzie was very much the live wire of the trio even at a ripe old age. Everyone in the neighbourhood called her 'Old Auntie'. Aunt Miriam gave me a newspaper clipping not too long ago. The short article was yellowed with time and as dry and fragile as dated parchment. The headline read, "Whirls Through Waltz at 92nd Birthday Party." That was Dad who danced with her, sashaying and segueing around the floor. Fifty friends and relatives had gathered for a celebration including two local fiddlers who entertained

211

the gathering with some lively trills and toe-tapping music. The softer strains touched a romantic chord in Lizzie and she felt a desire to loosen the tethers and swirl to a waltz once more, so she asked Dad to lead her through a two-step. The columnist went on to ask Lizzie about her health and recorded her reply: "Oh well, my family doctor drops in to see me occasionally, and he tells me that, apart from a noticeable bit of high blood pressure, I'm in good health. I have good eyesight–but of course I have to wear reading glasses. I hear well, eat well, I'm very thankful, and I'm a very happy old lady."

So out in the yard,
Jim grabbed the old dog
And he dragged him across
A big pine log.

He axed off the head,
The paws and the tail
And he stuck the four quarters
Snug into a pail.

With the pail on his arm
It's off he did jog
And to Mother Darby
He handed the dog.

It pleased Mother Darby
To see so much meat
That she brought out the bottle
Grey Jimmy to treat.

They shuffled the cards
And played hand after hand
For while the mutton did boil
The time seemed awfully bland.

Catherine Darlington's first son, Francis, married a girl named Chloe, who died while giving birth to Dad's mother, who was thusly named Chloe Maria. That was in 1876, thirty years after Big Roly was born. "A big, jolly, fat man who liked children," was the annotation beside his name in the family tree. Dad liked to tell how Big Roly went for walks pushing the baby carriage up and down the dirt road in front of the house when Dad's younger sister, Miriam, was just a few months old. Passersby waved and nodded their congratulations and Big Roly tipped his hat and returned the greetings with a smile and a look that was nothing at all if not pure unadulterated satisfaction. Dad always ended the story with a big grin and, "He was seventy-two years old and the proudest man in the county."

And then, Hughie Bisson,
The greedy old beast,
He longed for the mutton
And to have a great feast.

So down to the kitchen
So slyly he got
And he chewed on a rib
That stuck out of the pot.

And canny guy Jimmy
Thought Landon was long
When the steam from the kitchen
Began to smell strong.

When supper was ready
That ended the play,
And in a great hurry
Jim was called away.

He cursed and he swore
At his hard fate,
But he kindly told each
On him not to wait.

They ate all around
'Til they left not a pound
And the supper once over
The bottle went 'round.

Now they all did agree
It was a hearty fricot
But little thought they
It was Landon's Nero.

Dad smiled to himself, proud of his feat of remembering.

Now the anger is gone. There's just a sadness left at the years of hurt without knowing why and at the confusion that disturbed my senses, that made me wrestle with the devil, that made me live in a world of unimaginable depth, that opened my heart to God, that brought me an understanding of the human spirit, that brought me an angel who shows me where the love is. Every time.

Saturday, April 5, 1997.
First you hear the honking. Then the cries amplify into nasal shrieks. The noise startles and forces you to look up and search the sky. In the distance, line formations like scrawled hieroglyphics on a cave wall cut across the skyscape high above the land, colonies of air ants following a leader. Overhead, each becomes a tiny cross with wiggly arms. The Canada Geese and the Snow Geese are arriving back after their winter sojourn down south. Thousands of magnificent creatures are following the river to their resting and feeding grounds. Look at their synchronized movements. They sense when one of their comrades is tired and switch places during flight to give each other a chance to recover strength. Look how the sun catches the white on the Snow Geese! Splashes of silver sailing through the sky like glittering mirrored prisms trembling with intense movement. They'll rest on the river tonight. Tomorrow, they'll move into the stubby remains of last year's cornfields to nourish themselves on the roots before continuing their journey toward a northern summer habitat.

I'm going to visit Claire this afternoon. I'll have lunch with her and little Patrice. He's growing so fast. Eight years old now. Claire brought him with her when she came to see me in the hospital last year. I bought a Roald Dahl story for him yesterday—the one about the vicar of Nibbleswicke who has a strange speech defect that makes key words come out of his mouth backwards. He might greet his congregation with a blessing from Dog Almighty and, as a cure, he has to walk backwards for the rest of his life. I hope Patrice likes it.

Telephone......

It was Claire. She has a flu bug and isn't feeling well, so I'll not go to visit today. This sun will warm the countryside. It's a beautiful day. I brought two summer patio chairs down from the rafters in the garage and sat in the sunshine on the back deck for almost an hour. Spring air energizes. It's the irony scent of melting, decomposing and recomposing, the virile odour of birth, of blood and lust that seems to cast a spell. It wouldn't let me sit still any longer, so I brought out a roll of paper towels and a bottle of spray cleaner and washed windows at the back and front of the house.

Sunday, April 6, 1997.

A creamy peanut butter sandwich made with thick slices of homemade white bread. Spring rain is like that. Sure and steady. Reliable and emotionless. Or the smell of donuts frying on the stove when you enter the kitchen after being outside on a cold winter morning. A measured quiet rain tells you that everything is right with the world, as it should be. The wheel is turning itself, doing its part in the grand design, the rain providing the ingredients that will nourish the system and propel it along the curvature of the circle.

I can see a greenish tinge to the back lawn now. There's not much snow left after the nice days we've had, just a little in the bottom of the gulch beside me. I suppose there'll still be white patches in the woods, in the places where the sun doesn't reach, but a good rainstorm will melt whatever snow is left and wash away the spotty residue that settles on the outside of the house throughout the winter months. The wind sweeps in from the open fields to the west laden with dust and sand and deposits the lot at my front door.

Today is like an unexpected holiday. I have the whole day to myself. Mother isn't expecting me for lunch. She thinks I'm at Claire's because I told her I might stay overnight. I say that with a whisper. I'm not going to wash and dress for dinner when I don't have to. Just by not having to go, I can feel the Sunday pressure. I can feel the pressure that's not there today. Perhaps I'll go to the nursing home this evening for a short time, put the labels on her new file folders, and have her sign the income tax returns. But during the day I will have the whole time to be with myself and my story and my angel.

It's 3:30 P.M. The sun came out after the rain and it's hot sitting outside. I changed from jeans into shorts and a tank top. It must be twenty-eight degrees in this little corner of the deck. Imogen Cooper is playing wonderful piano concertos of Robert Schumann. It's as if he is sitting at the piano and laughing and crying all at once. The window of the studio room, where the stereo system sits in an oak cabinet, opens onto the patio, by my chair, and the piano plays on and on in a mixture of real and imaginary, painting a fantasy of sound. This sun feels splendid this afternoon; I'll not ply the past with indigestibles today.

Monday, April 7, 1997.
Nought could be done—nought could be said;
So—my Lord Tomnoddy went home to bed!
There was a Rotary dinner and antique auction this evening. Earlier in the day, the chairman of the fundraiser, Jacques, sent me a fax outlining the activities. He organized the whole event, including the ticket sales, and sent out invitations to three nearby clubs. My job was to conduct the opening and

closing ceremonies. The auctioneer handled the rest. My voice is still weak, but I have a portable microphone that makes speaking easier. I was late getting there. I phoned the treasurer to ask him if I could stop by his office to pick up some cheques because he couldn't leave work to attend. (It's income tax season.)

"Charles, it's Isabelle. Can you get some cheques ready for me?"

"Sure."

"I'll stop in to pick them up at twenty minutes before six."

"But it's twenty to six now."

"What's that? I don't think I heard you right."

"It's twenty to six now."

"Go on! I've got twenty minutes to five."

"I'm not joking. Honest. It's twenty to six. Did you change your clocks on the weekend?"

Griefus horrendus! "This weekend?"

"Right. Yesterday. Where've you been?"

"Here and not here, I guess."

"I guess."

"So I have no time to lose, do I?"

"None."

"Talk to you later, Charles. Bye."

I hadn't started to wash or change my clothes. I thought I had plenty of time to get to the school in LaViolette before the guests arrived at six. I called Jacques. It was ten minutes to six.

"Jacques, this is Isabelle. I've put myself in a fix. I forgot about the time change this weekend and am running an hour late. Can you greet the guests for me as they arrive?"

"Sure. I know pretty well everyone who's coming. Quite a few have arrived already."

"Thanks, Jacques."

I arrived at the auditorium in a fluster. *Like a blue-bottle fly on a rather large scale, With a rather large corking-pin stuck through his tail.* It was twenty-five minutes past six. Nonetheless, everyone seemed to enjoy the dinner, the camaraderie, and the auction; we made some money to put back into the community and it was fun being mistress of ceremonies.

My head is heavy now and aching slightly. I wish I had done a better job. I always stumble and trip over my words when I begin. I'll say something stupid until I get wound up. Then I'm okay. Once past the beginning bloopers, I love standing in front of an audience with a microphone and talking to them. Just love it.

Tuesday, April 8, 1997.

He's so thin. Too thin. Why was I so obsessed? What kind of a hold did you have over me, Vincent? I looked at him from a distance, out of the corner of my eye that looks inward, so to speak, the eye that stays awake at night wandering and wondering when I can't fall asleep. His new closely shaved haircut takes away the luxuriousness of the longish somewhat curly style he had been wearing. It did unmistakable things to me, that dramatic silver hair. I could see it on a leading man on the big screen, rumpled and unkempt, a few strands hanging over his brow, and oh so alluring. I watched him help me with my winter coat, watched the way he held it like a long cape, wrapping it slowly around my shoulders, making sure I was snuggled warmly inside. Then I felt the attraction, the sweetness, the attentiveness, the subtle haunting of his eyes–oh, those eyes!–that looked only at me and smiled. I was drawn to that mysterious nugget of genuine sensation, a little center of pure magnetism, a desire with shades of shame in love with recklessness, but still a desire, undeniable and mercurial, white-silver desire desiring desire.

Vincent telephoned. He was on his way to the office. I asked him how his stocks were doing since I knew he kept a close watch. His stockbroker was his best friend.

"I made a few changes. The stock market is uncomfortable again. It's hard to make any money the way it is, falling at the slightest whimper of change. The luckiest devil in the world is staying quiet these days."

"It's not simply a matter of the stocks being on a roller coaster, Vincent."

"What do you mean?"

"There's a larger dynamic."

"Isabelle, will you be at home this morning?"

"Yes."

"Good."

"Why?"

"We'll have to talk a little later. There's a call waiting and I have some work to finish up, then I'll stop in to see you. You can tell me then what you're talking about."

"I'm not sure I know what I'm talking about."

"You know. Catch ya later. Bye."

The illusion. How do I explain an illusion to Vincent?

It's searching for your own strength, but searching in the wrong places. It's looking to external sources to find fulfilment–to money, to business, the stock market, real estate, houses, fashion, makeup, fully equipped cars, computers, eroticism, rules and regulations, gadgets. The list is endless. We develop love addictions, business addictions, drug addictions, cutting addictions, alcohol addictions, food addictions, approval addictions, abuse addictions. We look to things and events that bring transitory pleasure but it's never enough, the high fades, and the quest for more and more goes on. The newly found happiness disintegrates into an emptiness. A hunger for fulfilment is still there. It's the energy of your spirit wanting to be listened to, wanting you to give it the things it craves–quiet, beauty, music, love, completion, glory. Feel that nugget of your soul's strength wanting to come alive. It wants to feel a boundless energy in a place where time doesn't exist. It wants you to live an expression of yourself that comes from the deepest part of you. Listen to the urges within you pushing you toward a place where your soul longs to be, a place where you can express your talent, the loves of your life, a place where you can create yourself. The setbacks, the difficulties, the struggles are speaking to you. Your soul is saying, "That's not where I want to be. You're in the wrong place."

And you are not just your body. It's beautiful and nice, but that's an image too, a temporal home. We sculpt our bodies for others to look at. We worship the perfect media images and the platforms of frivolity that the fashion houses create. Names like Cerruti, Dior, Georges Armani, and Gianni Versace inspire reverence. But without the strength of the spirit of your soul guiding the strength of your bodily image, you are merely inhabiting a physical form in this lifetime, unaware of its silent portent. But God is patient. He will wait for you to rediscover yourself. He'll give you all the time you need. Because, you see, thought is real. Physical is the illusion.

Well, maybe that's a bit too much right away.

I want to tell Vincent he doesn't have to struggle, nor does he have to fight to live.

3:00 P.M.

Vincent just left. I spoke as simply as I could. I was stuck at one point, didn't know what to say, so I asked Winona to help me, cleared my mind, waited, and the explanation continued. It was a tremendous concept to present to someone in a short time but Vincent took it all in. He didn't say a word, just listened. I have no idea how I explained it. Maybe being so tired helped because my logical and reasoning side that always tries to find the perfect words and put them into the best combination, didn't interfere with what was coming from my heart.

6:30 P.M.

I don't remember what I said. I went for a drive, picked up a few groceries and some more cat food for Toulouse, thinking the conversation might spin around in my head. I tried to remember: Vincent settled himself on the couch. He lay on his back to ease a muscular strain that had been bothering him and

I sat beside him on the edge of the seat.

"I'm so tired today I don't think I'm alert enough to justify what I had in mind."

"Just say it as simply as you can."

So I began with simple. "It's related to living, to our lives, to how we struggle and fight." But neither the words nor the sequence of the thoughts will come after that beginning. I remember being surprised that I was using such short sentences and so many. I thought, *What am I saying? This isn't how I planned to explain. He'll never understand this.* But it's gone whatever I said. No matter how hard I try, I cannot remember. The words had a life of their own as if they didn't come from me. They're nowhere in my memory. That little section of time doesn't exist any more and Vincent understood every word. Whatever I said made perfect sense to him.

I remember telling him how he would feel. I remember that part, "... the freedom, the lightness, the feeling that everything is beautiful and perfect. You will feel so much happiness that your heart will want to burst with love for everything and everyone, yourself included. And you will want to share that wonder with everyone, because you will feel so good."

"Oh! Yes!" His eyes were closed and he was smiling.

(I'm smiling now too, because I think Winona did the explaining for me.)

Vincent stood up to stretch. He seemed to be full, to have heard enough for one time. I couldn't tell from his face what he was thinking. It was expressionless, unreadable. He walked across the room to stand by my desk. A photograph of Dan and I when we were twenty–the summer we were living together in Toronto–was sitting in a polished copper frame of moulded irises on long stems. We were both young and attractive. I had been looking at old pictures trying to remember the past. Vincent picked it up for a closer look and replaced it without comment. I could tell he needed space now so I didn't add another word about the larger dynamic, as I had called it earlier on the phone. Vincent turned and we faced each other, our eyes locking. I felt a bonding, a melding, a rush of divine sensation. *It hasn't gone. It was just hiding!* I tried to turn the love magnet off. *Wait! Let those feelings go where they want to, let them play out the drama,* I told myself. For some time, we stood motionless in a long embrace relishing that sweet love, complicated and entangled as it was. Then Vincent left quietly to go back to the office.

Wednesday, April 9, 1997.

After four nights of not sleeping, I slept last night without waking until ten this morning. It's cold again. The sun is visible only as a white orb behind the thin clouds and there are snowflakes in the air.

Thursday, April 10, 1997.

Perfect day for a drive! Bright and sunny. I passed through the border customs into New York State and drove to Malone to have lunch with their Rotary Club. They're such a friendly active group. We talked about a joint World Community Service project–an orphan school in Africa–that several clubs in the area could sponsor jointly. I saw again those who had come to our Auction Nite last Monday. I love Rotary.

When I got home at five o'clock, there was a message to call the nursing home. Mother had fallen on the floor after therapy as she was trying to get from the bathroom into her wheelchair. The nurse sent her to the hospital for x-rays and the doctor discovered a break high on her right arm. He's going to let it heal in a sling. He also prescribed a ventilator for her congested breathing that has been difficult ever since she caught a cold earlier this week. She hauls in a breath, the air whining and wheezing as it enters her chest, then whistling and scraping on its way out like a toy-train. I telephoned her. She was sitting in her big armchair watching television, everything as usual, just a little more inconvenience and another pain to put up with.

Claire phoned in the evening. She's over the flu she had last weekend and invited me to her place for lunch tomorrow before my appointment with Léo, but I'd rather go when we can spend the whole afternoon together.

Friday, April 11, 1997. 5:00 P.M.

I'm having a hard time to wrap my head around this. I can't believe I'm really on the subject of goo and slime. I actually mentioned it to Léo. It's hard. I don't want to associate those things with my father because I thought he was the only one who cared for me.

Winona, if this is for real, I'm going to need a lot of support. I wasn't expecting that to happen today. The struggles and how each ended, that was supposed to be what we were going to talk about. I'm not sure how Léo brought me to slime. I think he was saying we had touched every area. I hesitated, hanging in some abrasive middle distance, a loose yet inescapable place, like quicksand. I wondered what I would get myself into, knowing the inevitability of the next few minutes, knowing that I had no choice, that I was as sure of saying what was in my mind as if the words had already been spoken and this was but a replay. I said quietly, "Almost every area. ... There is one area we haven't touched."

"Yes?"

"It's a fear, a fear of slimy things, of goo." Then I was delicately tiptoeing around questions. Léo didn't know anything about my father. I had never mentioned him.

I don't know if I can do this. Do I have to, Winona? I thought he was there

220

for me, understood me. He read stories to Anna and me. I don't remember but I know he did. I didn't go to either parent for comforting, didn't go anywhere for comforting. I wasn't supposed to cry, to need soothing. I see photos of him giving me a milk bottle. I always thought he cared for me, looked out for me. My dad could do no wrong.

I don't know, just don't know. It's too hard to imagine. When I think of slime my shoulder area squirms, my throat swallows. I had a dream last summer of a boy chasing me and taunting me with slimy goo that he let dangle over his open mouth. It horrified me, made me run and hide. Was there slime in my mouth one time?

I'm sorry for thinking these things. I don't know where they're coming from. Dear God. If there is something to those far-out ideas, from what even stranger place did that image come–the one in my mindspace of Dad dancing with my angel, saying that he was dancing for me? I was so happy the tears ran down my face because he was telling me that he knew I was hurt, and he was happy because I was understanding the hurt and had come such a long way. What does that mean now if he hurt me? How could he dance with my Winona?

This is a bit much. I tried to believe he supported me. I believed in a loving and caring father because he showed me how to do things. It is pretty weak, isn't it, the case for caring and support, just doing things, giving me a few dollars when the marks on my report card were good, teaching me how to drive the car sitting on his knee. He showed me how to build a wagon and helped me with the wooden wheels. I used to love spending time watching him at work in his workshop, but I don't remember any words of advice or consoling. When I wanted solace, I went to my room alone and looked at the sky. There was no communication. I told myself that we didn't need to communicate because my dad already knew everything I was feeling.

Some things I know and I know this is something huge. And I know I wouldn't be dealing with it now if I weren't able to. So, it's okay, Winona, if you say so then this is it. I tried to keep this area out of my life a long time. If you think I can handle it now, okay, I'll go along. I'll play it out. I'll try to let my feelings out about slime, goo. I'll try to give them the space they need without pushing them back down.

But, oh God and Winona, that would mean I had nothing, nothing, nothing when I was little. No. I can't believe that.

I took a break to watch a movie, *The Journey of August King*. It wasn't spellbinding, but the message was good. In 1815, August King went against the law, the white law, to help a slave girl keep her soul. And he found his own.

I'm still not finding it any easier to handle what has entered my thoughts since seeing Léo this afternoon. How can it be? An isolated incident flits through my mind. Mother asked me a few years ago, sort of shyly and quietly, if I remembered anything from grade one. She meant school stuff, learning. At least, I think that's what she meant. Anyway, I said no. I don't remember learning to read or to write or to add. I remember the teacher, Mrs. Charlton, my classmates, the seven school desks for grade one sitting in two rows on one side of the room, grades two and three beside us on the other. But I don't remember anything odd.

I don't think I'll get anywhere trying to remember. There's nothing involving my father. I can't imagine anything unseemly. Maybe it doesn't make any difference. There wasn't any love anyway. I wanted a nice tender feeling from at least one parent, but it wasn't there from either. It doesn't change a thing. There was no overt affection or closeness between any of us, never a hand reaching out to place it on another shoulder or arm in a loving gesture, my parents never touched each other in front of the girls. If love was there it was concealed, a forgotten commodity. Perhaps they enjoyed the comfort that comes from pulling on a favourite old sweater that no longer needs the care and attention that was once given to its maintenance. And Anna and I certainly didn't look out for each other's well-being; we were more like competitors checking to see that the other didn't have something that you wanted, annoyed at having to share.

You'll have to help me with this, Winona. I'm lost in that middle distance. I don't know which way to turn. Should I forget that idea of slime meaning something ugly? Or should I try to follow the slime to see where it wants to go?

But isn't it silly to take something so far when it's so improbable?

I don't know. I just don't know.

Saturday April 12, 1997.

I asked for a dream last night to help me understand. I didn't sleep well and had a weird dream in the morning that doesn't make any sense.

I was in what looked like a large public building. Several men were attending a class I was giving with another girl. I drew a daisy on the blackboard using a different bright colour to outline each petal, and drew a face inside each. The men were on drugs but I didn't know it. When they raised their arms to answer a question, a large bloody area appeared in each armpit that normally was not visible. They were going to die from this disease. Each went into a small room, the size of a closet, and closed the door. When a string was pulled that hung from the ceiling, a thousand ties, neckties, fell on each in turn and then tumbled to the floor. The ties turned into the floor, which then began to wash away.

I don't understand that at all.

If my father did anything that messed me up, then that too served to bring me where I am today. If I was sad, I believed he knew and he cared and that was enough. That was all I'd ever get. That was the way it was supposed to be. That was the way it was for everybody. You weren't supposed to be sad. If you were sad there was something wrong with you. So you had to be sad by yourself so no one would see. And you had to keep it inside so it wouldn't show on the outside. Then you were all right.

A stony silence dwelt in the home. No tears or great passions, no wild longings or ambitions, no indignations or terrors threatened to disturb family life. Instead, a lot of down to earth common sense and plain hard work created a bleak terrain. The winter clothes came out of the closets and went into the storage room; the summer clothes came out of the storage room and went into the closets. Every item was washed, starched, and ironed, even the dishtowels. The winter curtains came down, the summer curtains went up. The walls, floors, and windows were scrubbed and afterwards Mother baked cookies and iced squares. She sure was busy. Supper was always ready when Dad arrived home after a long day at work. When the kitchen was cleaned up she prepared the next day's activities for her kindergarten class while Dad read the newspaper. If you did your homework, got good grades in school, made your bed every morning, cleaned your room once a week, went to church with the family and sat in the same pew for everyone to see you were there, didn't raise a ruckus or antagonize the neighbours, didn't ask about money or sex and embarrass your parents, then you were okay. No one wanted to hear about scary nightmares or broken hearts or secret desires. Those things weren't real. They spelled trouble.

I didn't ask questions. It was impertinent to ask why because adults knew best. You didn't ask, you obeyed. I couldn't speak and no one spoke to me. It was hateful, ugly, if that's what happened, but that's the way it was. Emotionally retarded.

What kept me fighting? Because that's what I did, I fought to get away from those who were controlling and manipulating, shadowboxed with a tireless and unwavering urge to break loose, to throw away any chains around me. I didn't want to be another's creation or someone's possession like an ornament lending empty glory. I didn't want to be just a body. I had a quick mind and many talents but they weren't considered a boon or a blessing, they were just added attractions, bothersome to boot.

It seems there was more to unearth in that dream hole I was digging in the family backyard last summer. It was a deep one. I fell into it and kept on shoveling. It feels as though the safety valve, my backup reserve, my magic carpet that could do anything for me, my father, has been pulled out from under me. But I was hanging onto false pretences, believing in something that didn't exist, something that didn't have a life of its own, something I had fabricated myself. I was grasping at nothing. I guess that's why I felt like nothing. As soon as that nothingness would start to appear, I had to get away. I had to run as fast as I could to escape a fearful unknown. Fighting and fleeing that nothingness was a lifelong task. It hits me hard. I have no more questions. I've run out of feelings. I'm lost out in left field again, in the quick of no man's land, in the limbo of Middle-Earth.

7:30 P.M.

I went for my usual drive around by the rivers, returned the video, and rented another for tonight. I had thought of going to LaViolette this evening to watch the Figure Skating Club's presentation, but it began to snow late this afternoon and it's still snowing. The countryside is white again, all clean and picture-perfect, but I think I'll stay home and watch the movie.

The sun didn't appear today. The weather reflected my mood that wasn't sunny either. I hope Vincent calls soon. I would like him to be here right now, stand behind me, put his arms around me, kiss the side of my neck, and rock me, back and forth, back and forth, like he cares.

10:00 P.M.

I watched the entire movie, *Close Up and Personal,* with Robert Redford and Michelle Pfeiffer, but almost turned it off part way through. Strictly entertainment. Something to fill up a few hours. Until the last line hit home– "I'm here to tell the story." It was for me. Thanks, Winona. You gave me the answer to a question I haven't even asked yet. I needed to hear that message tonight.

I'm sorry for all these tears today. They're not entirely sadness. There's also an ocean-swell of relief, and a faint notion that I'm getting closer and closer to the end of a long nightmare.

Sunday, April 13, 1997.

I slept in this morning and didn't get out of bed until ten-thirty. I had enough time to sit and have a cup of coffee before meeting Mother for lunch. Afterwards, back in her room, I addressed the envelopes for the birthday cards she wants to send to her grandchildren and to her friend Phoebe. She likes to sign them herself. Even with the onset of Parkinson's disease and her arthritic deformed fingers, which lie almost at right angles to the rest of her hand, she's found a way to write. The letters totter and waver all over the page and are almost indecipherable but everyone knows her handwriting. "Look Harold, this must be a note from Verda. The dear old soul. I wonder how she's getting along." Anna's children love to see the shaky scrawl arrive on a card in the mail and proudly show it to their friends, telling them all about their special grandmother.

"Know what? *My* grandmother can paint pictures. Can yours? Know what else? Her fingers are all crooked! Yup. Crooked like, ... I can't do it with my hand. But you should see how crooked they are!"

The sling on her broken arm was too loose, so I refastened it, helped her to the bathroom, and arranged her dress so she could sit on the loo for a few minutes. *Circular time*. Time possesses the perfect symmetry of the circle. Past, present, and future are all contained within the one, revolving about itself. There's no beginning and no end, no marching on straight ahead in steady clear directions. That's all smoke and mirrors. The truth is that we're led around in circles, fascinated with the turning points in our lives, the turning points themselves forming the curvature of the circle. Time just is. It's just there, immeasurable, being a concept, recreating, recycling, playing the same tune over and over with a few variations. Instead of mother guiding daughter, here's daughter guiding mother. Why not friend guiding foe and foe guiding friend? Or lover and beloved? Betrayer and betrayed? Victim and victimizer? What does it matter that one has grown up and the other has grown down? The roles will alternate until we learn the lessons.

She wanted to lie down, so I followed her to the bed, removed her shoes, and lifted her legs as she lay back on the mattress. She seems comfortable enough and doesn't complain, but she must be swallowing a lot more pain than she acknowledges.

"I'll call in a few days to see how you're doing."

"Yes. Call me during the week. I want to have a little snooze now."

"Good. Bye, now." Before leaving, I gave her the buzzer to hold in case she wants to call the nurse, then went for a drive.

Monday, April 14, 1997.

The telephone hardly rings these days. They are peaceful quiet days where no one is after me. Thank you for being with me, Winona. You are kind to not let me experience this isolation alone. Thank you for the extraordinary love and well-being that is in my heart. Again, you showed me where the love is. And it's okay. My purpose is to tell this story.

There was a deep dark secret I had blanked out of memory. The clues are falling into place. I can remember every room of the little asbestos covered house that my father built in Bruce Crossing after we moved away from the place near the railroad tracks, except one. The living room had a big radio on a high table, where I'd lean on my elbows with my chin in my hands and listen to news of Santa Claus leaving the North Pole on Christmas Eve; the

225

dining room and the kitchen were in one larger room, separated by a fold-up play desk where Anna and I could sit and draw pictures, cut out dolls, colour, and paste; there was a white tin roll-top breadbox with a small round red handle and a yellow flower decal on the front that sat on the kitchen counter and wild animals used to jump out from behind it; Mum and Dad's room was next to the living room–Mum's school desk was set up by the window that looked out on the back yard; there was a long narrow bathroom by the back door; the basement was unfinished–Dad used it for his workshop and kept his wood-working tools there; upstairs on the left was Anna's room with two little beds because Aunt Willy stayed with us sometimes and her dresser was against the center wall. My room was to the right of the stairs. I can walk into Anna's room and look around at the slanted ceilings but I can't go into my room. I can't get past the door. There's an invisible shield across the doorway and it's so dark inside I can't see a thing, not even the window I know must be there. I remember my father laughed because I wanted to paint the walls and ceiling red. I know I had a favourite doll that I named Cecie. My father built two doll's cribs out of wood. He worked at them in the basement every night for months. They were play-size replicas of the real thing, even had a sliding side section. Mother sewed little sheets and matching pillowcases. One was for Anna, the other was for me. They were Christmas presents from Daddy. Mine must have been in my room for Cecie to sleep with me. I know I had other toys also, but my bedroom is a black space in my memory.

Everything looks different now, the early nightmares have a new angle. I was being watched intensely. It was a man's head but I couldn't see that it looked like anyone I knew. But it was bald, like my father, had big eyes, like my father. The face was angular and longish, like my father, had full lips, like my father.

Dear God.

The head was bodiless. I couldn't look at the body not even in a dream. The body was cut off. Whatever it had done, I was erasing it, didn't want to see it. I learned a way to survive, to fight what was confusing, to chew it up so well it didn't exist any longer. Feelings hurt you. There was no place for them to go. It was best not to show you had any feelings. They were dangerous. They might make you cry. Then somebody would ask what was wrong and you didn't know. Then you would look stupid. No, it was best to make everyone think that you were all right, that nothing hurt you. Don't let anyone get close in case an ugly confusion of messy thoughts would be touched and throw you off balance. *How dare you think something's wrong with me!*

A few of my friends had violent upbringings. They knew their past and could talk about it. I found it hard to imagine how anything so awful could happen to someone. It certainly never happened to me. My friends had reasons for being depressed and for unusual behaviour. What is my reason? I wondered. My family is ordinary. What's the matter with me? My willpower isn't strong enough to fight down the heathens inside. I have no staying power. I'm not controlled enough to keep the urge to escape, to flee somewhere, locked in a box. I'm too weak to fight desires that are stronger than I am, too weak to do battle with demons who became more insistent and angrier at me for not listening to their cry to be heard. The measures to keep them down became more and more drastic. It seemed I would never be free of torments–vomiting three or four times a day, drinking a bottle of wine before I could sleep. Even then the unconscious sleep would last only a few hours. The days began with telephone calls, more people wanting money, more problems at the Residence, another death, another empty room, more problems at the Manoir, kids vandalizing the building, the roof leaking, a fire, another financing refusal, another creditor wanting to be paid, always fighting, always struggling, always that angry dark fist in my head, that frog in my throat that blocked my windpipe, that would swell up and make me want to scream or cry. But I couldn't. That would be admitting defeat. They, an amorphous they of everyone, couldn't beat me. I would fight until I died. I reasoned that even if I died trying at least I would have lived.

It brings tears to my eyes to think of all the energy I put into fighting myself, fighting to keep an image intact, fighting to keep that box of confused and angry feelings closed tightly because I was too afraid to see what was inside. I was alone. There was no one, not one person, who I trusted enough not to cut me down and tell me I was imagining things, just looking for excuses. I wasn't strong enough, that's all that was wrong. I'll try to be stronger, tougher, and more diligent. I'll keep a watchful eye on everything. But I hated what the Residence had become, I hated what the Manoir had become, I hated sorting out other people's accounting messes, I hated myself for not having someone to love, for being alone. I was getting ready to die again, getting close to that point where living was just too painful and lonely. If I could die I'd be free.

I haven't spoken to anyone about what has happened. I have a big secret, but it's not the kind that is dying to be told. It's like suddenly being made okay, learning that you weren't foolish and weak and immoral after all. You were fighting against being pushed and used and put down, against not being cared for, against not being liked for yourself, against those who tried to make you into someone you didn't want to be. It's a big secret that belongs to me. And through it all was that tiny little core at the center of my being that fought to be allowed to live again, that had been shattered and had survived so many times it would never give up fighting me, until I gave up fighting it.

Tuesday, April 15, 1997.

A few birds have been chirping back and forth to each other since early dawn. They must be happy to feel the approach of more clement days. Their songs are filling me with a special energy, as is this warm low sun scudding through and scattering the morning haze like a foxy critter breaking into a chicken coop, birds skittering and feathers fleeing in all directions.

I picked up my mail at the Post Office yesterday. The box was jammed with letters including a notice from the government to file the corporation income tax returns for the two companies–the Ovila Street Residence and the Manoir. Good. They'll be cleaned up soon. I have to prepare the financial statements first but only the Residence business is lengthy to do.

I could never make myself sit down to work on them. My mind wanted to be somewhere else. I begrudged the time I had to spend on those accounting details, just moving numbers around to tell the government how much money I owed them. Even when there was a loss the government demanded a tax on the capital in the corporation. It was inane. I wanted out of that nonsense economy, the whole dry world of facts and figures and rules and regulations. Too many pieces are out of synch in that materialistic culture we live in that emphasizes productivity and efficiency above all else. Everyone is caught up in watching their stock portfolios and price-earnings ratios, surfing the Internet, jet setting with an expensive crowd dressed in silk suits and dresses, carrying laptops and shiny snake skin briefcases and Mont Blanc pens, meeting for cocktails before dinner and evening conferences. They're blinded by success images and sure that they have reached the peak of living in the 90's, confident that being constantly on the run to see this or that client, cellular telephone on stand-by, is of earth-shattering importance. They're caught in a whirlwind of activity, juggling a panoply of competing schedules, working long hours, creating a pantomime of hectic tension and pressure, but absolutely certain that what they are doing is meaningful because they're making money to pay off debts on house mortgages, car loans, the holidays at *the* resort places, the new computer system, the credit card. Their faces are keen with intention and drive to get ahead, to succeed in the business world, to be part of that glamorous network where wealth and power can disintegrate in twenty-four hours. They're making money and accumulating success trappings and wondering where the happiness is, wondering why they can't have everything, deciding they'll just have to work harder to make more money so they can retire early. Then there'll be time to be happy.

I want to talk to them. I want to say, Be kind to yourself. Slow down. Stop giving money such a high priority in your life. Listen to what your body is telling you. Don't tune out the longings you feel. Allow yourself the pleasure of feeling your secret desires and dreams. Touch the vault of treasures that awaits for you inside your memory. Give those precious gems space to wander in your thoughts. Let them be free and watch where they take you, notice where they want to go. That's where your soul wants to be. Put your energy on what your heart wants to do, something hands-on creative. Begin with something small to get a taste of this freedom, but do begin–that call to paint, to teach, to sing, to tell a story, to write one, to play an instrument, to help others, to plant a garden, to act on stage, to sew a dress, or a quilt, to start a family, to go to Uganda, to build a school, or a cabinet, or a car, or a youth center, or a new world. Discover yourself. Follow a dream. Make room for it in your life. The moment you to start to focus on what that little core of energy inside you would like to be doing, instead of how much money will be left in your bank account after you pay this month's bills, that moment will be the beginning of something unexpected and extraordinary.

I hope Vincent calls soon.

I wonder if one has to go through a trauma where one is broken and hits bottom in order to realize that what you've always been running after is what is in your heart, to realize that a desire to love and feel loved is not a sissy notion from great-grandmothers who held children on their laps and told them stories and legends of gods and goddesses, part human part divine, while rocking to and fro in a favourite chair. A land of wonder and imagination and infinite possibility spreads out before one's eyes, a land where the wisdom of the ages passes from soul to soul and love is the source of life, a guiding force of such power that Providence moves to create the dream when love is the spring that inspires it. The inspiration, the creativity of Einstein, Ramanujan, Pascal, Mozart, Zola, Shakespeare, Emerson, Gandhi, Picasso, da Vinci, Jung was fueled by the same genie who wants to guide us, each one of us, to heights of understanding and love and achievement, and will do exactly that when our hearts and minds are open wide enough to hear the call. We can live daily with that genie when we give up the fight to be in control of how we think we want our lives to be, when we quit trying to live an image, when we stop playing the society game of chasing fame and fortune and notoriety.

But do we have to survive a blockbuster, exchange breaths with death and defeat before we change our ways, before we start to think maybe something *is* wrong here, maybe something *is* missing, maybe there *is* something I don't understand? However the realization happens, whether it comes from the quiet explanations of a stranger or whether it takes an explosion for us to find out, that missing piece is always the same. Love. We stopped loving ourselves at an early age, we started doubting ourselves the moment we got to school and were submitted to intelligence tests and examinations and speaking contests and sports competitions. We were told that was the way of life; we were taught to abandon our instincts and intuitions; we were given messages that something is wrong with spending time getting to know your soul-spirit; we lost our ability to simply listen to ourselves; we were taught what society wanted. To be a good person, successful and smart, you had to be at the top of the prove-yourself values of our culture's measurements of worthiness. You had to win out over your classmates, beat your teammates, score high. If you were going to be anyone in this world you had to be at the top of the system. If you weren't, you told yourself you were stupid and incompetent and incapable and not up to scratch. And other adults, parents, who didn't understand the lunacy and inhumanity of the system either, probably told you the same thing.

We look far and wide for the answers to success and failure; we search for the key mix of external circumstances that will unlock the gates to glory. The simple dynamics hiding beneath the surface are ignored. Just possibly a successful effort had a humanitarian or ecological aspect to it, or a failed undertaking was becoming too greedy, had lost its soul. No one notices the simple justice that doesn't cost anything and is definitely not impressive to an expensive boardroom. A three hundred-page market study of facts and figures, all nicely displayed on grids and graphs in computer modules and flowcharts is something you can get your teeth into, something that can be understood and manipulated.

There is a simple justice. It applies to every individual, to every family, to every ad hoc group that is together for a reason, to every corporate boardroom, and to every government. It's love–love for yourself and for each human being. Whether love is there, in you, in your family, in your project, in your corporation, in your government, or whether love is absent, determines success in our world. Replace the competition, the quest for power and domination with cooperation, respect, and understanding, and then watch profits soar. That's when money grows on trees.

Watch a mind set that is centered on fighting and anger reorganize into a mind set centered on peace and happiness. Watch first what happens to a person of this nature. Watch a quiet confidence radiate to others that is incapable of being thrown off balance. Watch others draw themselves closer to that person and wonder what it is that's so special. Look at the smiles, the goodwill, the freedom that emanates, the sense of well being that others sense and want to feel themselves. Watch to see the difference one person can make in the world, a person who believes in natural goodness. Whether it's on a large scale or a small one, the same dynamic is present, a simple wonderful nugget of pure energy that contains God's justice–love. And it is infallible and doesn't cost a penny and has always been there.

Wednesday, April 16, 1997.

I called Vincent this morning but he wasn't at the office. I left a message for him to phone me. I wonder what he's thinking.

My pen isn't writing on its own like it did yesterday so I should be able to work on accounting paperwork today. I love so much to sit at my desk every morning and pick up my pen to write. My head fills with thoughts and my heart brims over with happiness. My fingers touch my face and feel that the skin is smooth, the smashed nose has repaired itself, the smile is genuine. Even when I don't have a lot to say, it's a real need for me to be in this place, open my mind to wondrous thoughts, and simply let the words stream through my pen onto the paper.

Vincent called at noon. He was controlled and overly polite on the phone. "Did you want something Isabelle?"

"I was anxious to know how you were doing."

"Oh, thanks for being concerned about me."

"So, are you all right?"

"I've been quiet after the sermon you gave me last week, but I have clients to see this afternoon and a dinner to attend tonight."

"So you're back in your groove."

"You might say."

"I just called to say hello, and ... I wanted to feel your arms around me. But I guess it's not the right time."

"But you know I'm there. You can feel my arms around you."

Hey! Wait a minute! I've heard that before. I heard it one afternoon last summer when I said to Vincent, "You were gone so quickly." He said it again. He says it like a line from a movie. The first time I swooned, this time I'm wondering where the truth is in that line. He's found a way to let himself off the hook so he doesn't have to respond to my expression of caring. He's playing a role in a movie. He's in an adventure. *Damn. Damn. Damn.*

"I can tell you're busy, Vincent, so I don't want to disturb you any longer."

"Right."

"I'll talk to you later. Bye."

"Bye."

4:00 P.M.

The drive around by the rivers and back home was a bit different today. I know how I'm told things now. Gently. Quietly. And it happened just like that—gently and quietly. I had just left the village, was driving along the highway heading northeast. A tape cassette was playing and I didn't like the song, the echo in the car was loud and hammering, so I turned the noise off.

It was quiet. Soon I was thinking of the earlier telephone conversation with Vincent, how I had told him I'd like to feel his arms around me and the canned response that followed. I thought of the last session with Léo and that I hadn't mentioned anything to Vincent about recent events. Then a dribble of saliva passed the wrong way in my throat and I started to choke and cough. I didn't think much of it, swallowing the wrong way happened often.

Soon there were other thoughts in my head. That drip, that trickle, is that what happened to me in that dark room I can't go into? Did he show me his thing in that room and let it come on me, on my skin, in my mouth, and some trickled down my throat and made me choke and cough and feel like I was suffocating? For sure, he would have told me not to tell. Maybe I swallowed some of the goo. Maybe that's what I was trying to throw up all the time.

6:30 P.M.

A bailiff just delivered the documents that will start the proceedings to sell the Manoir. A date hasn't been set yet, but it means I will be free of it sometime this year.

Thursday, April 17, 1997.

Couldn't fall asleep last night even though I didn't go to bed until midnight. I listened to the birds waking, then must have dozed between six and nine-thirty. I couldn't shut off the chatter, the mindless stuff, the tired stuff, the fear stuff, like paying bills, like the Residence not selling, like wanting someone to love, like doubting I can write a story, lonely stuff.

What is that restlessness that is still there this morning? Fear of repetition of the old ways? Of nothing ever working out? Of many things looking like a start, but eventually collapsing? I think that's what it is. It's a fear of hope dying on me again, hope to be free from disappointment and disillusion. I would plead, beg for something to work out so I could go forward. I would hope for the event that would allow me to come unstuck, that would allow my dreams to come true. The heartache continued with each refusal but hope is hard to squash. If one solution wasn't it, then it would be the next, or the next, on and on. It was a way of life.

That way of living was out of synch like I was. I was still an organizer, an administrator. If any of those projects in the Manoir had succeeded the acclaim would have appeased me for a while, but the restlessness would have returned because the same emptiness, the hole in my soul, would have been there still. I would have continued to shuffle papers and accounts and money and staff around. Again I would have managed to put myself where my feelings were safe from scrutiny, in the monetary world of business dealings. Even though each of the projects had a humanitarian aspect, I was still on the

232

outside looking in. My priorities were messed up. The mechanism that had closed my heart was still directing my life, still pushing me to be the super-organizer, looking for strength from an image of success, seeking but never finding, and living a sadness that came from the pain of not living from myself.

But then, the bliss. I discover that my miserable life has an artistry to it. There is another dimension of a sensitivity so delicate I'm in awe of the magnificence of the design, of the caring. Years and years of unspoken hurt are revealed to me little by little, tenderly. Feelings start to write themselves out the moment I sit with a pen in my hand. Quiet thoughts whisper to me as I'm washing my face in the morning, or standing under the shower, or driving along in the car, or doing the dishes, or watching the fire. A lifetime of confusion and pain expresses itself with an eloquence that brings tears to my eyes. My heart speaks as it never spoke before. It's bursting with a desire to reach out, to touch others, to reach out and touch their hearts that I know have been closed also by unspoken hurt. I've been given a gift of immense magnificence–my own soul. It fills the emptiness, overflows the borders, spills into life, and is beautiful, creative, intelligent, sensitive, and loving. And no one can take it from me.

9:00 P.M.

"Alex! So good to hear from you!"

He called this afternoon from his father's in California where he spent the winter months. I think we talked for almost an hour. I guess Dan will pay the bill. Alex was seething with frustration. He had bought a vintage truck and had been working on it all day trying to get it road worthy for the trip home.

"It's driving me crazy. So, I phoned you, Mom. Sounds funny, eh?"

"It does, Alex."

"You always helped me when I was stuck on something. How are you on trucks?"

"A wipe out. Completely."

"C'mon, Mom. You've got a trick somewhere."

"I can't help you with the mechanics, sweetie. I don't have a clue about what goes on under the hood."

"The problem isn't under the hood. It's a universal joint. But that's okay."

"All I can say is don't ignore the frustration, or sit on it, or try doing something else to make it go away."

"So, what do I do?"

"Give it space. Become quiet. Some words, or an image, or a person will come to mind. Then listen."

"But..."

233

"Stop fighting and getting mad at the truck, you'll only lock yourself into a knot. If you let it, the frustration will tell you something you need to know."

"But what about my truck?"

"Sorry, I got carried away."

"I want to be out of here by tomorrow afternoon."

"Go back to it after you've had a quiet time with yourself, after you feel good about an insight that will come to you. I bet that everything you were trying so hard at earlier will fall nicely into place."

"Sounds like a book I read about Zen on a motorcycle."

"I haven't read that book, but if that's what it says…"

"Sort of."

"Then it's true. There's another dynamic at work besides the mechanics."

"Good, Mom. I'll try. Thanks. How are you doing anyway? Things sounded pretty stormy the last time we talked."

"I feel a very special freedom, Alex. It seems that each episode since the accident has led me to touch the center of myself."

"That's wonderful."

"It's been an amazing magical mystical journey and I think I'm the happiest person alive."

"Mom, there's a tear in my eye."

How I love this child from my body who has a sensitive soul like mine.

Friday, April 18, 1997.

Appointment with Léo this afternoon. I look forward to these days.

Saturday, April 19, 1997.

"Did you know, Isabelle, that I had a car accident too?" It was Vincent. He came last evening and stayed until midnight.

"No kidding. What happened?"

"I was on a skiing holiday in the Laurentians and anxious to be on the slopes, so, to save some time I put on my ski boots before leaving the camp in the morning. I knew the way to the hill like the back of my hand and didn't see any problem driving with my boots on. The weather was good, I didn't anticipate any icy conditions, and I guess I was going too fast. An otherwise ordinary curve in the road turned into a devil of a twist and I couldn't manoeuvre the car around the turn. It slid off the side of the road, over a cliff, and fell twenty-five feet onto a frozen pond. The car was a total write-off. Broken glass was scattered everywhere, just like confetti, but I wasn't hurt. I didn't even have a scratch."

"Are you putting me on?"

Vincent smiled and shook his head, no.

"Not a scratch?"

"I think I did have a small cut here on my finger, but that was it."

"When did all this happen?"

"About two years before the ski accident."

"My God, Vincent, what is it going to take to make you look at yourself?"

A freak April snowstorm dumped a foot and a half of unsullied white cold outside. Vincent and I stood and watched through the windowed doors that look out onto the gallery and the back yard. The bright outdoor lights angled down from the roof of the house, illuminating the large spring snowflakes into a gigantic outburst of fireworks falling through the night sky. The snow had piled into foot-high perfectly arched mounds that spanned the length and width of the wooden porch balustrade like the inside portion of a long tunnel where snow had replaced air as the breathing medium. The distant village lampposts on the other side of the river glowed softly like faerie beacons shining a golden way through the fast descending snow. The absolute quiet of the wintry scene exuded peace. Heaven must be like that, I thought. Maybe not the snow, or the night, but the beauty.

"The snowy scene outside is just like love, Vincent. Love is all the things we see in front of us–beauty, peace, strength, grace, glory, passion, humility. And do you know what else?"

"No. What?"

"The physical sensations of our bodies loving is the same ethereal transcendental love being made physical, being brought down to earth."

"Isabelle, you say such things."

"That idea is thousands of years old."

"Well, there you go."

"What do you mean?"

"Takes something old to make me feel sad and happy at the same time."

Sunday, April 20, 1997.

I tried to walk into that room again this afternoon as I was driving. All was quiet and I thought it a good time to try to go inside. I can stand at the open door and look in, but still all I see is darkness, so, today, I tried to walk in.

After standing at the doorway for a few seconds, I took a step into the blackness, the room brightening to a certain extent as I entered. But instead of the darkness disappearing, I was the one who began disappearing. As my body was withering into an irregular patch of dim colours, I took another step into the foreboding and the farther I went into the room the more the outlines became smeared. The blotchy colours faded into a wavy grey voile that thinned into the shimmer of a heat wave, and then only feeling was left as I disappeared altogether like a dying star collapsing on itself. My body was in the room but it was nothing and I knew I was in there. It was as if I had become a black hole myself, a spot of intense energy that still communicated yet was so compressed no light could escape.

Monday, April 21, 1997.

Another session with Léo this afternoon. He nods his head when I tell him that I know I have to let go of Vincent, but I can't. I thought I was feeling a real love, a love that was beautiful and peaceful, a divine love. I was, I did, I do feel that love, that expansiveness, that effervescence, even when I'm alone. Even? Why do I say that? I'm more in touch with that special love when I am alone. I like being with Vincent, I feel his tenderness, but he doesn't tell me. I have to explain love to him. He's touched, holds me tight, but I have imagined it, haven't I? That's how I wanted it to be, so I wrote a love story of my own and told myself it was so.

It hurts again. I've been imagining again. He's using me, leading me on, nodding his head in understanding, marveling at the wild and wonderful things I tell him. I give him a way to keep up the charade while I stay stuck in the old stuff–trying to fill the emptiness with his willing and desirable physical love. What do I hope for? The impossible. That he'll recognize his cut-off self and change his life. For me. Sure. The moon is made of green cheese with a sprinkling of sesame.

Tuesday, April 22, 1997.

Sunny and warm this afternoon. I can barely wait for the nice weather to arrive. The grass is turning green on the parts of the lawn that sit in the sunshine. There's still snow left from that spring snowstorm last Friday, but it's melting quickly. I had to go for a drive again, couldn't sit still. The gremlins needed more space to frolic. Thinking that I'll be alone again makes me restless. But I never succeeded not to be alone, did I? Every relationship left me alone, never nourished, ate me up. I thought this one was different, I was different. After the accident I began to change, but I met Vincent a year earlier. So if I hadn't changed when the relationship began, what makes me think it was different from the others? I'm the one who changed and tried to change him. I'm having a hard time again. I'm tired, sad. I lost myself. Love was spoiled right from the beginning. Love, trust, confidence, sharing, caring–all those good things–ruined.

Wednesday, April 23, 1997.

Yesterday was a hard day. Murky. I couldn't even write my thoughts out, couldn't form a full sentence that made any sense. I thought of calling Léo. I wanted to say to him, *I'm panicking, Léo! I feel lost, afraid, alone. I'm afraid of that angry black cloud that is threatening to gather, the one that gets angrier and plunges me into that old darkness. HELP ME LÉO! HELP ME!* Last night I felt it coming back, the frenzy in the air, wild icy tendrils of dead breath, an unvoiced screech. I felt the nothingness cloud start to gather. I held myself tight, probably stopped breathing. Léo would have yelled at me, *"Breathe!"* I was wandering around in the kitchen because I was having such trouble to sit at my desk. I decided not to call Léo. No. I can do this myself. It's not going to happen again. *NO! IT'S NOT GOING TO HAPPEN AGAIN!* It was about ten o'clock. The telephone rang.

"Hi, Isabelle. How are you tonight?" It was Norman, the mayor of LaViolette.

"Just fine, Norman. How are you doing?"

"Fine too. I'm at a meeting at the municipal counties building and just had a phone call that a gang of young kids had gone into the Manoir."

"Not again."

"My wife had several calls from some neighbours who saw them go into the building. The police wouldn't go to investigate unless I called them, so I did, and they said they would check it out. I just wanted to let you know."

"Thanks, Norman."

"What's happening there now?"

"The two boys who are interested in the building, Jean-François and Louis, haven't finished their business plan."

"Not yet? It's taking them a right good while, isn't it."

"They're looking into the government plans to see which sections of their project are eligible for guarantees before handing it to the banks. They tell me they're going as fast as they can. They're worried that someone else might buy the building because Monsieur Jeanneau is having the Manoir sold by a sheriff's auction."

"I thought he might. When's the sale?"

"The date hasn't been set yet, but Jean-François and Louis have at least several months to get it together."

"Let's pray for the best."

"Yes."

"I have to get back to the meeting, Isabelle. Let's keep in touch. What happens to that building is important to the town."

"For sure. And thanks, Norman. I'll call the S.Q. to ask them what they found."

A few minutes later, "Bonsoir, Sûreté du Québec."

"Hello, this is Isabelle Carberry. I'm the owner of the Manoir in LaViolette. I've had a phone call that some young people were going into the building."

"Yes, Madame. We are there now. An agent will call you back with a report."

The telephone rang at eleven o'clock.

"Mme Isabelle Carberry?"

"Yes."

"This is Constable Alain Laferrière from the Ste. Philomène Sûreté du Québec. We were requested to go to the Manoir this evening."

"Yes, I'm aware. Norman Brennan, the mayor of LaViolette, spoke to me earlier."

"Everything is quiet there now."

"Good. What was going on?"

"When we entered the building we found six young boys, all around age fourteen, sitting on a sofa on the second floor. One was smoking a cigarette. They were just talking and left without any fuss when we asked them to leave the premises."

"Those boys have nothing to do in that town."

"We do have a problem with under-aged repeat offenders for petty crimes."

"Do you?"

"Very much so. There are too many for the size of the town and there's no ready follow-up or counseling available."

"But before they're into that situation shouldn't there be something more for them to do?"

"Definitely, that would help. Kids need a lot to keep them interested and off the streets."

"If someone would give me the money, I would organize a youth center with a big gymnasium in the Manoir tomorrow."

"That would be an ideal spot for it."

"I tried for three years to get a project going in that building. I've lost a lot of money so far and I hit my head against a brick wall every time I tried to find funding."

"That's too bad. Especially, for the young people. Small crimes turn into big ones."

"So they do."

"It hurts not to be able to do something."

"Don't I know it."

"Well, good luck anyway."

"Thanks for looking after things tonight."

The pressure had stopped building inside my head. I wasn't able to sort out the tangle, but someone or something wanted attention. That threatening blackness had spoken to me as surely as if it had taken me by the shoulders and shook until my teeth fell out.

Thursday, April 24, 1997.
    There's a love that's coming from nowhere. It's nowhere and everywhere. It's spilling out from inside me. It's gushing into me. I don't feel alone, I feel full. I don't feel an empty place, I feel a marvelous vigour that's very strong and quiet. It fills me with farsightedness, softens and strengthens at the same time. Just like the springtime and this bright blue sky this morning. Think I'll go outside.

Friday, April 25, 1997.
    Tired.

Saturday, April 26, 1997.
    Slept a bit. Book Club today.

Sunday, April 27, 1997.
    Tired again this morning. Our Rotary Club is putting on a fundraiser brunch today. Last evening, I worked outside picking up broken branches that littered the ground after that heavy April snowstorm a week ago. Almost all the light had drained from the sky before I put away the lawn tools. I read until midnight, but still didn't sleep.

Monday, April 28, 1997.
    No energy today. I tossed and turned fitfully until four o'clock then must have dozed for a few hours after that. I was so tired when I went to bed last night that I was sure I would fall asleep. I got home from the Rotary Brunch around four in the afternoon, changed into jeans and a T-shirt, and worked outside again. Dugan arrived out of nowhere. I was emptying a wheelbarrow load of twigs at the back of the lawn, turned around, and there he was by the back steps to the house, standing stock-still, looking straight at me. He wandered around checking out the yard.
    "Do you want some help, Isabelle? I could go home and get my chainsaw."
    "I wouldn't mind some help."
    "I can cut the bigger branches into smaller pieces so you can move them to the back more easily."
    "I'd appreciate it, really I would, because I didn't know how to get rid of the big limbs that fell."
    "Good."
    "But, Dugan, I'll tell you right now, I'll not go out with you."

239

"That's all right. I can help you, can't I? We were neighbours once."

"I suppose."

"I'll go and get my chainsaw. I'll just be a minute."

Ten minutes later, Dugan was back with his chainsaw and a can of gas. We chatted while we were working.

"So, you won't go out with me?"

"I'm having a rest from men."

"Why?"

"Just doing it."

"You don't do that for any old reason at all."

"I guess not."

"So what's your reason?"

"I've been seeing a therapist for almost a year now…"

"That so?"

"I've spent a lot of time trying to find myself."

"I knew you were lost."

"How come?"

"Most people don't behave the way you did."

"Let's not get into it."

"All right."

"I've never had a good relationship."

"That started with your father."

"What do you mean?"

"He probably abused you."

"Dugan! How can you say that?"

"I'm not so stupid."

"I don't remember anyway."

"He was a womanizer."

"You never even met him!"

"Your poor mother. Didn't you know?"

"No."

"Ask anyone in town. They know how much he liked women."

"I've never heard of such a thing."

"You're mother shouldn't have left you alone with him when you were little. Men fantasize. They go crazy when they don't have sex."

"Speak for yourself."

"Doesn't your therapist take you back in time so you can remember?"

"You mean hypnotism?"

"Yeah. Going back into early memories."

"We've never talked about it."

"You should remember so you can be free. Until you do there will still be doubts in your mind."

"Let's talk about something else."

"Sure. What do you want to talk about? I'm free and easy to discuss anything."

"Anything else, then."

"I'm retired now. Did you know?"

"No."

"Yep. Got the time to myself. Anytime you need some help or feel like going out for dinner… I'm there, just a call away."

"Thanks, but I get along just fine on my own."

Dugan sawed the broken tree limbs into sections and stayed to help drag them to the back of the yard where later I could throw them into the gully. He set aside a pile of the larger pieces that were usable as firewood and left after we had done a fairly good job of cleaning up. I went to the village to rent a video, fixed a quick supper of cold chicken and warmed-up broccoli, and installed myself in an easy chair in front of the television. The telephone rang.

"Hello. Dugan Begley here. I just called to say have a good evening."

"Hello, Dugan."

"What are you doing?"

He could hear the voices in the film, so I couldn't bluff. "I'm watching a movie."

"Oh, that's nice. Well, goodnight."

"Goodbye, Dugan." *Phew!* I was sure he was going to ask me if he could come over and watch it too. I went back to the movie. Two minutes later, the phone rang again.

"Do you want me to come and watch the rest of the movie with you? I'll bring a bottle of wine."

"No, thank you, Dugan. I'd rather be alone tonight."

"Just thought I'd ask."

"And thanks for helping out."

7:30 P.M.

It was good to see Léo this afternoon. He helps me to find some sense, or else he reassures me that I'm not insane. He listens so intently. I can be confused in front of him and he just watches. I can feel two ways about the same thing, he just takes it in. I can talk about the nothingness cloud, the two faces everywhere, the deceit, and the madness, but I don't talk about my angel. I did mention her once, but he acted like she was an imaginary friend I had created because I was lonely. I never spoke about her again.

Tuesday, April 29, 1997.

I don't have the energy to write this morning. I don't feel the flow, but I can work on the taxes and other paperwork that's hanging around. It's beautiful this morning. I'll put on some music. That Fauré and Debussy CD that sends my thoughts floating to imaginable worlds should be nice in the background as I'm working on those...

Claire came to the door. We sat at the kitchen table and chatted over coffee for two hours. I told her about the past few weeks.

"I guess it stays with you for life."

"I've heard that said, but, Claire, I don't believe it. It's not an albatross around my neck, I feel a relief and a freedom because finally I'm walking in my own skin."

Later in the afternoon, I drove into the village to mail off my income tax returns, parking my car in front of the General Store across the street from the Post Office. A young boy about sixteen years of age spoke to me as I walked out of the building and waited a few seconds before crossing the street to my car on the other side. He was with a gang of his buddies. They often congregated on the sidewalk in front of the Post Office after school was out to have a smoke and a few laughs.

"How do you do, Ma'am. Do you have a loonie for the bus to Montreal?"

"Yes, I think so. Come to the car across the street. I don't have my purse with me."

He followed me to my car, his friends watching.

"So, you want to go Montreal."

"Yes, Ma'am."

"Do you live here in Wakeham?"

"Yeah, I stay around here but my mother's in Montreal."

The day was sunny and the air pleasant, but the boy seemed cold. He was holding himself.

"How much money do you have?"

He took the change from his pocket and started to count, "One dollar, two dollars, and ten, twenty, twenty-five, thirty-five, thirty-seven cents."

"You might need more than that to get to Montreal," and I handed him a five-dollar bill.

The boy didn't speak for a few moments while he fingered the coins on the palm of his hand, as if he was trying to figure out how much change to give back to me. Then he looked up, "Thank you." A wonderful smile lit up his face.

"You're welcome. Have a good day!"

He started to return to his friends who were watching the incident from across the street but changed his mind, turned, and walked back towards the

General Store. His friends saw the blue bill exchange hands. One had a big grin on his face and seemed to be the cocky one of the bunch: "Hey, Lady! Will you give me five dollars for a bus ticket to Montreal?"

I pulled out of the parking space into the street. As I drove by in front of the group, he yelled again, "Hey! What's your name? We want to thank you!"

I drove home to finish another tax return thinking of that boy's face and the smile that gave him a spark of feeling good like he had found a note for a new bicycle in his Christmas stocking instead of a potato.

Wednesday, April 30, 1997.

Thank you for today. I slept last night. I feel as unsinkable as a buoy bobbing on the water, as high as an elephant's eye. The biggest smile is on my face. I worked on some paperwork then went for a drive in the sunshine. A few minutes after I arrived back home, Dugan knocked at the back door.

"Hello there. Been for a drive, have you?"

"Dugan, what do you want?"

"Don't get testy now."

"Well, I don't like you watching to see when I come and go."

"What do you mean? I was just driving by."

"Okay, okay.

"You mean you still don't think we're perfect for each other?"

"Please, Dugan. The answer is no. I can hardly believe you're serious. Are you?"

"Am I what?"

"Serious. About thinking we're perfect for each other."

"Why not? You mean you don't think so?"

"Well, I can't say it any clearer than a plain no."

"I can ask, can't I?"

"Is that why you stopped in?"

"Not exactly. I just wanted to tell you that I'll drop in tomorrow to pick up the rest of the wood."

"That's fine. Come when it suits you."

"Do you want me to finish cleaning up the yard?"

"No thanks, Dugan."

"Hey, I had to ask, didn't I?"

"That's all right."

"Bye, then."

"Bye, Dugan."

May

"What we live is necessary to be lived."
James Hillman,
The Soul's Code

Thursday, May 1, 1997.

A dishrag furry with fungi, or one that's been wrung out, hung on the clothesline in the sun, and hardened and contorted into a misshapen board. That's what I feel like today. I didn't sleep well again last night. I can't shut off the head noise that rattles on as steadily as the clatter and rumble of the steel wheels on a slow-moving train on a set of rusty tracks. It's the uncertainty. I'm sure of it. The not-knowing. Being held in suspension as if I've no control over my legs to take me anywhere. As if I could kick to my heart's content, wear myself out with the kicking, without the slightest consequence. As if my will has as much say in the matter as one of the cows in the field next door or a soggy bun.

Everything is up in the air again. I like that, don't I? I like having everything certain, not having to be spontaneous, wanting to know when my house will sell, where I'll be living, wanting my story to be finished before I begin, wanting everything to be finished before I begin, not wanting to risk failure again, afraid, and tired, tired. I see a dichotomy too, because only part of me likes a fixed routine. It's a safe place to retreat to where everything is arranged, nothing changes, and questions aren't asked. It's hard to make decisions when you don't know how you feel inside so when everything outside is in place, it's safe. I'm safe. When you're confused, you want an anchor to hold onto. But that part of me is only around sometimes.

Another part can hate exactly the same schedule I had been comfortable with the week before. I had to force myself to concentrate on something that earlier I had worked away at quietly and as unquestioningly as a clam. Suddenly, I didn't want to be there, I had to escape the monotony, felt trapped and attacked, shackled in place, bound with fetters.

Another part likes to participate in the daily routine, feels a depth and pleasure in the constancy of simple things, doesn't look for safety or escape as an avoidance measure, is enthused about living, wants to be part of it, and wants to share its well-being with others. That's when I'm feeling good.

There's another part still: the part that needs to express itself and be creative, the part that tunes into that dimension that is so rich with insight and ideas that they seem to come from somewhere beyond me. This part of me

245

knows such joy and happiness in that realm that I long for the sweet satisfaction that comes from doing those things that issue from that special place. This part gives me strength and freedom and dignity.

I'm going to stalk this restlessness. Last night I was worrying about where I would be in the summer, thinking that I'd like to be right here in this beautiful back yard surrounded with the peace and tranquillity and happiness that I had searched for in all the wrong places. The whirling dervishes nattered at me, *But you won't have any money. How will you be able to look after cutting the grass at the Manoir? Or pay the mortgages?* I finally stopped the incessant grumbling by concentrating on and repeating each word of a litany–*Strength, grace, courage, humility, compassion, wisdom. Strength, grace, courage, humility, compassion, wisdom.* Why didn't I learn to do that years ago? Then I just thought, *Strength and grace. Strength and grace,* over and over again until four-thirty in the morning and the movement of light and sound in the room washed away the remaining night.

Sunday, May 4, 1997.

My story is with me once more. Last night in bed, I started to reread what I had written and I'm starting to like it again. For a while I was afraid of it.

Monday, May 5, 1997.

"You tell me, Isabelle, about all these dramatic and hurting things as if you're giving a news report," Léo said to me today. It's becoming clearer that I'm supposed to write about what's inside because I can't say what I'm feeling. This afternoon, I tried to sit back in the hammock chair in Léo's office, relax, and feel in touch with myself. I couldn't do it. I spend hours here on my own sitting back, closing my eyes, and just letting thoughts wander into my mindspace, sometimes in a helter-skelter fashion, sometimes inviting a particular thought then following it to a conclusion. But with Léo watching, I couldn't get into the acquiescing mood that permits a free-flowing conversation. I couldn't ignore his eyes on me that felt like two blinding stage lights beamed right at me, exposing who knows what flaws. Spotlights are unforgiving and harsh on complexions that want to look younger than they are, revealing every zit and red blotch and then more, and I felt the same inscrutable unwelcome intrusion seep into my innards. When I sat back into the padded sling, unfolding my arms and placing them on the chair-rests in an attempt to do what I thought I ought to be able to do, the idea was in my head that somebody was going to poke me in the stomach. Then vague thoughts of that nightmare where my father was coming to get me started to get stronger and clearer, and I thought if I didn't put a stop to the sequences rolling by in the front of my skull behind my eyes, there might be images from my old bedroom and that was the end of trying to sit back and let go.

Léo asked a simple question, "How are you feeling right now?" I couldn't answer. I didn't know where to begin. A blind stubbornness was in my head, a squeezing pressure. It refused to move like an irascible ogre hiding and waiting under a folktale bridge. That's all there was in my mind–an impatient emptiness. I didn't know how I felt. I felt nothing, perhaps a little tightness in my stomach, a slight constriction or indigestion, but I could not answer.

I stammered, "I-I-I-I don't know. Okay, I guess. Fine."

Léo is willing to help me, to be with me when I remember, but I can't drop my guard when he is watching. Earlier it was all right for me to talk to Léo about the past because I had already written it down, had already brought back the torment, and worked through the trauma on paper. But I'm a blank if I have to explore something with Léo that I haven't already worked through. I'm too overwhelmed with a multitude of feelings like a flock of crows massing above Vincent Van Gogh's cornfield, to make sense of any one, and I can't say a word. But if Léo had given me a piece of paper and a pen, I could have written what was going on inside me as easily as sipping a glass of cool lemonade on a hot day.

What do you think, Winona? One minute I felt that I didn't have to relive the early drama because I had already lived the madness of it during my life. I knew what it would feel like, so what was the point of reliving it? The next minute, I felt I did have to know what happened, otherwise the not-knowing would continue to haunt me.

I fought that madness in my twenties. *Get away from me! Leave me alone!* My hearing turned into distant voices that seemed to be caught inside trees, then, when they escaped, they rushed by with sighing sounds, whispers in the dark, or cries in the night of my baby calling to me. The light in the room wavered and grew dim. I'd squinch my eyes and strain to see through empty voids, knowing the void wasn't empty, then an eerie feeling would lighten my body as if it was a crisp autumn leaf buffeted by the wind. Sometimes the obscurity was complete for a few seconds, my legs wouldn't work, I couldn't put one in front of the other. Sometimes I fell and passed out, my body rigid with spastic muscles. One Ottawa psychiatrist thought I was epileptic and I took dilantin for quite a while. When the madness would catch me at home, I got down on my knees ahead of time so I wouldn't fall when I needed to get to the bathroom, holding my head with spread fingers to get through that aimless insanity that was becoming part of my life, that I wouldn't let anyone see.

Not having an outlet made me interiorize. With the years, the parts of myself that I didn't want to know anything about grew into a sizeable mass, became more and more difficult to camouflage, or bury. Eventually, the solitude forced me to write out what was inside. Or, perhaps I should say, the solitude allowed me to write. That was my way of handling the avalanche of emotion, but Léo doesn't see it that way. He thinks I should be putting on a vocal display of being devastated, disgusted, angry, and resentful. He appears to think if I don't rant and rave those feelings will stay inside and foment. But I know that, if I do remember, I'll be watching from afar. It will be a relief for me to know, like turning the last page of a book.

Thanks, Winona. Now, I know I have to remember, for the freedom. Dugan was right.

Neither will I see myself as a poor victim. I'll see an opportunity I was given, I'll applaud and be thankful for a wise, enduring, and skillful gift, not from a disturbed and chaotic world, but from a caring and purposeful world that helped me to understand the human spirit.

Wednesday, May 7, 1997.

"So how have you been, Isabelle?" Anna asked as we drove to my house from the nursing home. She had been in Montreal on business for the week and came out to Wakeham to spend an hour with Mother and give her a Mother's Day present. I had walked over to the Home since I knew she was short of time and I wouldn't have seen her at all if I hadn't made the short trip myself. She was driving me home.

"Oh, fine. Quiet. The Caisse knows I can't pay the mortgage on the house in LaViolette, so I'm waiting for developments."

"Good."

"Anna, do you remember your room in Bruce Crossing?"

"Sure. Why?"

"I've been trying to remember our rooms and I can remember yours but not mine."

"My ceiling was sloped on both ends of the room and there were two little beds. One was for Aunt Willy. Up against the inside wall there was an old brown bureau. My room didn't have a window, but yours had one."

"I thought so."

"Do you remember how we chose whose room was going to get painted first?"

"Spooky! We sent big yellow Spooky the cat up the stairs to decide."

"And the four of us waited at the bottom cheering him on."

"Poor Spooky didn't know what the commotion was all about."

"He stopped near the top step, turned around, looking bewildered, as if he'd never seen us before, then sat down."

"And he wouldn't go any farther until we stopped making so much noise. I remember how Mum laughed. She didn't usually laugh so naturally."

"You won. He always went into your room anyway. I wonder whose idea that was."

"I'm sorry. I guess you were too little to object."

"You wanted the whole room painted red. I don't remember from back then, but Dad kept reminding us. He thought that was pretty funny. A red bedroom."

"Do you remember anything else about my room?"

"You had a big bed. And there was a little wooden rocking chair that Grandpa gave you. I think he made it himself, as a Christmas present. It sat in one corner."

"Oh? I don't remember it at all."

"Well, the time's getting on and I'd better head back to Montreal to catch my flight home. It wouldn't do to miss it. I want to spend some time with the kids before they're back to school tomorrow. Take care, Isabelle. I hope things work out for you."

I'm feeling a little lost, or shut down, stifled like a wheel that has left the paved surface and is running through sand. Perhaps the whole mess is a product of my imagination. It has gathered weight like the sand accumulating on the spokes of the wheel, convoluted, whirling. Anna seems so normal, busy with her work and her young family. Mother seems so ordinary and sweet. So does Dad when they remember him. He is, or was. They all are. It makes me doubt my sanity.

Thursday, May 8, 1997.

Vincent telephoned at noon.

"Hello, Isabelle. How have you been?"

"Just fine, Vincent. What have you been up to?"

"I've been real busy lately. I don't remember the last time I called. When was it?"

"Must have been mid-April."

"That long ago? There's been one project after another, a new one everyday."

"Have you spent any more time by yourself?"

"No. I'm okay now. I don't need to."

"Vincent, you're playing games with me."

"What do you mean I'm playing games?"

"You tell me you want to relax and slow down but you don't do it. You had a good start, but I guess you had nothing else to do at the time."

"Isabelle, we should talk once a week."

"Perhaps."

"At least once, maybe twice a week. What do you think?"

"I don't believe that will ever happen."

"No? Like I've been telling you, I won't have as many responsibilities at work pretty soon and I'll be able to see you more often."

"You're here and you're not here."

"Isabelle, we'll have to talk later, there's a client waiting and I have to go. I'll call you soon. Bye."

"Bye, Vincent."

That was interesting. I didn't feel a tug when I heard his voice at the other end of the line. No intimate tug. Perfect. Part of me would like to believe that the erotic passion was more than just an adventure to him or a good drag on a pipe. It does hurt to think it was so shallow with no more substance than a mirage, quick and fluid. I'd like to hear him say that he really did care for me, but I have a feeling he'll disappear now that he didn't like what I said.

Friday, May 9, 1997.

I drove to LaViolette this morning to mail a thank-you letter to a local farmer who had donated several cans of maple syrup to the Rotary Club for a drawing. On the way home to Wakeham, pictures of my old bedroom began to form in my mindspace. I caught myself before I blanked the images out altogether, old habits die hard, thought for a brief second about what was to happen, then said to myself, *Okay. Come. It's all right. I'll look this time.*

Father is standing in white underwear and holding my head against him while I sit on the edge of a big bed. He's quiet and doing things, showing me things, rubbing my stomach, my throat, my mouth with slinky fingers. He's getting mad and holding my face harder against him. I'm scared. It's hurts. I gag and spit and cough. He tells me never to tell anyone. It's our secret.

Is this real or am I imagining?

I shake my head and blink. Pictures re-emerge. He gets into bed behind me. Fingers crawl on me, touch my stomach. I cry without making any noise. I'm scared. I hate this. I want him to die. The thing spills on me. I feel sick.

Sunday, May 12, 1997.

Yesterday, I didn't write. It was a Rotary day. The Foundation Walk for our district was in Montreal this year. We walked six miles around the streets of downtown and through the old quarter of the city. I met new people and saw old friends. They come from various towns and cities of Quebec, Ontario, and New York and any get-together is always an occasion. We introduce ourselves as if long lost acquaintances, then keep on talking until an interruption imposes. It's so different from living in a small closed community where talk reverberates as if in a glass bowl.

Four of us walked together along Saint Catherine Street. It was a perfect day to be walking, sunny and neither hot nor cold, the flirtatious atmosphere of Montreal bursting with dust and lust. Several street artists and musicians were plying their trade on the sidewalk between University Avenue and Mansfield. A troupe of chalk-faced mime artists in black and white chequered body suits turned and twisted their lithe forms in dramatic renditions of Happy and Sad. A little farther along, a young dark-haired fellow was playing a violin and started into a lively polka tune. The District Governor gave me a nod, spread his arms out wide in the air asking me to join him, and started to dance a few steps. I flowed into his outstretched invitation and we twirled to the melody of several bars of alpine music in the midst of the Saturday afternoon crowd along Saint Catherine Street! What fun!

Tuesday, May 13, 1997.

Very tired. I dozed a little after the birds' noisy waking hour but my head was elsewhere the rest of the morning. I lay down for an hour and a half when I returned from an afternoon appointment with Léo. I didn't sleep, but I rested. I ventured a precious topic with him today. I was unsure how to present it.

"Léo, have you heard of Plato's daimon?"

"I'm not familiar with the term. How do you spell it?"

"D-a-i-m-o-n."

"Doesn't ring a bell. What does it mean?"

"It's a Greek word that means the genius or the genie, the soul-spirit, the breath-soul, the animal spirit, destiny, or fate. Goethe called the daimon 'the power of nature'. James Hillman has brought it into a modern context."

"James Hillman?"

"He's an American psychologist. He lectures internationally and has written twenty-some books."

"Do you know what branch of psychology he follows?"

"He's a Jungian analyst."

"I'm not aware of him. If he's not dead yet, he's probably not included in current study curricula."

"Too bad. You ought to read what he says. He's like an ancient voice chatting casually about life today. He could be Plato's reincarnation."

"So what does Plato have to do with 'daimon'?"

"He tells the Myth of Er in the final chapter of *The Republic*. It's a story of how each of our souls is given a unique daimon before it incarnates and each has chosen a fate that we will live through on Earth. However, when we come into this world the memory of the agreement that took place in that other dimension is forgotten and we believe that we arrive into our earthly environment with nothing. But the daimon, our soul-companion, remembers

251

what is in our character and awaits the experiences that will activate the soul's mission. So, during our lifetime, it guides and prods us along towards our destiny."

Léo didn't seem interested in pursuing the topic so I let it be. It's a habit—tossing out a barometre to measure the static in the air, testing to see how open someone's thinking is, testing for acceptance or rejection. There's a part of me that Léo doesn't know. It's the real me, the most important part of me now, the part I shelter from criticism as if it was a flower too delicate to be exposed to harsh weather. If I told Léo how I live daily with my angel, how she inspires me, how she leads me, protects me, talks through me, writes through me I'm not sure how he would react. I fear Léo has been indoctrinated with the leveling influence of statistical rationales that makes the norm into the Good and the Right, that makes mediocrity a god, the docile average the ideal to strive for. It makes the unusual that is above and outside the norm into deviance and sickness. Communicating with an invisible angel borders on insanity according to current psychological belief where all behaviour is based on heredity and environment. There's no room for daimons or angels or souls or mythology, the essential mystery, the great indefinable that operates in our lives.

Wednesday, May 14, 1997.

This afternoon I went for a long drive to feel the sunshine and just let my thoughts go wherever they pleased. I guess they'll settle somewhere when they're ready.

Thursday, May 15, 1997.

My eyes didn't want to open this morning, narrow crescent moons, stymied banana republics, and, once open, they stare stupidly like the rigid eyes of a statue. I didn't sleep any night again this week until after the birds were awake and chirping in loud refrains. Last night, I listened to music and did aerobic dancing until two in the morning, hoping I'd be tired enough to sleep, but it didn't work. I cried in the middle of the night, long hiccupy sobs. I wanted someone to love. I didn't want to be alone any more. I talked to God.

"Hello God. It's me again, Isabelle. How are You tonight? I'm having a hard time right now. I'm sorry to be running to You with problems but I know it won't always be like this. Would You please help me to understand whatever it is you're trying to tell me by keeping me from sleeping? If you're trying to show me that I don't want to be alone any more, it's working. I do want to be with someone, to share my days with someone. I can see a peace there now. Before I couldn't see myself being able to write and think to myself, as I like to do, if someone else was around, but something is missing when I'm alone. I can feel the beautiful raptures of being in that timeless dimension of pure creation; I can cry out of sheer wonder at the marvels of the universe; I know the happy delights of ecstasy; but I would like to share all of these things with someone who loves me. I've searched for love all my life, God. It doesn't make any sense that I shouldn't find someone who will love me, or that I shouldn't be able to give this love inside me to someone else. Does it?

"I'll wait for your answer, God. Perhaps that's not what's keeping me awake at all. I don't want to be a nuisance and I know I can be pretty tiresome always trying to figure out what You're doing, so, thanks for listening. Goodnight, God."

Friday, May 16, 1997.

I'm at loose ends today, floundering without an anchor, as impressionable as cookie dough. My head isn't alert enough to deal with financial statements and is too dull to work on my story. I wonder if I'm really supposed to write this story. It seems so trite today. Who would want to read that old stuff? Maybe the wandering and doubting has something to do with the fatigue. I wish I could sleep. I'd be okay if I could get some good natural sleep. At least I got some exercise today cutting the grass at the front of the house and raking more twigs and dead foliage off the back lawn. I called Claire, to ask her if she felt like going to see a movie at a theatre. She can't today. She's getting ready for a garage sale tomorrow at her house, so perhaps we'll go to the theatre at the beginning of next week. I'll drive over to her place at nine in the morning to help her out for a while. A book I had ordered arrived in the mail today, *The Web of Life,* by Fritjof Capra. Guess I'll sit and have a look at it.

Saturday, May 17, 1997.

It was sunny, cold, and windy this morning for Claire's garage sale but that didn't stop a crowd from arriving before eight o'clock to be the first to pick through the loot and find the best buys. I worked outside this afternoon ripping out noisy weeds and turning over by shovelful the moist ground, smelling dark and rich and sensual, in the flowerbeds. George cut the rest of the grass with his tractor lawnmower while I was at Claire's. The apple and cherry blossoms will soon be in full bloom and the tall willows are beginning their Rastafarian hairstyle, long greenish-yellow dreadlocks, their branches as yet only delicately furnished so that the dark filigree of the bark shows through the fresh spring colour. It really is a beautiful spot.

Monday, May 19, 1997.

I soaked in the bath for three quarters of an hour last evening, the pads of my fingers and toes like soft soap when I emerged. That seems to help my back. It's sore after working outside in the damp earth as if the dampness had traveled through my hands, up my arms, around to the back of my neck, and down my spine. I turned the light out around ten because the yawns forced my eyes closed and I couldn't see what I was reading, but I still couldn't fall asleep. The birds started calling to each other an hour before dawn; I listened to them, then slept for a few hours until Toulouse meowed at me. It was early for him. He usually waits until I get up but his water dish was empty.

Tuesday, May 20, 1997.

This thing of not sleeping is wearing me out. What is it, Winona? I'm holding something back and I don't know what it is. Can you tell me? I asked God but I still don't know. I'm tired at night when I go to bed. I roll and stretch and twist trying to find the most comfortable place, sit up to blow my nose, pound the pillow, subside back down under the covers, change positions, wonder if I should turn the light on and read a while, but end up just lying there trying to relax. Then I can't try any more. And I start to get mad. That finishes any idea of falling asleep for that night, if there was any thought of it in the first place. I'll see Léo this afternoon. Perhaps he can help.

Wednesday, May 21, 1997.

You know how the birds raise such a ruckus in the pre-dawn, Winona? I guess you do. But anyway, it starts with cheery warbles from the robins, then the sparrows chime in with long sweet whistles that speed up to a trill, the mourning doves add a slow *Oh-woe-woe-woe*, but then the crows arrive with their high-pitched nasal *caw-caw*-caw, and the owls and pigeons join in with a whole series of deep *hoo* notes that ends in a loud scream! Over and over again! As if they had been given an assignment to wake up the world! Well, I didn't hear their noisy ritual this morning. I must have fallen off to sleep in the middle of the night. That's not so bad. If I were alert and rested I'd want to work with my story. It's cool and cloudy again today, not tempting me to putter around outside–a perfect day to do book work and to organize the mess of papers on my desk and the kitchen table.

Thursday, May 22, 1997.

"All right, Isabelle, here's what we're going to do." Good ol' Dr. Gregory. He's been my doctor for the past twenty years and has always been there for me. I was so fed up yesterday I called the medical center and asked his secretary for an appointment to see him today. I walked across the street to the hospital at two o'clock this afternoon. "I'm going to be a dynamic psychotherapist for you. Come to see me again in two weeks and tell me whatever you want to, whatever is on your mind. I'll listen as an outsider and tell you what I think you should do. Your body sends you messages. Physical symptoms bring attention to a part of yourself that wants to be recognized. All forms of illness, even not sleeping, demand something new from you. The challenge is to find what it wants. Here's a prescription for some Ativan. It's a muscle relaxer and should help you for now to get some sleep. I don't think there's anything physical that's keeping you awake. I think once you put everything behind you, you'll sleep."

And I did sleep last night, straight through from nine-thirty to eight-thirty this morning. I slept, but I don't feel the creative alertness that comes with natural sleep. It's the difference between swimming in a deep clear lake and a milky green pond–you don't jump in the pond unless your wallet falls in, but you swim in the lake for the pleasure it brings. It's another day to work at cleaning up papers.

Friday, May 23, 1997.

I worked on government reports this morning and drove into the village at noon to mail the six letters I had prepared. It was a beautiful day. Early this morning, the bright sun on the back yard made the lawn sparkle like green sugar crystals on shortbread cookies. I'm anxious to plant flowers but it's still too cold. This afternoon, I gassed up the lawnmower, cut the lawn at the front and sides of the house then went for my usual drive around by the rivers.

The fragrance of rose water perfumed the air. I put my head back, closed my eyes, and cried for my little girl and myself. The ethereal music of James Galway's flute played softly in the background. My head leant against the high back of the bathtub and my arms floated on the warm scented bath water. Winona put her arm around me. I looked into my mindspace and saw my head resting on Winona's soft breast, her head leaning down on mine. I spoke to her, *I'd like to put my arm around little me, I'd like to hold me when I was three or four and the horror was happening.* So I did. I put my arm around little me and hugged. *You poor dear child. You must have been so afraid, so full of hate, and so wanting to die. How did you manage to ignore what was happening? At least you didn't take it. You fought. You hollered as loud as you could but I couldn't hear for the longest time. I didn't know how to listen.*

Tuesday, May 27, 1997.

I'm sitting on the back steps in this glorious sunshine listening to the melodic vignettes of a sonata in A by Gabriel Fauré. Light and resonant sounds wander through the open window like wood-nymphs in a sultry summer forest. Romantic and magical notes paint sketches of the quest for love and completion, the heightened responses of just being. I feel guilty that I can sit here and luxuriate in the magnificence of life right here in my backyard, guilty that perhaps I should be working at accounting in an office somewhere, making money. But it's so peaceful right here there's no place I'd rather be.

I called Mother at one o'clock this afternoon: "Would you like to go for a drive to see the apple blossoms?"

"Oh, I'd love to. But I'll miss cards if I go out."

"It's up to you."

"Okay, I guess it would be a good idea to get some fresh air."

"I think so."

"What time do you want to go?"

"I'll pick you up at two o'clock."

We followed the highway that stretches along the top of the hills in the middle of apple country. The blossoms were later this year than other years. The showy sight won't be at its best until next week. After an hour of traveling the familiar country roads, I headed back towards Wakeham. All was quiet, so I thought I'd start a conversation.

"Do you remember how old I was when I went to the hospital to have those two molar teeth pulled out?"

"You went to the hospital to have your teeth pulled? What hospital?"

"The hospital in Cornwall. We were living in Bruce Crossing at the time. I remember lying on a thin white pad on a high steel table and somebody covered my face with a gas mask."

"Oh?"

"I can still sniff that mocking ether. When I woke, my mouth was filled with loose plump slippery flesh that I touched with the tip of my tongue and tasted horror. It reeked of raw chopped meat and root rot. After that I used to be sick whenever we went for a drive and Dad stopped at a gas station to fill up."

"I remember you getting sick in the car, but I don't remember your teeth being pulled out." *I'll not go any further. That's far enough. She doesn't need to know what I know.* "I was in that hospital myself a long time ago. It was for a hysterectomy after one of you girls was born."

"It must have been after Anna was born. How long after she was born?"

"Oh, I don't remember, not long after. Then when I got home I had to keep my feet up because I had phlebitis in my legs."

"How long did they keep you in the hospital then for a hysterectomy?"

"Probably about three weeks. They don't keep you long now."

We had arrived in Elmo Station, ten miles from Wakeham, so the topic came to halt while Mother looked around at the buildings she recognized from earlier times. Once out of the village and on the highway home, Mother changed the conversation and immediately the air was charged with tension.

"You should have a nine to five job with your wonderful education. You could make lots of money."

"Mother, we've been through that."

"Well, maybe when the Residence is sold you'll get some money."

"I won't get anything from the sale. The town will get any taxes owing and the Caisse will take its mortgage. The building won't sell for much more than the value of the loan without a business operating inside. If there is anything left it will go to the real estate agent or the Caisse, whoever sells it."

"I thought once you bought something it was yours."

"What? Well, it is, but Agnes took the business away. It was worth forty-five thousand, and it's gone."

"Well, I hope you'll get something when the Manoir is sold."

"No, nothing."

"Gad! So you should get a job."

"I don't want to work in an office handling paperwork. I've tried and I can't. The brain concussion affected me and won't let me work on numbers more than two or three hours at a time. I can't concentrate any longer than that on book work. The figures won't stay in my head and I start to get a headache."

"Well, what can you do?"

"I can write. I always wanted to write but I had trouble to express myself. I was sick inside." I hesitated then threw it out to get rid of the words as quickly as possible: "Dad abused me when I was little."

"He did not!"

"He came to my bedroom in the middle of the night. It must have started when you were in the hospital. I blanked it out, didn't remember at all until just lately, but it all falls together now."

"That's just your make-up. You live in another world sometimes."

"I must have been confused and scared but I couldn't go to you. I didn't know what I was cursed with. I thought I was inflicted with some kind of mental disability that confused things. Didn't you ever wonder why he went on binges?"

"Work was too much for him. He was too old to take on a new job at sixty."

"How blind can you be? You always protected him, tried to hide him if was drinking! You behaved as if you didn't know."

"You're not going to put that in your book for everyone to read, are you?"

"It has to be there."

"Well, you sure know how to hurt someone."

I was glad we had arrived back at the nursing home. I helped Mother from the car into her wheelchair and pushed it through the automatic doors into the building, over to the elevator to take us to the second floor, and back to her room. She sighed, "I might as well die now. There's no reason to live. I hope my next breath is my last."

I didn't reply. Mother hadn't looked at me once. I had glanced over at her several times as I was driving and talking, but she stared straight ahead out the car windshield, as if stunned by words that didn't make any sense to her, that couldn't possibly be real. I took her sweater off and hung it in the closet on the right hanger and in the right order.

"Isabelle, what's the name of that place where we ate one time after the doctor's appointment?"

"Salaberry Chicken?"

"No, the other one."

"Zellers?"

"Yes, that one. Do you think if I cut a piece off the grey slacks that I can't wear and take the swatch with me, I could find another pair of slacks to match? The grey jacket is still as good as new."

"Probably. What are you going to do now?"

"What time is it?"

"It's twenty minutes past three. Do you want to lie down?"

"No, I'll sit and read until supper."

"Okay. I'll be here at eight in the morning on Friday for your doctor's appointment."

"I'm sorry if I hurt you."

"I think we spent a lot of time hurting each other."

Every night in my bath now, I put my head back and close my eyes. Soon little me appears. I put my arm around her and give her a hug, hold her close to me. *It's okay now. You're okay and I'm okay too. You poor little sweetheart, I love you. Can we be friends now?*

Friday, May 30, 1997.

I brought Mother to her doctor's appointment at the regional hospital in Salaberry-de-Valleyfield this morning. Afterwards, we toured the stores in the shopping mall and she found some new clothes that she liked. Mother was in a pink mood and chatted away in a sweet and light voice. "Oh, there's bathing suits. Look at all the colours. Summer must be on its way for sure. Do you want a bathing suit? I'll buy you a bathing suit."

"No thanks, really, Mum, I don't need one."

"Oh, and look at all the plants! I've never seen so many blooms. How lovely! Do you want some more flowers to plant?"

"Thanks again, but I still have some that I haven't put in the ground yet."

"Well, I'm ready to go home now. If we leave soon I'll get in on the tail end of lunch."

As we were driving, Mother's comments cantered freely. I just listened, not wanting to get into another confrontation.

"Oh my, aren't those trees beautiful? I wish I could paint them but these old hands aren't good for anything anymore. … We had the most wonderful times when Dad took us camping, didn't we? Eating outside around a picnic table. Washing our faces with cold water first thing in the morning. A campfire under the stars every night, at least, when it didn't rain. We each had a book and we used to read by the Coleman gaslight until we were too sleepy to keep our eyes open. My, those were good times. You always helped Dad put up the tent."

A truck whooshed by us going over the speed limit.

"Oh, that bad truck! Well, I hope he gets what he deserves."

The Reaper had just reprinted an article from its archives, where I had gone out west with a delegation from the village on a twinning project. I was nineteen. Mother had read the newspaper yesterday and reminded me of the event. "Just imagine. It was thirty years ago when you and the French girl went out to Winnipeg. What a wonderful experience it must have been for you. Your first airplane trip."

"Yes, it was. I was the youngest of the group and I really enjoyed it."

A feeling that I didn't like had been gradually creeping into me as a vine will encroach on the less robust specimens in a flower box until it has the entire space to itself. A disquieting sense of uneasiness clambered on top of the good times making the memories shimmer and tremble in an unsteady light, the faint brilliance taking on a shadowy dimension of heavier proportions. Mother had been badly hurt too, years ago. Her first two babies died, her two sons. Jimmy and Johnny. I found photographs of them in the drawer of the old secretary desk that I used to play in and asked who they were. Mother told me, in a quiet way, that they were my brothers and they had died when they were little—one at birth, the other at six months. She'd carried each boy the full nine months, had buried two babies and grieved twice before I came along. The sun was in my eyes and I squinted from too much glare and pain buzzing like an electric fence to keep the cows in the field. After the deaths, control became a watchword, control of tears, of traitorous emotions, of smiles, of laughter, control freezing a stiffness into her lips and chin, wary, remorseful, and plaintive. The baby boys were buried in the United Church cemetery in Bruce Crossing. Two little flat stones inscribed with their names, one for each, marked the small graves. Jimmy and Johnny. I used to repeat the names to myself. They were my brothers. I wondered what they would be like. I loved them. I imagined how they would look after me and I, them. I didn't know what Mother's thoughts were. She never mentioned it again, as if the matter had been forgotten, or, more likely, if the deaths weren't spoken about they were out of harm's way. But rumbling somewhere deep down, there had to be a disturbance, a necessity demanding to be heard, keeping the ache alive. There's no other way. It's a law of life. Part of Mother must have been buried with her two baby boys, that part not accounted for, forever accumulating its due and awaiting its rightful recognition. When Dad took me away from her she must have buried another part. No wonder she protected Anna. And what remained of herself.

June

"Forgiveness means that you do not carry the
baggage of an experience. ... When you forgive
you release critical judgment of yourself as
well as of others. You lighten up. ... If one
person grieves at his or her experiences while
another is able to laugh, who is the lighter?
Which is harmless? The heart that dances is the
innocent heart. The one that cannot laugh is
burdened. It is the dancing heart that is harmless."

Gary Zukav,
The Seat of the Soul

Sunday, June 1, 1997.

"Hi Mom, it's me."

It's Alex! Whenever I hear that quiet soft greeting, my heart somersaults
into the telephone, jumps into a headstand, and, still springing and leaping,
it goes into a whole series of revolving acrobatics. Then it races at top speed
to the other end of the line and puts its arms around him in a big hearty
squeeze.

The blur in my head isn't quite so dense this morning. I slept a little better
last night, dreaming and waking, waking and dreaming, and didn't get out of
bed until nine-thirty. Snippets of a dream, one from a few years ago, like
insistent flashbacks, have been scurrying through my mindspace since early
morning. ... I found the dream in my notebook. It was the 9th of November,
1994. I didn't understand it at the time, but it makes more sense now.

It was deep winter. Mum, Dad, Anna, and myself had gone away for a
week long holiday. Dad drove the car into a large vacant parking lot. High
snowbanks were piled around the edges of the lot turning the space into a
huge white outdoor arena. Dad parked the car at an angle, the front end facing
the tall mounds of snow, taking two spaces instead of one. It hadn't been
snowing in the dream, but the car, a brown sedan, was covered with snow, as
was everything else in this bleached wilderness. I got out and started to clear
it away with a long-handled brush. As I was cleaning, the car and the snow
grew bigger and bigger, inflating like a rubber whale. Soon, what had been
a few inches of the white stuff was transformed into a few feet and I couldn't
reach high enough or far enough. Anna got out of the car to see what was

happening. The dream ended.

Snow whitens, camouflages, covers the rough places.

There was another dream two nights after the snow dream. It was short and unspectacular, just one banal scene in a large residence, like a reception center. I thought it was a seniors' complex because that's what I was working on at the time. But the place was deserted. There wasn't a soul around. The high-ceilinged central lobby was vast with yellowed painted walls as if time had been the factor in choosing the colour, similar to the LaViolette Manoir, and the floors were littered with children's toys–dolls, trucks, fire engines, colouring books, wagons, craft tables–but no children were there to play with them.

Perhaps all the dreams about young people were trying to bring attention to my own childhood. I thought I was supposed to build a Youth Center, but maybe the children in the dreams wanted me to look at my own little girl who was hurting just like the ones I was dreaming about.

Monday, June 2, 1997.

Do you sleep, Winona? I mean, where you are, do you need to sleep? Sometimes I try to fool myself into falling asleep. I got up twice in the middle of last night and walked around the house for a while, trying to mimic the usual routine of feeling tired, yawning, stretching, going to bed, and sleeping. It didn't work. At four in the morning, the birds began their chorusing in anticipation of the new day and, soon, the angular light of dawn had intruded on the still dark of the night and the room was filled with changing shadows. I watched the light forms play for an hour then went downstairs to make a pot of coffee.

The telephone rang at nine-thirty this morning. It was Charles, the treasurer, reminding me to bring the special fine money I had collected for him at some earlier Rotary meetings. It was a perfect sunny day, the kind one could write a song about if you didn't live in the country where, at the beginning of every June, the blackflies will eat you alive if they find a patch of exposed flesh. It happens every year when it's time to plant flowers–a sunny day in spring beckons you outside to feel the warmth of the afternoon, compelling you to sink your hands into the soft cool earth and wiggle your fingers in the rich compassionate dampness, the little beasties hovering about, just waiting for you to arrive with your undefiled flesh. They made a meal of me for several hours this afternoon, several hours of slapping, whirling a garden spade in the air, spitting and spluttering to send them away from my nose and mouth, and rubbing the bugs out of my eyes and dirt into them. At five thirty, I went inside to organize myself for the Rotary supper. I tried to camouflage the dozens of tiny red welts on my face and ears with concealer make-up, but the result looked like a bad paste-up job. I washed it all off, applied a little beige coloured cream to soften the blotches, and left for LaViolette, letting the fly bites testify to an early June afternoon spent in the outdoors.

Wednesday, June 4, 1997.

I'm not writing much these days. I don't have the spark that makes me get what I'm feeling down on paper, the muse that streamlines the thinking words into the written words is taking a holiday. Yesterday, I was happy to just dig in the earth, pull weeds, and clean the flowerbeds. Sometimes the simple things are the most fulfilling. I planted deep blue pansies in the afternoon, a wonderful velvety colour.

Jean-François and Louis arrived for a visit last night. They're rolling once more and are full of young enthusiasm for their project. And now, a group from the municipal regional counties is serious about wanting the building to use as a central to house their own offices and the local government-funded organizations. I showed a group of nine people through the Manoir last Saturday morning. Some kids, probably a teenaged gang, have ransacked all four levels of the structure, writing on the walls, upending whatever could be upended, throwing papers and junk into the center of the floors, dropping soda cans and smashing the middle with their feet into thwarted boats. A dirty mess, is an apt description of the godforsaken building. Once over the initial shock of the destruction—they gave a group shake of their heads in amazement and disgust—the strong lines are still there, underneath the damaged exterior. The paint has begun peeling off the walls and ceilings. It hangs in curvaceous strips that eventually fall to the floor in a puddle of cracked chips. You have to look hard to see past the bad to the good, very hard indeed, but it is there.

Thursday, June 5, 1997.

Soiled and pampered. I sat in the bath last night for forty minutes. My back was tired and my muscles were stiff from sitting on the grass and pulling weeds. This morning, I cleaned two more flowerbeds and added fresh earth so they would be ready for planting. There are snapdragon and dahlia blossoms in the back yard now. I set them out this afternoon. Then, in the early evening, when it wasn't so hot, I cut the grass in front of the house. Afterwards, I went to the nursing home. Mother wanted her bureau drawers and closet rearranged from winter to summer.

One would think I should sleep, but no, it doesn't happen. Last night my body was tired, like it is tonight, and relaxed from the warm bath. My mind was empty. There was no chatter ricocheting about in my head and having a conversation with itself. I was comfortable lying in bed holding onto my pillow, free from worry and at peace with myself. I listened to the birds singing happily to each other in the half-light of dawn–they calm down to a reasonable level of sound after the early blast has achieved its effect. The air in the room was cool from the fresh night breeze as I had left all the windows open so the heat of the day could escape. I really don't understand why I can't fall asleep. Léo thinks I'm still keeping some anger inside.

"Isabelle, do you think you can talk to the anger?"

"I guess I could try."

"It has something to say."

"If it's angry I'm not sure I want to hear it."

"Just trying to replace uncomfortable feelings with beautiful music and paintings or just creating a nice space around yourself, does not deal with the outrage. It's still there somewhere in your body."

"I've let go of so much already, I didn't think there was any left. In fact, it's discouraging to think of uprooting another drama. I don't want to even think of it. Anyway, I don't think there is another one."

"Perhaps you're not angry with anyone else anymore."

"Pardon?"

"Perhaps you're angry with yourself."

"Myself?"

"That's why it's so hard for you to see it."

"But I've been feeling so well, so good about coming to an understanding of the past."

"You have been very close to your self lately. No doubt about it, you've opened areas that had been locked for a long time. But now that they're open, perhaps there's still a hurt waiting inside that wants to come out and needs some of your attention."

"It's true, I'm good at burying what hurts."

"And distancing yourself from it."

"Yes."

"By the way, how's Alex these days?"

"He's busy cleaning the campsite, installing the docks along the shoreline, getting everything in order for the season. I talked to him last weekend. Why do you ask?"

"You haven't mentioned him for a while and he seems very precious to you."

"That he is."

"Well, our time's up today. Next time that restlessness strikes, Isabelle, try to listen carefully to what you're feeling."

"I'll try, Léo."

Anger frightens me because it reminds me of the black hole. It accumulates, festers, fumes inside, tightens, torments, and turns into disease and death. It circulates in your system like a killer venom. Anger comes when there's hurt. I don't want to hurt anymore. I'm tired of hurting. I see the violence, the pain and confusion in war and fighting. It's the same hurt, the same pain but on different levels–a country's pain, anger, intolerance, desire to kill, and an individual's pain, my pain, my anger, my want to kill, to die, because I'm hurting inside. It's the anger that kills. Anger is out to get you. I don't want its ugly tentacles inside me and the only one who has the power to send it out of my body is myself.

Friday, June 6, 1997.

I drove to the Town Hall in LaViolette this morning to bring the architectural plans of the Manoir to Rodney. He's part of the new group that is interested in using the Manoir for regional community services. When I got home there were two messages on the answering machine. The first was from the insurance agent asking about renewing the insurance on my house. The second was Mother, saying, "It's Mum. The cheque arrived."

I went over to the nursing home in the evening to find her sitting forward in her big armchair, eyes riveted on the television screen.

"Such a good movie, *The Sound of Music*! I've seen it five times now and it still makes me cry."

"It is good. The Von Trapp children. Liesel, Brigitta, Kurt. The little one is Gretl. I forget the others."

"There were seven. And the Captain. And Maria."

"*How do you hold a moonbeam in your hand?*"

"The Mother Superior sang that. It was lovely. ... So, you got my message. I don't like those machines."

"Yes. You did fine."

"It took the lawyer long enough to get things settled."

"It has been a while since Aunt Emma died."

"More than two years."

"I thought as much."

"This is the last payment, so I decided to split the amount three ways and give each of you girls a third."

"You did?"

"I hope it will help you out of your mess."

Mother motioned to her portable writing desk. It was still sitting in the center of her room where she had been working at it. Papers were scattered in disarray on the top: a long legal document, envelopes, a bank passbook, a chequebook, three signed cheques, and a pen. I picked up a cheque written in her own squiggly letters that was made out to myself for an amount of ten thousand dollars.

"I don't know what to say. ... Thank you. ... It did come at a good time. ... Thank you again. And thank you, Aunt Emma."

"I want you to take my bankbook with you and deposit that cheque of Emma's. And I have a few little jobs for you to do before you leave."

"Okay. What would you like me to do?"

"Take my blue jacket from the back of the closet, will you, and put it on a hanger closer to the front. The girls always mix my clothes up. They're never in the right order."

"All right."

"The plants are needing water. And can you refill my small bottle of hand lotion? I can't manage the big one."

"Sure. I'll start with the plants."

I treaded delicately while completing her small chores as if the sheer weight of my presence could shatter a fragile moment, or a single misplaced word could disintegrate the precious truth of an understanding as rare as a blue gazania into a mere glimpse of tenderness. Then I left for home where I burst into tears, humbled and thankful.

Sunday, June 8, 1997.

I slept at the beginning of the night but woke at two in the morning. I had been dreaming, got out of bed, and came downstairs in my nightgown to eat some ice cream and I pressed a dollop against the roof of my mouth with my tongue, holding it there until it melted, thinking the cold might dull the nature of the dream residue that was swimming in my head. It was the middle of the night. I wanted to go back to sleep. A sticky negativity wiggled and squirmed inside. *Don't bother me! Not tonight! It's too late! I'm sleepy.* I took another spoonful of ice cream remembering what I told Léo, that I would listen the next time the disturbance made itself known. So I put away the ice cream, sat down in a chair by the kitchen table, closed my eyes, became very quiet, and emptied my mind of all thoughts, left a blank space. I didn't push the feeling away, I let it come into that blank space and I started to look at it with my inner eye, looking and feeling at the same time. Not wondering. I didn't want any wondering and speculating thoughts to interfere. I wanted to keep a neutral territory where anything could happen, unbidden by myself.

The first thing I felt was resistance. I felt a little longer and recognized avoidance, the avoidance of something unpleasant. *Okay,* I thought. *This could be unpleasant for you too.* It was knotted and unhappy like a tangled skein of knitting yarn, but I knew I was feeling the emotions of a person not a thing. Far in the distance and slightly out of focus, an image started to form. Any second I expected to see a fallen priest extending his arms out to me, or death's handmaiden slowly approaching, or seven grandmothers pointing and waving their fingers. Something had been unbridled but was still hesitant, gathering life force, garnering form, preparing to act and to elicit response but not certain of where the danger lay. As it came closer, it was moving. It was alive, right now, tonight. It wasn't coming from the land of the dead, it wasn't an incriminating grandmother, or a moralizing priest, or a death scout. It was a bundle of distraught emotions that had begun to kick. It flared up and died down like a candle flame in a drafty room. Closer now and clearer, like a photographic lens being adjusted, little legs trashed about and small arms punched the air as if throwing off a heavy blanket. It was a baby. Perhaps... Dear God. Perhaps... It was my baby! My very own. And I heard a sound, a tiny wail, like a lament in the wind, a baby's cry. My baby. My baby was crying. To me! Calling out to me! Oh, God. After all this time. *Alex! Dear sweet Alex. Can you ever forgive me?*

Monday, June 9, 1997.

My mind was clear when I went to bed last night, the wakefulness wasn't agitated. Nothing was batting itself around and keeping me awake. I breathed deeply letting the lightness of the air flow down into my lungs then into the rest of my body. My breathing became slower and soon I didn't notice it. Instead, I felt the beginning of that delicious swirl that used to let me fall gently headfirst into deep sleep as if the foot of the bed had been tilted upwards and I was slipping off the end into oblivion, a limp sack. *How wonderful! It's going to happen tonight! I'm going to be asleep in ten seconds! I can hardly wait!* But as soon as the spiral began to carry me downwards and backwards into that long tunnel, something halted its slide at the last minute. The descent went only so far then stopped, so that I couldn't enter that luxurious deep space of sleep.

There's a Rotary meeting tonight and I have some planning to do this afternoon in preparation for it. Also, I'm going to call Alex today.

Thursday, June 12, 1997.

I'll see Léo this afternoon. I'm so tired I don't feel like going. It will be hot in the car.

6:00 P.M.

Léo was waiting for me when I arrived at his office at three o'clock.

"Léo, I think this is the last hurt."

"Perhaps it waited so long because it was the deepest pain of all."

"I hurt Alex."

"I think, Isabelle, that you never allowed yourself to believe that you had

267

been wounded."

"I don't know. All I know is that it hurts."

"You kept a festering sore inside for years and years."

"I couldn't look after him."

"Maybe you were afraid to be a mother."

"And I'm disgusted with myself."

"You didn't want to be like your own but you didn't know how else to be."

I nodded my head while my face twitched with emotion.

"Didn't you know any other mothers your own age?"

"No. ... I-I was alone, a newcomer in Ottawa."

"What about the people at work?"

"None of them knew me so I put on an image that I was completely in control of my life, that it was perfectly all right if my child wasn't with me, and that I was perfectly all right as well."

"Did you have anyone you could talk to?"

"I had a lot of friends, but I didn't let anyone close enough to have a real friend."

"There was no one in your family?"

"No."

"No old friends you could call?"

"No one I felt comfortable enough with. I'm so angry at myself I don't know if I'll ever get over it."

"Tell me how it happened."

"It's a long story."

"I'll listen."

"What hurt at first was having to take Alex to a babysitter while I worked. Dora lived in the same apartment building, so it was handy to bring Alex to her in the morning and pick him up every night after work. Some time later, she told me that Alex was biting the furniture and that he cried often for long periods of time, sometimes the entire day. When I questioned her about the other children, she said Alex was the smallest and the others played games with him, treated him as the baby, and made him sit in a basket while they lugged him around. I could tell Alex was disturbed. Sometimes he would hold himself rigid and tremble. Dora tried to tell the others to leave him alone but they wouldn't listen. The older children were supposed to be moving away but no one knew when. I continued to leave Alex with Dora, asking her to watch the other children more carefully. There wasn't anyone else I knew of nearby who would look after him during the day and I couldn't afford a private babysitter. But it hurt me every day to hear him cry when I left him at Dora's apartment.

"Then the daycare at the university began and I brought Alex with me on the city bus. He seemed better but would still cry and cry when I left, and wouldn't play with the others. He kept to himself. I knew he was like me and didn't like a lot of noise and commotion around him. Again, it hurt to leave him there all day where I knew he was unhappy.

"One day I received a phone call telling me Alex was sick and I left work to take him home. I don't remember if I called Callah or if she happened to call me, but she said she would rather look after him at the farm during the week than see him in a daycare. I felt better knowing that he would have peace and quiet and attention. I knew Callah was eccentric but she was open, talked easily, and would spend a lot of time with him.

"Then I was hurt because Alex wasn't with me, but I thought it hurt him too much to stay with me. After a while, I didn't like going out to the farm to see him on weekends because I wasn't his mother any more. My comments about raising him weren't welcome. I felt like an intruder, a guest. He would run and climb on Callah's knee instead of mine. When I had to leave, he would cry and hold onto me, and it hurt so much that I tried to be the brave one, to not let myself feel anything. I always left with a big smile, 'It's okay, Alex. I'll see you next weekend. It's okay.'

"That's when I started to wear a veil over myself. I couldn't spend time with something so painful and something that I had no power to change. I busied myself with the union debate, with Ariff's radio program, with the Staff Association, with men. I had more men friends than I did women. The radio shows were taped on the weekends and often I would miss going out to the farm. I forget when it started, but Callah's husband, my ex father-in-law, started making advances, pushing me in the corner, touching me, so I hated even more going out to the farm. ... Dear God, I was trapped wasn't I?"

"Do you think you did to your son what was done to you by your parents?"

I swallowed a lump of air that felt like a basketball. "It looks that way."

There's more. There is. It does look that way, but there's more to it than that, much more, said Winona. I know the tone of her thoughts now.

Friday, June 13, 1997.

I looked at the clock at three in the morning and let myself sink back into the mattress. I felt good this morning, relieved. That ever so sensitive spot that had been denied acknowledgment for decades had been recognized. I had abandoned my son, my baby, my child when he was so young. I could never use that word 'abandoned' but that's what happened. It was a tender touchy spot that I had protected, banished away into a lonely corner, and could never think about in any depth because it was too painful, too stressing to even

269

consider giving it a stage on which to walk and talk. I couldn't have lived with myself if I put words to what I had done to him. Words made it real. They would have made me admit that I had left him, rejected him, his own mother.

Outside, a cleansing life-giving rain, a needed rainstorm after a hot dry spell, parallels the cleansing I feel inside myself.

Saturday, June 14, 1997.

I've gained a little weight. There was a prize ceremony at the high school in LaViolette last evening and I went to present three scholarships on behalf of the Rotary Club. I feel stuffed into my dress suit that feels a few sizes too small.

Yesterday's rain cooled the air. A few wispy and faraway clouds are floating near the sun in an otherwise clear blue sky. It's sunny and beautiful again, but not so stiflingly hot.

Monday, June 16, 1997.

Twenty-five members came out to the Rotary meeting tonight. I had called an executive meeting before the regular supper meeting because there were financial matters to wrap up before the year-end. Last fall, I remember finding a double meeting difficult. Too many details had to be processed quickly one after the other during three hours, and the blow to my head had jiggled my brains. They objected with headaches if I forced them. But that's gone now. There's only one meeting left in my term as president, on June 30th.

I hope I can calm down enough to sleep tonight, because tomorrow I'm going to Willow River to see Alex.

Thursday, June 19, 1997.

It's raining today, a nice quiet warm rain. It began in the middle of the night, around two o'clock. The thrumming sound woke me and I got out of bed to check that the windows were closed. Back under the covers, I listened to the steady pitter-patter of the drops on the roof and the windowpanes–a primordial sound that rocks the infinite–then fell asleep. The doorbell chimes made me jump at eight in the morning. It was Farley, an old school friend.

"Mornin', Isabelle. I hope I'm not calling too early."

"That's okay, Farley. It's time I was up anyway."

"Rosemary and I are planning a barbecue back at the farm for my sister's birthday on Saturday."

"For Jolene?"

"Yes indeedy. She's turning fifty and we realized there are quite a few of you still in the area who were in school together and are reaching the big five-O this year."

"Remind me about it. Hard to believe, isn't it? I don't feel like an old person."

"Either do I, and I hit the half-century mark a few years ago. Goes to show you how fast you can change your perspective once you're in the middle of something."

"Flexible, aren't we?"

"I think that's a good thing."

"Ditto. So, you're having a party for us?"

"Nothing fancy. Rosemary is fixing some casserole thingumajigs and I'll cook hamburgers and steaks on the grill."

"How many of us were you able to get in touch with?"

"Around fifteen."

"No kidding? That's super, Farley."

"Do you think you can come?"

"I'd love to, but what time on Saturday?"

"Most are arriving in late afternoon and staying on into the evening. It's nice sitting under the trees at the side of the house."

"For sure it is. You've got a real nice spot there."

"If it turns cool we can move inside, but this morning's rain is just a shower--the heat-wave we've been having is here to stay awhile yet."

"Rotary has planned a Fiddle Contest this weekend at the high school in LaViolette."

"Goldarn it, that's right. I saw the notice in *The Reaper*."

"We're trying to raise funds for service projects. Perhaps I can go to your party during the break between the afternoon and evening competitions."

"You should be able to manage it. The farm is only a fifteen-minute drive from LaViolette."

"Sounds like fun. I haven't seen some of those school chums for thirty-three years."

"That long?"

"Not since we finished grade eleven at old Wakeham H.S."

"I can hear the giggling and the yakkity-yak already."

"Oh, c'mon Farley. Your ears will get so hot trying to hear what we're talking about, we won't know if the smoke's coming from you or the steaks are burning."

"Well, maybe. But I'm still up to playing a few tricks, you know."

"Are you? Who would have thunk that?"

Farley laughed. "You girls had better watch yourselves."

"You'd be in trouble if we welcomed the attention."

"Oh, sure."

"What would you do then? Maybe we like it and you'll have to run with your tail between your legs."

"That'll be the day."

"Okay. We've been warned. … I'll give Rosemary a call to ask if she needs any help."

"I think she's got everything organized, but give her a call anyway."

"I'll do that. Thanks for the invite."

Talk about never a dull moment! A constant stream of people were milling about the farm in Willow River on Tuesday. Alex's half-sister, Denver, and her girlfriend, Amy, are living in the house until Dan and his entourage arrive in two weeks to spend the summer months at the lake. Denver and Amy are both sixteen, both have long blonde silky hair, both are tanned, and both have Barbie doll figures that were well displayed in short shorts and tight jerseys. The Willow River boys were smitten. The telephone rang as soon as the girls were in the house and rang again whenever the receiver was replaced.

A school buddy, Cole, is helping Alex to build a play-gym in the campground, cut wood for bonfires, and keep the grass mowed and the hedges trimmed. He's staying in another bedroom upstairs in the once-grand old farmhouse. Another fellow, Jared, had just separated from his wife and was searching for a new place to settle, so Alex had told him he could stay at the farm until he got things straightened out. He was supposed to be moving in next week. With a little over one hundred lots rented for the summer season, there were usually one or two or three campers in the front yard waiting to request permission to borrow a tool or to report something broken that needed fixing.

"I've got so many demands on me right now, Mom, there's never a moment's peace."

"That's not hard to understand. This place is like Grand Central Station."

"I'd like to have a little time to myself now and then."

"Don't wait for the piece of straw that will break your back."

"True enough. There are other things I'd like to be doing."

"I've never seen such a busy place."

"Nana left this to me, but I don't want to spend my life running a camp and trailer park."

"What would you like to do?"

"I'd really like to teach philosophy to children."

"What a terrific idea! Get an early start on how to develop concepts instead of memorizing facts."

"Right. Like curiosity and questioning."

"And creating."

"And problem solving…"

"Using intuition instead of the so-called historical reality in school textbooks. Putting one and two together to have something meaningful instead of half-baked recitations."

"The technocrats and philistines won't like that very much, but it has to come about somehow."

"How exciting, Alex! I think you have plenty of time to prepare because it will be a while before the schools change their curricula."

"It is becoming better known. There are some private schools that teach understanding before facts."

"I've heard of that."

"Unfortunately, most are still stuck in the old methods, especially the public schools. They're dinosaurs."

"How true. The old ways don't work any more. … I sound like the captain on Star Trek."

"Just look at the drop-outs and suicides and the violence. It's so obvious something has to change, and it can't be a backward change for more draconian and disciplinary measures."

"I agree."

"School is the place to develop a young person, not to alienate him or her."

"Right on, Alex. Everyone has a special talent of some sort. The schools ought to be a place where you can begin to discover yourself, where you can get in touch with those areas that spark your interest."

"Yeah. Instead of shoving in as much information as they can, they should try to draw the individual out of himself, help him to express himself. That's what I would have liked. I hated school."

"I know. The whole system needs an overhaul. Everyone fights over who's responsible and the crisis marches on full speed ahead."

"It excites me so much, Mom, I want to be ready when the change does happen."

"There's such tenderness in you."

"What?"

"Integrity."

"Mom? I've no idea what…."

"That's okay. I was just talking to myself. Do you want to go back to school?"

"It's been on my mind."

"Are you thinking of finishing that philosophy degree you were working on?"

"I am, but, right now, I don't know how I could manage it, money wise."

"I think it will all come together for you, Alex, in its own time. Just keep heading in that direction."

"I will."

"It sounds like it's for you."

"I don't think I could get rid of the idea even if I tried."

"Right there in the back of your mind like a bun ready for the oven, is it?"

"Always."

"I'll help you all I can."

Alex and I went for dinner in the dining room at the Lakesider, just a little farther along Willow Park Road. I told him what was on my mind, how the most painful thing I had to face was abandoning him when he was little.

"I wanted to live with you, Mom."

"Dear God. And I needed you with me."

"I know how it happened that I came to live with Nana and Gramps, but I didn't know I was biting the furniture. ... But it's okay now, Mom. They were good to me. Nana was pretty frustrating because she worried big time, especially as she got older, but I could still love her."

We both had tears in our eyes.

Friday, June 20, 1997.

It was good to see Léo this afternoon. After a little more than a year, it feels like an end to therapy is approaching. The intense heart of the drama seems to have passed. Previously, the sessions were mainly urgent and anguished monologues where Léo sat back, rarely interfering except to offer an encouraging word to keep up the flow, his eyes and ears fixed on me. Now, the tone of our encounters has changed to conversational.

"I'm glad I was able to be there with you, Isabelle, during a very important part of your life."

"It's me who thanks you."

"I understand now why you were always holding onto yourself, hugging yourself, because I look around and I don't see anyone supporting you, holding you up. You're holding yourself up."

"I guess that's the way it's always been." I thought of Winona, thinking how wrong I was to think I had always been alone, how she had always been there for me, even without my knowing it. All I had ever needed to do was realize she was there and ask her to help me.

"I think we can talk about other things now."

"Such as?"

"On-going self-discovery, for instance."

"Interesting."

"What do you think about carrying on with weekly appointments for a while?"

"Sounds a bit much. I don't think I could handle that."

"It's up to you."

"I'd really like to have some time to wind down before starting into something else."

"Take as long as you need. You know where I am."

"Thanks, Léo."

Saturday, June 21, 1997.

Hang Man Reel. Rubber Dolly. The Rotary Fiddle Contest began this morning. *Mocking Bird.* Old feet and young feet are tapping to the music all day long. It's infectious. A lot of work goes into organizing the weekend, but all goes well. A former fiddle champion and his wife are staying at my house tonight. They've gone to bed already and will leave early in the morning to go back to LaViolette to visit with the friends they've met who have a common passion for the violin. I drove over to Farley's farm during our supper break to see my old classmates from school. There was so much catching up to do that two hours wasn't nearly enough, but I had to be back in the gymnasium by seven to record the stepdancers' and fiddlers' performance scores for the evening competition.

Monday, June 23, 1997.

A glorious weekend! I'm so excited! Never would I have thought that it would happen like that. But first things first.

Yesterday, Laurent, one of the Rotarians, introduced me to his brother, Hugo. Towards the end of the afternoon show, Laurent asked me to join Hugo, himself, and his girlfriend for something to eat during the supper break. We went to a deli in town, ordered four specials, and chatted away to each other while we ate, sometimes in English, sometimes in French. Hugo didn't say very much. Laurent did most of the talking. During the remainder of the evening Hugo stayed near the desk where I was working while the last of the finalists performed. Then the time everyone was waiting for–the grand finale. Fifteen fiddlers ran on stage with their instruments. After the first few strains of *Orange-Blossom Special*, the audience was on its feet. The accompanist's hands were rollicking over the piano, chording heavily, whomping the keys to keep up with the chorus of violins. Deafening applause. A flurry of fingers went on a merry escapade up and down the keyboard. *Devil Reel.* The fiddles joined in. Then ten dancers streamed on stage, their feet tapping and clacking. Shouts of '*Hooray!*' came from the crowd. Everyone sat down to watch. Shoes whirled, clicked, clattered, and thumped. Crazier and crazier. All at the same time. It sounded like a freight train had entered the gymnasium. The building rocked. "Encore! Encore!" *Maple Sugar*. The spectators were on their feet again, cheering and hollering. *Big John McNeil*, the tune to end the evening. Another thunderous performance of twenty flying feet rapping and slapping the wooden stage in time with the fifteen fiddlers. Standing ovation. "*Bravo! Bravo!*" Hands waved and clapped in the air. Shrill whistles ricocheted off the cement block walls. It was over until next year. I looked around the room. There were tears on the faces in the audience.

When everyone had left we had to clean up the school and leave it in good order for Monday morning classes. The men took the stage apart, dismantled the sound system, and mounted long ladders to take down the ceiling decorations. I went around the gym collecting the cutout musical notes–they were blue and yellow–so we could use them again next year. Hugo helped me to remove the staples and tape we had used in fastening them to the wall. He is quiet and listens and is very nice. I said things to him I wouldn't ordinarily say to someone I had just met.

"Thank you for helping me with these things."

"Ça me fait plaisir."

"You seem much handier than I am at taking out the staples."

"I'm a carpenter."

"That explains it."

"You must be tired after working all weekend."

"I am."

"It's been two long days for you."

"Right, and I haven't been sleeping lately."

"Oh?"

"No, I don't sleep well."

"Why not?"

"I know it's psychological, but it's passing now. I've gone through a difficult period with a psychotherapist."

Hugo looked at me with a question mark written all over his face.

"My life has been a little out of the ordinary."

"Nothing wrong with that."

"No, but I tried to kill myself a few times."

I wouldn't have said anything like that to just anyone. I must have been testing him, throwing that at him to see how he would react, to see if he would think I was barmy or deranged somehow. I was surprised at myself but he just listened. Later, after the school had been tidied and our equipment removed, he walked with me to my car in the parking lot.

"Isabelle, you can say anything to me. Ce n'est pas plus grave que cela.

It's not any more serious than that."

"You're right. It's not."

"Will I see you again?"

A whirring dynamo whizzed into my thoughts and blurred any reason that may have tried to get past it. I had been telling Léo and myself that I wanted a little quiet time now to live with the past behind me and here was Hugo standing right in front of me, hardly two feet away, not allowing his gaze to drift from my eyes, and expecting an answer to a question that disturbed my good intentions and put me on the spot. But I found myself speaking anyway, "Yes, I think so."

"Good. I'll call you tomorrow around four-thirty in the afternoon after I finish work."

As I left the parking lot, I could see the lights of Hugo's truck following me in the rear view mirror. Just out of LaViolette, he turned north off the highway and headed to the nearby city of Salaberry-de-Valleyfield on the south shore of the Saint-Lawrence River. I continued home to Wakeham, wondering all the while about this unexpected twist of fate and how I felt about Hugo. I said I would see him again, but it hardly seemed to be me who was talking and I don't want to lead him on if I really don't want a relationship. I don't trust myself yet, doubt my relations with men, and question my motives. On the other hand, my heartstrings play a different tune, they're revving up a symphony orchestra. And I know now not to fall into that old trap of doings–reasoning and planning and deciding. *Okay, this is what I want,* the monologue went. *This is the way it should be. The time is right, everything is in place, so it's the perfect moment for something to happen because I'm ready* right *now.* And then the waiting began. *I mustn't have done it the right way. I should have an answer by now. What are they thinking? They've come across something they don't like. Not again. What if it doesn't work out? What'll I do next? What if I missed something really important? Whoa. It's not my fault. No way. I've done my bit. But why doesn't it show up? I'll never get ahead at this rate....* God and Winona know better than I know myself what I need and they always seem to want for me what I want anyway.

Tuesday, June 24, 1997.

Hugo telephoned yesterday as he said he would and came to Wakeham in the early evening. When he arrived, I was in the backyard sitting on the ground beside a young shade maple loosening the earth around the sapling with a hand spade. Hugo squatted beside me, took another garden tool that was sitting on the grass, and turned the soil with me. We sauntered around the large expanse of green lawn commenting on the surprising privacy, stopping to touch the tender new growth and smell the budding flowers. Toulouse had been sitting quietly and patiently in a corner of the yard not far from the house. Hugo spied the fluffy white bulk watching our meanderings and pointed in his direction. "Look who's keeping an eye on us!" Once he had Hugo's attention, Toulouse fastened his big copper eyes on Hugo's, cocked his ears forward, and strode over to where we were standing. Long bushy tail straight up in the air and keeping his glance steady, he took one delicate cat step after another, stopped a few feet in front of Hugo, sat, aligned his front paws perfectly one against the other, and waited to be acknowledged with a pat on his head, a simple act of fondness with which Hugo was more than willing to oblige him.

Hugo left around nine o'clock in the evening just as the sun lowered itself over the horizon leaving the luminous dusk air in all its sweetness to transform the remaining daylight into a silken summer darkness that soothed and cradled a yearning wrapped in velvet. Last night, the son of Venus, astride the back of a lion and playing on a lyre, tamed the fierce savage and the beast turned his head to listen to the harmonious chords.

Friday, June 27, 1997.

Hugo came to see me every evening this week. *Thank you dear God and sweet Winona. Thank you for loving me.*

An angel whispered in my ear. I looked in my mindspace to find Winona and there she was, waiting for me. I took her hands and we danced in a ring. So did my little girl. One would have thought we were in a fairy woodland or a mid-summer meadow with bits of flowers clinging to our hair, dancing and leaping like forest sprites. Everything spoke to me that I was free, that after all the lessons and obstacles of the past years I was free now to go wherever my daimon would lead. The only thing I couldn't do was find myself all over again. Happiness and sweet, sweet love reached out to touch every living thing, the bloom, once more, on the rose on the vine.

And then I took Mother's hands as she sat in her wheelchair. She was a teacher. Her past was my past and all that had happened to her had happened to me. Whatever had made her angry had made me angry as well. Our present reality lies where it is true in our minds, but there are other realities that turn the thieved into the thief, the betrayed into the betrayer, the ingrate into the grateful. The sore ceases to generate poison when you put a stop to the hurting and allow your wound to become your gift. Healing the raw tender place is the greatest reward you can give to yourself, and to others. As I watched, little me vanished into me, Hugo was right where she had been, and put his arm around my shoulders. Then Alex was standing in front of me in his tall youthful strength, his hands reaching out for mine, and we held each other close. I lifted my head from Alex's chest, opened my eyes, and there, in my line of vision, at Winona's side, was Jake dressed in his old plaid shirt and baggy pants. Quiet as the air around us, he continued to look at me, his arms hanging loosely by his sides, the familiar worn cap dangling from the fingers of his right hand. And those same divine creatures of thirty years ago who sang songs at my wedding burst into heavenly choruses once more as the words that passed through my lips were spoken directly to him: "It's all right now, Dad. You can dance with my angel again." And, this time, unmistakably and irrevocably, the sounds were songs of love.

Part Four

The Throne of Necessity

"Love is the secret key; it opens the door
of the divine. Laugh, love, be alive, dance,
sing, become a hollow bamboo and let His
song flow through you."

Bhaghwan Shree Rajneesh

Tableau Vivant

July tiptoes in silently and barely noticed. The first few days of the month
are hushed and of modest midsummer temperatures. Then the sun blazes with
such an intensity that when one steps out from under the coolness of the
shade trees one is reminded of a Baked Alaska, a quivering swell of dessert
wizardry, a cloud of hot meringue blanketing a chilly nugget of ice cream and
sending thrills running through the unsuspecting body.

Isabelle is sitting on the back steps looking at the resplendent scene about
her, the joy in her heart bouncing on a beam of sunlight, dancing about,
bounding, leaping, bursting, joy outdoing all of the other senses for sheer
purity. Love is in the air. All seems so perfectly simple, so beautiful and
peaceful in the aura of the bright sun shining radiantly in the clear blue sky.

Magenta surfinias cascade past the edges of hanging baskets. The fresh
green of the newly cut lawn disappears from in front of her eyes as it rolls
over a gentle slope at the end of the yard and enters the tiny forest glade on
the riverbank. Dense foliage keeps the light from the tangled and thorny
undergrowth, making the young saplings reach higher and higher in their
yearning for completion. The river beyond is languid; not wanting to disturb
the tranquility of a summer afternoon, the odd ripple on the mirror surface
simply casts back the sun's glorious energy in packets of brilliance.
Magnificent willow trees with giant trunks seem to breathe like living beings;
from time to time a slight zephyr makes the lithe and slender leaves stream
gracefully from far-reaching boughs as if to embrace the pillar of strength at
the center.

A twelve-foot high cedar hedge bounds the perimeter along the east side
of the lawn creating a private interior court. Flower gardens claim the space
as their own in front of the thick greenery. Splendid rose bushes sheltering
new buds under the leaves, lofty blue spikes of delphinium flowerets,
precious pink cosmos blooms on long feathered stems, bursts of flamboyant
dahlias in vivid oranges and clear pastels, well-mannered riots of yellow and
white garland chrysanthemums, bewitching pink and purple cornflowers,

283

ballets of lacy white alyssum, cavalier geraniums in rich royal scarlet, charming velvet pansies in shades of the deepest indigo, pompous zinnia buttons in chartreuse armour with fiery sprays at the center, and playful yellow-throated snapdragons–together, they throw a profusion of light and colours into the air.

Lush fruit trees have discarded their blossoms in May and now prepare for new birth. Tall windblown pines, scraggy and unruly branches covering the top two-thirds of their trunks, grow alongside a dilapidated fence of weathered cedar pickets and mark the west side of the lawn. Clinging vines and creepers twist in merry tendrils from post to post. Across the fence is farmer Séverin's grassy meadow where his Holstein cows amble at their leisure up and down a water-worn ravine, their great milky udders swaying ponderously to-and-fro as they move about. A streamlet in the bottom of the gully trickles its way towards the river. Silvery streaks flit from tree to tree. The music of birdsong rejoices the day. Sweet fragrances waft into the air. Tremulous butterflies caress the faint breeze. Gleams of sunlight dance. The joys of nature's lavish abundance and a delicious freedom pour forth from this little acre that is hidden away at the edge of the village.

Isabelle's thoughts carouse merrily in the wonder of it all. Love tickles her soul. And then Demeter turns the summer season into the harvest festival. The days are still ripe and wanton but at night there is a chill in the air. Summer's frivolous noise quiets down and the earth's new secrets murmur. It seems that Nature has already revealed her magnum opus for this year then the romantic blooms of autumn appear in a new splendour until a hard frost signals the end like a glowing ember spurting to life before fading into dry ashes. Asters cluster in starry showers. Windflowers weave rich tapestries on the ground. Marigolds throng in bushy mounds of florid brilliance. Baby's breath droops in delicate tresses. Hardy hibiscuses unfurl in bright pinwheels throughout the gardens. Billowy clouds of frosty lavender flowers tumble in great waves over rockery and footpaths. Magenta-purples, rose-reds, lavender-blues, clear pinks, and pale lilacs mingle with the chorus of fall leaves to provide Nature's encore.

The countryside blazes with the reddening foliage. Shimmering leaves run riot in full daylight against the blue of the sky and burst into passionate displays of intoxicated Nature.

Flaming crimsons, vibrant yellows, rich oranges, earthy russets, green bronzes, and liquid golds revel in unrestrained freedom, in a boisterous gaiety the mere sight of which provokes one to sudden exclamations. *Oh! Would you look at that! Oh! Did you ever see anything quite like it? Oh! And look over there!* Tiny openings in the patchwork of leaves permit the sunlight to filter through in bands of sunny dust that dance with the shadows on the ground. Forest floors are covered with lacy woodland ferns, short thimble pines, tangled thickets, briar bushes, tufted spongy mosses, flat-capped toadstools, fairy mushrooms, strawberry trailers, tiny liverworts, yellow lichen, and crumbling leaves. Bramble, bunchberry, and moosewood shrubs bear fleshy clusters of small ripened fruits.

During these days of fall riches, furry squirrels and chipmunks, working constantly to store away their winter provisions, dart here and there under the trees filling their cheek pouches with hazelnuts, beechnuts, butternuts, chestnuts, and acorns. In the depths of the woods, grand antlers on white-tailed stags approach their finest display in readiness for yearly mating rituals. Every species of bird and insect chant in harmony the voluptuous notes of autumnal songs. Young balsam firs with soft spread-out needles; big-tooth aspen with trembling leaves; poetic sumac draped in brilliant red, dark burgundy organs raised in salute, a seedy toast of woodland wine; fragrant clumps of bushy cedars; graceful ash with silver-grey trunks; wild chokecherry with limbs thrust open to feel the wind blow through them; and elegant dogwood adorned in leafy waves, dominate the middle range of the opulent forest growth. Giant sugar maples, straight white birches, colossal oak, native linden, lofty pines, and mighty spruce tower above the others. Seen from a distance, the dark conifers and bright hardwoods lay a mottle of light and colour on layer after layer of the rounded hills that edge the valley, ancient hills of granitic rock uplifted during the continental shifts millions of years ago and then smoothed by receding glaciers.

Elsewhere in the lower regions, gardens bulge to the borders with maturing melons and squashes. Great orange pumpkins like small full moons seem to roll across the level acres of tired soil. Golden-rayed sunflowers have attained their height and now lower their heavy heads. Pastures rustle with wildflowers gone to seed. Silky white down from milkweed and thistle plants scatter through the air at the first breath of wind. Cornfields stretch high. The sun-baked stalks dry in the bright crisp air. Long narrow corncribs, their wire sides groaning with the plenitude of deep yellow cobs that fill to capacity, stand tall and proud in front of the azure sky. *Jay, jay, too-wheedle, too-wheedle*–the raucous calls and loud whistles of noisy blue jays are familiar sounds around the corn bins where the handsome birds in their crested plumage pick up the fallen kernels and transport them away to a winter hiding place behind a piece of tree bark.

In another corner, old apple trees with twisted limbs and gnarled bark are so heavily laden with delicious fruit that their branches bend over to touch the ground. Tapered mature pears are suspended like precious ornaments from leafy boughs of greenery. Shady retreats harbour knotted bunches of wild grapes on vines that climb at random over the tops of hedges and bushes to reach the unfiltered light. Plump cherries swell with sweet juice and hang thickly together like dark rubies. A mourning cloak butterfly, soon to hibernate for the cold months, balances on a colourful Virginia creeper and unfolds its wings to gather the warmth of the afternoon sun. Waxwings, starlings, and grackles, drunk with the abundance of luscious fruit and berries, fly headlong into window-glass that dazzles in the sunshine, wobble a moment in the air to get their bearings, then turn about. A sensual musk, the subtle fragrance of mellow fruit and drying leaves, perfumes the autumn air. And there, in the midst of it all, the old river meanders on in unconcerned mockery of all that tries to stand still.

With the changing of the leaves and the shortening of the days comes hunting season and Hugo drives into the wilderness of northern Quebec to hunt moose with a bow and arrow. Isabelle passes every waking minute of each day he is absent working on her story, giving it form and substance, grateful for the gift she has just untethered, and bringing alive the myth that has shaped her life.

The Manoir is sold at the beginning of December. The sale takes place in the tiny fieldstone registry office in LaViolette. The county sheriff conducts the public auction in the two-room building, which is only large enough to handle ten people at one time. It isn't necessary to hold the proceedings in a larger space since Monsieur Jeanneau is the only buyer who appears at the sale. Isabelle begins bankruptcy proceedings not long afterwards.

Christmas is a happy season spent with Hugo. On Christmas day, he trundles Mrs. Carberry's wheelchair through the ice and snow and up the outdoor stairs into the Wakeham house for a Christmas dinner of turkey with all the trimmings. Later on in the day, three of Hugo's brothers and sisters and their mates arrive to share in the holiday cheer. The small group gathers in front of the fireplace in the living room for a relaxed evening of conversation, food, and drink. Alex is in sunny California. He left a month ago because Dan turned fifty years old in November and Alex flew south for the celebrations. He will stay with his father until the awakening land calls him back up north in the spring.

January of the new year ushers in the ice storm of the century. No great rolls of thunder resonate through valley hollows announcing the coming; no howling wind screams its virtue around doors and windows; no blinding flashes of lightning sizzle with revenge in a darkened sky; nothing whatsoever of an untoward nature that one might expect to precede such a major event comes to pass–the simple truth being that one evening a cold rain begins to fall and it drizzles on and on throughout the night and the following days without letting up. A slow and steady warm front has worked its way towards Quebec from Texas while, at the same time, a cold front moves in from the Arctic. When the two air masses collide, the warm air rises and passes over the cold. With no wind to disturb its pattern, the system remains anchored in place and drops its deluge below.

In Wakeham, the freezing rain begins to patter and tock on the windowpanes on late Sunday evening, January the fourth, 1998. It continues for six days. During that time there are no spells of sunshine to thaw the ever-thickening layers of ice that coat everything it touches. Power lines begin to strain and break under the load on Tuesday. By Thursday, four million people in southeastern Ontario, southwestern Quebec, parts of New Brunswick, upstate New York, and New England are in a power blackout in the middle of a frosty winter. Transmission towers topple. Hydro poles snap in two. One after the other they fall like matchsticks, strewing the countryside with curled wire like unraveled holiday cellophane. Roofs and entire buildings collapse, unable to bear any longer the weight of the tremendous build-up of frozen water. Every power line, every tree branch is wrapped in perfectly rounded gauntlets of ice.

Life comes to a halt in order to live again. Authorities request that businesses close their doors. Neighbours share firewood, make communal meals on outdoor barbecues in the middle of winter, huddle around fireplaces or candles, and open their homes to those who are in a worse position. Communities pool strengths to help each other. Emergency shelters are hastily organized in every village, town, and city.

The army is mobilized. Military trucks carrying sixteen thousand Canadian soldiers in green fatigues roll into the stormed regions of Ontario, Quebec, and New Brunswick. Operation Recuperation is the largest domestic military effort in Canadian history. The ice storm troopers help hydro crews repair downed power lines, clear roads that have been littered with broken branches, trim trees, pump water from flooded basements, run soup kitchens, rescue frightened pets, trek door to door canvassing the occupants, and transport the sick and elderly from frigid homes into public shelters. Firefighters, police officers, hydro workers, military personnel, municipal authorities, and volunteers work together around the clock to lend a helping hand to thousands until the power returns, which, for many, is not until a month later.

The sun comes out in a week's time and temperatures plummet to bone-chilling levels. A full moon shines brightly on the twelfth of January above a blackened landscape reminiscent of a war zone. The normal winter quiet is shattered by the sound of ice-coated tree limbs crashing to the ground. Some people choose to walk in the middle of the streets to minimize the danger of falling ice. Others wear helmets. Schools remain closed until the structures are cleared of layers of icicles pointing downward from rooftops like long silvery swords. Children skate over the open fields during the unexpected holiday. Convoys of vans filled with thousands of cords of wood make their way to Saint Césaire, a municipality south of Montreal that is situated in the heart of the storm where the most havoc has been wreaked. Much of the wood comes from the Saguenay, a region of Quebec that has itself experienced a similar outpouring of support from far and wide during a flood disaster two years earlier.

Trainloads of generators are sent from Ontario and the western provinces. At the request of the mayoress, railway workers drive a locomotive onto the streets of Boucherville to provide emergency power and warmth to local shelters. Large corporations, small businesses, and individuals from across the continent and the world send gifts of blankets, generators, batteries, bottled water, diapers, milk, food supplies, and cash into the devastated areas to be distributed to those in need.

The rural areas are hit the hardest. Some dairy farmers lose whole herds of cattle when portable generators fail to provide sufficient energy to ventilate the barns and run the milking machines. Unused to irregular milking times, the cows develop mastitis, a killing infection of the udder. Without a constant supply of fresh air, cattle, pigs, and sheep suffocate. The carnage is scooped into waiting bins for the dead by great mechanical shovels. Twenty million litres of milk have to be dumped in the first week of the storm since processing plants are unable to operate. Syrup producers count their losses as maple bushes are decimated. The dense overhead canopy is thinned. However, the sun's rays can now reach through to the forest floor giving new life to the young trees.

The woods throughout the vast storm region are transformed into fairy-tale structures of crystalline winter beauty, illusive woods of glacial softness that seep cool and ashen into your soul, soft as silk, cool as death. How colourless and soundless is this stealth, this seeping artful extraction from eternity. The sun dances in sparkles of white light to a continual crackle of divine music. Slender aspen, birch, and young poplars are forced to bend to the ground in graceful humility, the outermost tips of their branches frozen in the snow where they touch the earth and remain bowed prisoners until the warmth of spring releases the icy hold.

Tall spruce and pines are decapitated, their crowning tops falling sixty feet to the ground. The weakest limbs of the maples and elms are severed, their flesh ripped open in the struggle to survive God's justice leaving a zillion daytime torches flashing across the land, streaks of light against the dark winter bark like a herd of white-tailed deer in flight, like beacons of divine language. Many tongues utter at once, "Stop! Look! Listen! I will speak to you if you will listen. Can you not see the soul in action on Earth? Can you not see where the glory lies?"

The torch parade is an ancient festival performance of runners passing on the light of knowledge, the wisdom of God. He is asking for our attention in a chaotic chorus of opposites–the strong and the weak, the beautiful and the tragic, the worst of weather and the best of people, the visible violence and the invisible grace, the torn flesh and the spirit within. Hidden in the center of our beings, as it is in all of nature, is God's gift to us: the power to heal, to recreate ourselves in our intuitive images, to remember who we really are.

After the ravages of the ice storm, a buyer for Isabelle's house expresses his interest in acquiring the property and signs a deed of sale. She and Hugo work daily for three weeks packing boxes and moving furniture. The last day in Wakeham, Isabelle arises early, in the hush of dawn, to witness the first glimmer of breaking light turn into the violet interval that deifies the daybreak. The strange power of those transient moments, those dim half-tones that quietly pervade the languishing darkness, the blending of something ancient and something futuristic, impress upon her a special intimacy and she watches until the sun rises over the tops of the trees. A little later, Hugo will arrive with a trailer behind his truck to bring the last load to his place in Salaberry-de-Valleyfield. Before leaving, she wants time alone to say thank you to the house at 33 Simmian Street for sheltering her with its strength while she lived within.

She called it her sunshine house. It was pale yellow with green shutters. Rays of golden light entered through all the windows in cathedral streams while the sweet strains of James Galway's flute and Mozart's concertos filled its space with the music of the spheres, uniting forever the mortal with the immortal. Rich and delicate colours put beauty and harmony on its walls in tones that flowed into painted borders of cascading flowers or ivory etchings of Greek vases.

Outside, the silent ice sculptures keep a vigil poised in dignity. Long after the storm, the destruction is still frozen in its dance, an enduring statement from the earth. Once again, it speaks of death and life, of renewal. It speaks of quiet magnificence, of terrible beauty. It speaks of all things that proceed from an eternal necessity. It speaks of the new day where God is whitening the dawn.

The End

ACKNOWLEDGMENTS

Grateful acknowledgment is made to the following for permission to reprint already published material:

Epigraphs:
p.147 Gregg Levoy, *Callings*, c 1997 by Gregg Levoy, Harmony Books, New York, 1997.

p.157 Thomas Moore, *Care of the Soul*, c 1992 by Thomas Moore, HarperCollins, New York, 1992.

p.245 James Hillman, *The Soul's Code*, c 1996 by James Hillman, Random House, New York, Toronto, 1996.

p.261 Gary Zukav, *The Seat of the Soul*, c 1989 by Gary Zukav, Simon & Schuster, New York, 1989.

Grateful acknowledgment is also made of the following quotes that were used within the text:

p.31 "God is not dead nor doth He sleep."
From *I Heard The Bells on Christmas Day*

p.33 "The ghosts of evening tune again their lyres and wander singing in a plaintive band down the long corridors of trees."
F. Scott Fitzgerald, *This Side of Paradise*

p.99 "The devil's most devilish when respectable."
Elizabeth Barrett Browning, *Aurora Leigh*, bk.vii

p.100 "The music soars within the little lark, And the lark soars."
Elizabeth Barrett Browning, *Aurora Leigh*, bk.iii

p.109 "How do I love thee? Let me count the ways."
Elizabeth Barrett Browning, *Sonnets from the Portuguese*, no.43

p.117 "Sing me a song of a lad that is gone,

Say, could that lad be I?
Merry of soul he sailed on a day
Over the sea to Skye."
Robert Louis Stevenson, *To S.R. Crockett*, XLV

p.118 "In the land of Nod, on the east of Eden."
The Bible, Genesis 4:16

p.127 A "silent spot, amid the hills,
A small and silent dell!
...'Tis a quiet spirit-healing nook!"
Samuel Taylor Coleridge, *Fears in solitude*

p.131 "Sometimes a scream is better than a thesis."
Ralph Waldo Emerson, 1803-1882

p.215 "Nought could be done–nought could be said;
So–my lord Tomnoddy went home to bed!"
Richard Harris Barham, *The Ingoldsby Legends*
Hon. Mr. Sucklethumbkin's Story

p.216 "Like a blue-bottle fly on a rather large scale,
With a rather large corking-pin stuck through his tail."
Richard Harris Barham, *The Ingoldsby Legends*
The Auto-da-Fé